UNLOCKING THE MYSTERIES OF BIRTH AND DEATH: BUDDHISM IN THE CONTEMPORARY WORLD

UNLOCKING THE MYSTERIES OF BIRTH AND DEATH: BUDDHISM IN THE CONTEMPORARY WORLD

DAISAKU IKEDA

Foreword by Professor N.C. Wickramasinghe
Department of Applied Mathematics and Astronomy
University College, Cardiff

Macdonald

A Macdonald Book

First published in Great Britain in 1988 by
Macdonald & Co (Publishers) Ltd
London & Sydney

British Library Cataloguing in Publication Data

Ikeda, Daisaku
  Buddhism and life.   294.3
  1. Nichiren Shoshu
  I. Title
  294.3'928   BQ8415.4

  ISBN 0-356-15498-X

Photoset in North Wales by
Derek Doyle & Associates, Mold, Clwyd
Reproduced, printed and bound in Great Britain by
Hazell Watson & Viney Limited
Member of BPCC plc
Aylesbury Bucks

Macdonald & Co (Publishers) Ltd
Greater London House
Hampstead Road
London NW1 7QX
A Pergamon Press plc company

Contents

Foreword

Buddhism: A Philosophy For Our Times – An Historical Perspective

Chandra Wickramasinghe

Wherever we care to look we are surrounded by a plethora of destructive symbols. They vary in scale from the gun to the nuclear weapon; from strife and violence within small social groups to discord between nations that might eventually engulf the whole world in war. The horrors of terrorism show up with ever-increasing frequency in every corner of the Earth; and the great ideological divide between the United States and the Soviet Union still exists. Against such a background it is not unduly difficult to become convinced that we are perilously close to self-destruction. And this destruction, if it comes, will not be confined to the human race; rather does it threaten the extinction of all higher life-forms that inhabit our planet.

Our eventual salvation, however, must depend on the emergence of a collective sense of sanity – an Enlightenment – within our species. As individuals we are endowed with an instinct for self-preservation, but in the larger demographic groups of the modern world such an instinct has no place. Instinct has to be replaced by a self-preserving philosophy of life embodying some form of religious or moral code. For centuries in Western Europe such moral values were provided by the Christian religion, and indeed Christianity proved to be a powerful civilizing and preserving force. Although such ethical principles evidently failed to prevent wars, they were on the whole adequate to secure happiness for individuals in society and to ensure the survival of mankind.

The influence of the Church began its decline in the latter half of the nineteenth century. Consequently there was an erosion of our long-cherished Christian ethical values, an erosion that has continued to the present day. Whether one likes it or not the great Christian Ethic that has been such a preserving and civilizing influence has effectively vanished, leaving behind a society that is distinctly a-religious and even amoral. The dangers that face such a society, armed with nuclear weapons but stripped of moral values, are stark and real.

The choice we now have is either to revive the old Christian values, or to adopt new sets of moral values, perhaps better suited to our times, that would serve to maintain the social systems we so cherish. In the present crisis it is perhaps no surprise to find more and more individuals in the West turning for solace to Eastern philosophies, philosophies in which peace and compassion are accorded pride of place. Buddhism is a supreme example in this category.

Buddhism has an immediate appeal to the intellect. It seeks solutions to problems of the world by means of understanding those problems at a deep and fundamental level. The understanding is sought mainly through a process of meditation and self-analysis. Such a process would inevitably lead to the transference in some degree of self-interest and self-preservation to the benefit of much larger social groups. A deep concern for one's own inner peace and tranquillity is quickly transformed into an equal concern for all mankind, or even for all living things. Thus arises the Buddhist refrain, 'May all living beings be happy!'

In its original form Buddhism may be seen as a pragmatic philosophy worked out by an Indian Prince Siddharta Gautama (563–483 BC) some 2500 years ago. As a royal prince, married and with a young son, he had enjoyed all the regal comforts that befitted his station. But such privileges did not make him blind to the intensity of human suffering that he witnessed around him. One day, at the age of 29, riding in his chariot in the royal gardens, he is said to have witnessed four sights: a decrepit old man leaning on a stick and shaking all over, a sick man, a dead man and finally a monk in calm repose. He began to ask questions about what he saw, but he could not find answers that satisfied him. He was indeed so deeply moved by what he saw that he rode out at night to renounce all worldly pleasures and to lead the life of an ascetic. For six years he tried many forms of asceticism, including self-mortification and fasting, but to no avail. Finally he retreated to meditate under the shade of the sacred Bo-tree, seeking to find his own solution to the problems of life, disease, suffering and death. His eventual enlightenment is said to have come after 49 days, after which he came to be known as Gautama, the Buddha – the Enlightened One. The philosophy that emerged from this enlightenment was at once simple and profound. It touched upon all aspects of life, the cause of suffering and the nature of human relationships as well as the nature of the world in which we live. It was as all-embracing and comprehensive as any philosophy could be. An important point to note is that this enlightenment was not regarded by Gautama Buddha as a miraculous event. It is presented as a state of mind at peace with the world from which objective knowledge quite naturally flows. It is a condition that every single human being could aspire to and reach to varying degrees in his or her own lifetime. For the remainder of Gautama's life until his death at the age of 80 he travelled widely in Northern India preaching his doctrines and making millions of converts.

The teachings of Gautama must be viewed against the background of pre-existing traditions of Hinduism, the religion to which Gautama himself was born. His philosophy could be seen as a form of protestant revolt against the tenets of orthodox Hinduism. Yet, certain basic Hindu concepts were taken over essentially unmodified, for instance the doctrine of Karma, the inexorable law of cause and effect whereby actions in the present life are thought to have consequences in future reincarnations. Another ancient Hindu concept was the belief that the world abounds in ignorance and misery from which the wise and the pious should endeavour to escape. Where Gautama differed in a fundamental way from Hindu ascetics of old, however, was the manner in which he sought salvation. His own experience had led him to conclude that excessive self-denial such as fasting practised by Hindu ascetics was futile in furthering this cause. Gautama advocated the so-called 'Middle Path', the path that lies between austere asceticism on the one hand and extreme self-indulgence on the other. Furthermore, revolting against long-established Hindu traditions, he rejected the caste system, asserting that all human beings are equal in their potential to accomplish salvation.

Gautama's first sermon at Benares embodies two fundamental pronouncements of Buddhist philosophy: The Four Noble Truths, and alongside it an exposition of the Noble Eightfold Path. The Four Truths are enumerated thus:

(1) Suffering is an essential component of individual existence
(2) The cause of suffering is a craving or attachment for objects of sense
(3) Release from suffering involves the elimination of craving
(4) The elimination of craving is achieved by following the Noble Eightfold Path.

The Noble Eightfold Path itself implies an ethical code of conduct and self-discipline summarized as: right knowledge, right resolve, right thought, right speech, right action, right living, right mindfulness and right concentration.

The ultimate goal to be achieved in Buddhism is seen as freedom from the cycle of birth and re-birth reaching finally the state of impersonal reality known as Nirvana. So much is commonly accepted as the bare essentials of Buddhist philosophy derived most directly from the historical facts relating to Gautama Buddha. The details of practice and the specific interpretations given to scriptures, in relation to subjects such as the Nature of the World, have led to the emergence of a diversity of Buddhist sects.

For some 2500 years Buddhism has been a major civilizing influence throughout much of Asia and the Far East. The graceful spires and domes of temples in Sri Lanka, Burma, Thailand and Japan and the murals and sculpture within them bear impressive testimony to the influence of Buddhism upon the art and architecture of these lands. Two centuries after the death of Gautama Buddha his religion had spread across much of Northern India and had just reached the shores of Sri Lanka. Buddhism was deemed to be the state religion of India during the reign of the great Emperor Asoka from 269–237BC. The Buddhism in India at this time, and that which came to Sri Lanka in the latter half of the third century BC were, in their most pristine forms, the religion as preached by Gautama himself. The scriptures that expound these original teachings are contained in the *Tripitaka* (the triple basket), a document that was compiled by Indian monks well before the dawn of the Christian Era. The original version of Buddhism is known as Hinayana Buddhism (Buddhism of the Lesser Vehicle), and it is this version that is preserved almost unchanged in modern Sri Lanka. Buddhist doctrines of a generally similar form are also preserved in Thailand and Burma.

In India, however, the dominance of Buddhism over Hinduism was not destined to last. The original Hinayana form, which concentrated almost entirely on individual salvation and was virtually free of ritual, gradually incorporated certain aspects of devotional temple worship associated with Hinduism. Already in the first century AD a group of Buddhist monks began to adopt a new and widened interpretation of the teachings of Gautama Buddha. The emergent form of Indian Buddhism took upon itself the cause of salvation of the entire human race in addition to concern for the individual. Because of this wider scope it came to be called Mahayana Buddhism (the Buddhism of the Larger Vehicle). In general the Mahayana Buddhist would aspire to the status of 'bodhisattva', that is to say one who would eventually become a Buddha. The new Mahayana Buddhism had a more popular appeal and spread rapidly across India and abroad to Tibet, Korea, China and Japan. Whereas Hinayana Buddhism did not change with time in any essential manner in the places where it became established, Mahayana Buddhism on the other hand continued to evolve and take on a diversity of shapes. In India, however, due in large measure to the Islamic invasion, Buddhism was eventually reabsorbed into Hinduism and effectively disappeared as a separate religion around the year AD1300.

Wherever it spread, Buddhism brought with it high moral precepts – tolerance, non-violence, respect for the individual, love of all nature and an abiding belief in the equality of all men. Buddhism was first introduced into Japan in AD538 from Paikche, a kingdom in Korea, and shortly afterward in the year AD594 the Prince Regent Shotoku Taishi (574–622) declared Buddhism to be the religion of the State. The form of Buddhism was of course Mahayana. The earliest school of Buddhism (the Tendai school) to be established in Japan was based on the 'Lotus Sutra', a Mahayana text written in India around the second century AD. It claims to contain Gautama Buddha's teaching in its absolute purity. Gautama himself is presented as an eternal being surrounded by arhats, gods and bodhisattvas. Recitation of the sutra is deemed an important part of religious conduct and the ultimate objective of a devotee is the attainment of the state of Buddhahood. Subsequent developments in Japan involved the inclusion of a succession of other texts such as the 'Pure Land Sutra', which was also written in India in the second century AD. In this latter sutra the declared aim is to establish a pure or happy land free of evil where human beings enjoy longevity, achieve a state of freedom from worry, a state from which they might easily transcend to Nirvana. From the year AD538 to AD1200 many divergent sects of Mahayana Buddhism came to be established in Japan and have flourished at various times.

In the present book Daisaku Ikeda deals mainly with a form of Buddhism that evolved in Japan in the thirteenth century AD. Its founder, Nichiren (1222–1282), the son of a humble fisherman, became a monk at the age of 15.

Nichiren became confused and frustrated by the many different paths to salvation that were being offered by the various sects and schools of Japanese Buddhism. Emulating the great master Gautama, he decided to seek a solution for himself through meditation. Nichiren accepted the Lotus Sutra as containing the true teachings of Gautama. In addition he stressed the importance of espousing Buddhism to free the nation from evil and unrest. Nichiren's seemingly practical solutions brought him very many followers, and the Nichiren school continues today as an important Buddhist sect in Japan.

The present book is one of a series in which Ikeda expounds Buddhist philosophy mainly of the Nichiren school stressing its profound relevance to the problems of the present day. In these books we are shown that Gautama Buddha's thoughts about the world are in remarkable accord with discoveries in modern science. In Buddha's analysis of the mind, for example, modern discoveries in psychology would seem to have been anticipated. More impressively perhaps, in his analysis of the Universe recent developments in astronomy have been similarly anticipated. The Earth as a planet around a sun, the sun a star amongst billions in the galaxy, and the galaxy being one of many billion galaxies finds unambiguous expression in spirit if not in literal detail. In the *Visuddimagga* it is stated that '... as far as these suns and moons revolve shining and shedding their light in space, so far extends the thousand-fold universe. In it are thousands of suns, thousands of moons ... thousands of Jambudipas, thousands of Aparagoyanas ...', the latter references being to extraterrestrial abodes of life. The billions of galaxies discovered in modern astronomy could be identified with statements such as in the *Vajracchedika* referring to the entire Universe as '... this sphere of a million, million world systems'.

Since the modern scientific viewpoint is derived from the application of the methods of empirical science, one might wonder how the same results could be reached without recourse to such methods 2500 years ago. The answer must lie in the still mysterious and unproven powers of meditation. If we are creatures of the Cosmos would it not seem reasonable that we have an innate knowledge of its nature somewhere deep within ourselves? The basic facts relating to the Cosmos could be viewed as essential components of our own true nature. The universal aspiration to Buddhahood contained in all forms of Mahayana Buddhism implies that a form of omniscience is hidden within each and every human being.

The Buddhist attitude to an omniscient God outside ourselves is on the whole negative. In this sense Buddhism can be regarded as being distinctly atheistic. In neither Hinayana nor Mahayana Buddhism is a Buddha or a Bodhisattva conceived of in any way as a god possessing extraordinary creative or omniscient powers; nor is any other such entity identified or postulated. This lack of a central God-figure might indeed be seen as a positive attribute, for men have been known in the past to fight bitterly to defend the gods they believe in. It is quite remarkable that Buddhism has spread across vast tracts of Asia and has maintained itself in many countries without recourse to religious wars or crusades. Buddhism is a philosophy that enshrines peace, compassion, selflessness and universal love as fundamental virtues. Peace to conquer the world, Enlightenment to dispel ignorance and to understand the true nature of the Universe. What better philosophy could there be in the decades that lead us into the 21st century?

Introduction

We all desire happiness, and yet happiness always seems to be just beyond our reach.

Numerous philosophers have tackled the question of happiness. Their conclusions have, I believe, without exception been incomplete because, however many books might appear telling you "how to be happy", human beings are on the whole still beset by the same problems as their ancestors. The poor seek wealth, the sick yearn to become healthy, those suffering from domestic strife would rather have harmony, and so on. However, even if we do secure wealth, health and a happy home life, we will still inevitably find ourselves confronted by problems in other areas. And, even if somehow we fashion circumstances such that they apparently satisfy all the conditions necessary for our happiness, how long can those circumstances be maintained? Obviously not forever: none of us can avoid the illnesses and slow weakening of the body that accompany ageing, and still less can any of us escape death.

Problems, however, are not in themselves the fundamental cause of unhappiness: according to Buddhism, the real cause is not just that we have problems but that we lack the power and wisdom to solve them. Buddhism teaches that all individuals innately possess infinite power and wisdom, and reveals the process whereby these qualities can be developed. In addressing the problem of happiness, Buddhism focuses not so much on eliminating suffering and difficulties, which are understood to be inherent in life, as on how we should cultivate the potentials that exist within our own lives. Strength and wisdom, says Buddhism, derive from *life force*. If we cultivate sufficient life force we shall be able, not only to withstand life's adversities, but to transform them into causes of happiness and joy.

1

If this is to be our goal, however, we must first identify the principal sufferings that exist in life. Buddhism says that there are four universal sufferings: the suffering of birth, the suffering of sickness, the suffering of old age, and the suffering of death. No matter how much we would like to cling to our youth, we cannot prevent ourselves from gradually ageing with the passage of time. However hard we try to maintain good health, we will eventually contract some disease or another. And, more fundamentally, however much we abhor the thought of dying, the longer we live the closer we come to the moment of death – although, of course, it is beyond our power to know when that moment will come.

We can recognize various causes – biological, physiological and psychological – for the sufferings of sickness, ageing and death. However, in the last analysis it is life itself – or, rather, birth into this world – that is the cause of all our mundane sufferings.

In Sanskrit suffering is called *duhkha*, a word which implies a state fraught with difficulty in which people and things do not accord with our wishes. This condition is said to derive from the fact that all phenomena are transient: youth, health and even our lives cannot continue forever. Here, according to Buddhism, lies the ultimate cause of human suffering.

Shakyamuni Buddha's motive for renouncing the secular world is outlined in the story of the four meetings, found in many Buddhist scriptures. The young Shakyamuni, known as Prince Siddhartha, was confined most of the time to the palace by his father, King Shuddhodana, so that he would be shielded from worldly suffering. However, as he emerged from the east gate of the palace one day, he encountered an old man, withered with age, tottering along with the help of a cane. Seeing this man, Shakyamuni realized that life inevitably entails the suffering of old age. On another occasion, leaving the palace by the south gate, he saw a sick person and realized that sickness, too, is a part of life. A third time he was leaving via the west gate when he saw a corpse; this "meeting" led him to grasp the reality that all which lives must eventually die. Finally, one day as he was going out through the north gate, he encountered a religious ascetic whose air of serene dignity awoke in him the resolve to embark on a religious life.

Eventually, after he had dedicated himself to various religious practices, ascetic and otherwise, for a number of years, Shakyamuni attained enlightenment, gaining freedom from the sufferings of birth, sickness, old age and death. Determined to lead other people to this enlightenment, he set about preaching, and came to be known as the "Buddha", a Sanskrit term meaning an "enlightened one" – one whose wisdom encompasses the ultimate truth of life and the Universe.

If we truly understand the things that the Buddha realized, we find that neither the four sufferings nor any of the other sufferings derived from them have power enough to topple us into the abyss of despair and misery. This is because, as we acquire the wisdom to penetrate the true aspect of life, we simultaneously establish a stronger, higher self which enables us to overcome all sorts of worldly adversities and to enjoy our lives to the fullest, transforming all sufferings into a source of limitless joy.

It is generally held that, immediately after his enlightenment, Shakyamuni preached the doctrines of the four noble truths and the eightfold path. The four noble truths are:

- the truth of suffering
- the truth of the origin of suffering
- the truth of the cessation of suffering
- the truth of the path to the cessation of suffering

The truth of suffering is that all existence in this world is suffering, as represented by the four sufferings we have noted as inherent in life. The truth of the origin of suffering states that suffering is caused by selfish craving for the ephemeral pleasures of the world. The truth of the cessation of suffering is that the eradication of this selfish craving ends the suffering. And the truth of the path to the cessation of suffering is that there exists a path by which this eradication can be achieved: the path is traditionally interpreted as the discipline of the eightfold path. This latter is composed of

- right views, based on the four noble truths and a correct understanding of Buddhism
- right thinking, or command of one's mind
- right speech
- right action
- right way of life, based on the purification of one's thoughts, words and deeds
- right endeavour, to seek the true Law
- right mindfulness (always to bear right views in mind)
- right meditation

The four noble truths and the eightfold path were directed chiefly to those disciples who had rejected secular life and were wholly engaged in Buddhist practice; they reflect the basic attitude and approach underlying Shakyamuni's early teachings, which concentrated on predominantly negative views about life and the world so that he could awaken people first to the harsh realities of life and then to the inexpressible spiritual experience of nirvana. These teachings, which encouraged the negation of all desires, would, if carried out to the letter, inevitably lead to the negation of the desire to live. The fundamental solution to human suffering in this world, they stated, lies in the eradication of earthly desires – that is, all manner of desires, impulses and passions arising from the depths of our lives. By following the teachings we can sever our ties to the cycle of birth and death and attain the state wherein rebirth in this world is no longer necessary to us – that is, we can attain the state of nirvana.

These teachings may have been applicable to and beneficial to Shakyamuni's monks and nuns, but they were extremely difficult for lay people to follow. However, his original determination was to save every human being on this Earth. For this reason, he travelled back and forth across the region of the Middle Ganges, expounding his philosophy. But lay people, even if they wanted to achieve

4

nirvana, must have found it not just impracticable but actually impossible to abandon all earthly desires. They had families to support, jobs to do, and other everyday affairs that demanded their attention. For them, while nirvana might be an ideal, there was no way that it could be an attainable goal. Yet somehow Shakyamuni's wisdom and compassion always reached the ordinary people who, obviously, had many problems which they lacked the means to solve. Had this not been the case – had Buddhism been helpless to save ordinary people – then it would never have achieved any status higher than that of an intellectual pursuit. Shakyamuni counselled people, and inspired them with hope and courage so that they could overcome their various sufferings and enjoy the prospect of a brilliant future. For example, he spoke about a pure land far away from this world where, by following his teachings, people could be reborn free from all desires. Those who inhabited this pure land, he explained, would be strangers to any suffering or fear.

Just as he encouraged his monks and nuns to observe his many precepts and follow the eightfold path in order to attain nirvana, Shakyamuni taught his lay believers to be faithful to the teachings he expounded so that they could be reborn into the pure land. However, in actuality, neither the eradication of desire nor rebirth in the pure land is an attainable reality. It is impossible to blow out the fires of desire and interrupt the cycle of birth and death – because desire is inherent in life, life is eternal, and birth and death are the inescapable alternating aspects of life. Nor is it possible to reach a pure land that does not in fact exist. Both nirvana and the pure land were metaphorical devices that Shakyamuni used to train and develop the understanding of his followers.

Looking at all this another way, the teaching concerning nirvana was directed towards personal emancipation through the realization of ultimate truth, and that concerning the pure land was directed towards the salvation of the people at large. These two emphases are representative, respectively, of Hinayana (the lesser vehicle)

5

and Mahayana (the great vehicle) – the two major streams of Buddhism. However, these two emphases were later integrated in the Lotus Sutra, which we shall discuss at some length in this book. This sutra makes it absolutely clear that there are two aspects of Buddhist practice indispensable if we are to attain enlightenment. One is directed towards perfecting ourselves, in the sense that we realize the ultimate truth and develop all the potentials inherent in our lives, and the other is the practice of leading other people towards that perfection.

The Lotus Sutra also reveals the true meanings of nirvana and the pure land. According to the sutra, we do not have to put a stop to the cycle of birth and death in order to enter nirvana; rather, nirvana is the state of enlightenment in which, as we repeat the cycle of birth and death, we come to terms with it, transforming it so that it is no longer a source of suffering. Similarly, we do not have to abandon all desire in order to attain nirvana because earthly desires can be transformed into a cause of happiness and, further, into enlightened wisdom. Moreover, the pure land does not necessarily lie beyond death: we dwell in the pure land here and now if we believe in the Lotus Sutra, which reveals that we can transform this world – full of suffering and sorrow as it is – into a pure land full of joy and hope.

Some Fundamental Doctrines
How exactly does Buddhism provide the solution to the fundamental problems of life and death? By taking a close look at each of the four sufferings – birth, sickness, old age and death – this book seeks to illuminate the truth and wisdom that enable us to sail calmly over the troubled sea of worldly suffering.

It might appear on the face of it that people today are inclined to avoid facing the problems of old age, sickness and death. This is not really the case. Of course, fear of such things is nothing new – it was probably shared by our earliest ancestors. However, what seems different about people's attitudes in this current age is the expectation that medicine and technology will provide the means to prolong life while holding the symptoms of ageing at bay. But such an expectation is itself a product of modern humanity's enormous fear of the realities of old age, sickness and death. This fear has, over the centuries, provided the impetus for the development of medical science, but science and medicine have today reached a stage where, by creating the illusion that all physical illness is at least in theory curable, their very existence is a part of the cause of people's apparent refusal to face these timeless and universal problems.

At no time in the past has science been in a state of such rapid advance. As a result, humanity has adopted a blind belief in the powers of science and technology, and has forgotten to regard the problems inherent in life also from the viewpoints of philosophy and religion. Observing the state of affairs in the world today, I cannot help but feel that, while it may be true that contemporary philosophies and religions may have neither sufficient power nor sufficient profundity to illuminate the underlying causes of suffering, people are not putting enough effort into the struggle to come to grips with the fundamental problems.

From the perspective of ultimate truth, earthly desires and the problems of life and death are not seen as obstacles that must be eradicated, as taught in the Hinayana teachings. Instead, earthly desires are regarded as something that can be transformed into enlightened wisdom, and the sufferings of birth and death as means whereby we can attain nirvana. The Lotus Sutra takes this one step further, setting forth the principles that earthly desires *are* enlightenment and that the sufferings of birth and death *are* nirvana. In other words, there can be no enlightenment apart from the reality of earthly desires and there can be no nirvana without the concomitant sufferings of birth and death. These pairs of contrasting factors are innate in all our lives.

The great Chinese teacher T'ien-t'ai (AD 538-97) employed an analogy to explain the above principles. Suppose there is a bitter persimmon. By soaking it in a solution of lime or buckwheat chaff, or by exposing it to sunlight, we can make the persimmon become sweet. There are not two persimmons, one bitter and the other sweet: there is only the one. And the bitter persimmon has not turned sweet through being sweetened with sugar. It has become sweet because the inherent bitterness of the persimmon has been drawn out and its inherent sweetness has been allowed to emerge. The catalyst, the intermediary that helped the transformation along, was the solution or the sunlight. T'ien-t'ai likened earthly desires to the bitter persimmon, enlightenment to the sweet persimmon, and the process whereby the sweetness was brought out to Buddhist practice.

If we are fully to understand these important doctrines we must comprehend the Buddhist teachings, which illumine life's multifaceted dimensions. In order to clarify the teachings' substance we shall, later in this book, discuss two major doctrines, that of *ichinen sanzen* (that life at each moment possesses three thousand realms) and that of the nine consciousnesses. These doctrines represent the pinnacle of Mahayana Buddhism. Instead of negating desire and life in this world they accept the realities of life as they are and reveal the way to transform them into a cause of enlightenment. The profound doctrine that earthly desires *are* enlightenment teaches that one should not try to eradicate desires, or to regard them as sinful, but should elevate them in an attempt to achieve a nobler state of life.

The same may be said concerning the sufferings of birth and death. The Hinayanists' wish not to be reborn reflects their misunderstanding of the true nature of the sufferings of old age, sickness and death, which are of course incumbent on us from birth. Yet this misunderstanding, and the resulting sense of despair or defeat, are in Buddhist terms delusions – because these sufferings are inherent in life. Once we are awakened to their true nature, by contrast, they become instead vehicles whereby we can attain happiness.

For a correct understanding of the Buddhist view of life, the concept of the Ten Worlds is indispensable. The first six of the Ten Worlds derive from the idea of the Six Paths, an ancient Indian paradigm concerning transmigration: these six worlds, or paths, are Hell, Hunger, Animality, Anger, Humanity and Heaven. It was thought that the particular world or realm into which unenlightened people were born was determined by the things they had done in their past lifetimes, and that people endlessly repeated the cycle of birth and death in these six worlds. Even if born into the highest world, Heaven, one could not stay there long; when one's good fortune was exhausted one would fall back into a lower state of existence.

Transmigration in the Six Paths can be likened to moving from floor to floor inside a six-storey building shut off from the outside. The storey corresponding to Heaven is at the top and beneath it are the storeys representing the other worlds, all the way down to Hell, on the ground floor. Each floor is connected to each of the others. People are confined in this building, going up and down forever. Even though they may find comfort on the upper storeys – Heaven and Humanity – they cannot remain there indefinitely.

But the people of ancient India loathed the thought of this endless cycle with its implication of an ephemeral world in which nothing was stable, and longed to rid themselves of the fetters of karma which bound them to the mundane world. They sought a way of escaping from the cycle, and Shakyamuni Buddha offered them, in his exposition of the four noble truths and the eightfold path, the promise of an exit. Or, at least, he appeared to do so. What seemed like an exit from the transmigration of the Six Paths was in actuality a door leading to Buddhist truth.

Our world is itself a manifestation of the Six Paths: to try to escape from it is futile, and cannot lead to enlightenment. However, this was a matter beyond the understanding of the people and so, as an expedient, Shakyamuni at first taught that, by extinguishing both desire and life itself, people could escape from the cycle of birth and death.

Buddhism refined the concept of the Six Paths, explaining that they exist not only as external worlds but also as internal states. For example, Animality represents on the one hand animals or their world but, at the same time, the condition of life in which we humans are motivated solely by instinctive

9

desires. Summarizing this view of the Six Paths, the medieval Japanese Buddhist master Nichiren Daishonin (1222-1282), of whom more will be said later, writes:

> When we look from time to time at a person's face, we find him sometimes joyful, sometimes enraged, and sometimes calm. At times greed appears in the person's face, at times foolishness, and at times perversity. Rage is the world of Hell, greed is that of Hunger, foolishness is that of Animality, perversity is that of Anger, joy is that of Rapture [or Heaven], and calmness is that of Humanity.[1]

As long as we dwell among the Six Paths we are largely controlled by the changing circumstances of our environment. However, if in the midst of transmigration among the Six Paths we can achieve the requisite wisdom and insight to comprehend the true nature of our own lives, we can manifest the life of Buddhahood – the supreme jewel in the depths of our being. To do this we have to enhance our wisdom and make strenuous efforts to gain access to a higher condition of life, one that transcends the six lower worlds. Buddhism identifies three further worlds between the six lower ones and the condition of Buddhahood: these are called Learning, Realization and Bodhisattva.

The state of Learning is a condition in which, through learning and study, we awaken to the impermanence of all things. The state of Realization is a condition in which we perceive the impermanence of all things through our own observation of natural phenomena, such as the fading and shrivelling of flowers or fallen leaves. The state of Bodhisattva is a condition in which, through compassion, we devote ourselves to helping others, performing altruistic actions on their behalf. Concerning these three conditions, the Daishonin states:

> The fact that all things in this world are transient is perfectly clear to us. Is this not because the worlds of the two vehicles [Learning and Realization] are present in the world of Humanity? Even a heartless villain loves his wife and children. He too has a portion of the Bodhisattva world within him.[2]

10

The Tenth World

If we add the three higher states of life to the lower six we have, obviously, nine different conditions, ranging from Hell to Bodhisattva. These are called the Nine Worlds, and they constitute the varying conditions of common mortals. Beyond these Nine Worlds, which are innate in all common mortals, there lies the highest state of life, embodying the four enlightened virtues of eternity, happiness, true self and purity. This is Buddhahood. However, this state exists only as a potential in people's lives unless they develop it through the *practice* of Buddhism. When we manifest this great potential the nine life conditions of common mortals are not extinguished, as was traditionally thought, but, instead, all fall under the influence of Buddhahood. In this way the nine life conditions all contribute simultaneously, in their various ways, to the construction of happiness for ourselves and others.

Buddhahood is, in short, the condition of absolute and indestructible happiness. By contrast to this, "normal" happiness is really only relative happiness: wealth instead of poverty, health instead of sickness and peace instead of conflict are all examples of relative, not absolute, happiness. That is, relative happiness depends on necessary conditions. The moment one of these conditions disappears, our happiness is shattered; and, if the loss is a serious one, we experience despair. So, no matter how fully we may be endowed with such things as wealth, financial security, a happy family and a good job, such happiness can in no way be regarded as everlasting. Moreover, even the fact that we are well off in this sense, because it is subject to comparison with the conditions of others, can be a cause of envy or jealousy and so in itself lead to unhappiness. Such finiteness and uncertainty are inherent in mundane happiness and characterize life in this world.

By contrast with such fleeting, relative happiness, the absolute happiness of Buddhahood is unaffected by circumstantial changes or difficulties. In other words, although absolute happiness does not imply freedom from sufferings and problems, it does indicate possession of a

11

vibrant, sturdy life force and the abundant wisdom to challenge and overcome all the sufferings and difficulties that we may encounter. If we make such a condition our own we can lead our lives with unassailable confidence. Buddhahood is also furnished with a deep compassion for others and an inexhaustible merit, both of which dignify our lives. That is, all of the elements that enable us to lead truly humane lives are contained in the state of Buddhahood.

To reveal and embody such a supreme state of life is called "attaining" Buddhahood, and is the ultimate goal of Buddhist practice. Even so, aiming solely at our own enlightenment is not in accord with either the way or the spirit of Buddhism. Mahayana Buddhism expounds the importance of teaching and encouraging other people to seek enlightenment and of devoting ourselves, in unity with others, to Buddhist practice. That is, we should practise both for ourselves and for others: these two facets of Buddhist practice are each as necessary to each other as the two wings of a bird. In view of this principle, our efforts to improve society and the environment are a natural reflection of our internal efforts to attain Buddhahood. In the Buddhist view, life and its environment are fundamentally one, or inseparable. Thus, while Buddhists are trying to attain their own individual enlightenment, they are at the same time striving constantly to bring peace and prosperity to their respective societies and countries – indeed, to the world as a whole. To establish lasting peace and prosperity throughout the world is the underlying purpose behind the spreading of Buddhism throughout society.

Manifesting one's inherent Buddha nature, then, provides the fundamental solution not only to the four universal sufferings of birth, sickness, old age and death but also, more broadly, to all other sufferings too.

Nam-myoho-renge-kyo
Nichiren Daishonin writes:

> The four faces [of the Treasure Tower] represent the four sufferings of birth, old age, sickness and death. These four aspects of life dignify the tower of our individual lives. By

12

chanting *Nam-myoho-renge-kyo* through birth, old age, sickness and death, the fragrances of the four virtues [eternity, happiness, true self and purity] are made to issue forth [from our lives].[3]

The Treasure Tower, an image that appears in the Lotus Sutra, is a huge tower adorned with seven kinds of gems. It represents the solemn dignity of human life, and stands as a symbol of the lives of those who manifest their inherent Buddhahood. As the Daishonin states, by chanting *Nam-myoho-renge-kyo* we can transform the four sufferings into the four virtues emanating from the depths of our being.

Nam-myoho-renge-kyo, as we shall discuss later, indicates the ultimate Law of life and the Universe, and hence constitutes the cause for all beings to become enlightened. More specifically, *nam* is an expression of devotion, and *Myoho-renge-kyo*, the title of the Lotus Sutra, is used as a name for the ultimate reality. The Daishonin interprets the Lotus Sutra in its entirety as dedicated to the clarification of the Law of *Myoho-renge-kyo*. Such principles as that earthly desires are themselves enlightenment and that the sufferings of birth and death are themselves nirvana, as well as the doctrine of the Ten Worlds and their mutual possession (i.e., that each of the Ten Worlds contains within itself the potential for all the other nine), are all based on the teachings revealed in the Lotus Sutra, which is thus a work of central importance to the whole of Buddhism.

All the teachings expounded by Shakyamuni are recorded in the form of sutras. The number of sutras is enormous, and for this reason they are often referred to collectively as the eighty-four thousand teachings. Each sutra was taught to a particular disciple or group of disciples for a specific purpose. But the Lotus Sutra alone contains the full, perfect revelation of Shakyamuni's enlightenment. In view of this sutra's unique position, then, all the other teachings can be understood on the one hand as only partial revelations of the ultimate truth to which Shakyamuni was enlightened, and on the other as preparations for the exposition of the Lotus Sutra.

This unique sutra denies that Shakyamuni Buddha attained enlightenment for the first time during his lifetime as Siddhartha in India in the sixth century BC. Instead, it reveals, he had actually been the Buddha since the inconceivably remote past. This teaching points to the truth that Buddhahood has existed eternally in the lives of all people; in other words, to attain Buddhahood does not require us to become in any way extraordinary beings, merely to make the effort to manifest the Buddha nature latent in the depths of our lives.

The ultimate purpose of Buddhism is to enable all human beings to realize the true nature of life. This truth, although it is alluded to in many of the sutras, cannot be fully revealed in words. Shakyamuni Buddha himself realized it not through words but by devoting himself to many kinds of practice, and finally by engaging in meditation under what is now called the Bo, or Bodhi, Tree. However, even before he attained enlightenment, both the ultimate truth and the wisdom to perceive it were present within his own life: what he did was to bring them forth, thereby breaking free from the fetters of desire and illusion. When he tried to convey this truth to other people he found it impossible to do so completely through the medium of words. So, as he expounded his teachings, he helped his disciples fully understand them by prescribing various types of practice; likewise, we today can attain enlightenment only by assiduously devoting ourselves to Buddhist practice. For this reason, both practice and study are equally indispensable: it is impossible to attain enlightenment either by practising meditation alone or by studying the Buddhist teachings alone, because both are necessary.

In the Lotus Sutra Shakyamuni expounded the ultimate truth of life. However, although he used thousands of words to describe it, there is no single word or phrase that can be used clearly to define it. Shakyamuni expected that his disciples and his future followers would realize this truth through devotion to the practices he had prescribed. However, these require tremendous patience and effort, a fact which in turn demands that one place complete belief and trust in the Buddha and in his teachings. But for a person to follow this path involves renunciation of secular life and the devotion of all of his or her time to Buddhist practice. For this reason, for centuries the only people able fully to engage themselves in Buddhist practice were monks, priests and nuns. Lay believers supported them financially and materially, thereby accumulating much good karma for themselves, but for the most part did not hope to attain enlightenment in their present existence.

The ultimate truth expounded in the Lotus Sutra was crystallized in universally accessible form by Nichiren Daishonin, the great Buddhist master of medieval Japan. The orthodox tradition emanating from him is called Nichiren Shoshu; it is this stream of Buddhism that our lay organization, the Soka Gakkai, exists to propagate. The Daishonin in effect opened the way for all people to attain enlightenment, or Buddhahood. He made this possible by clarifying in words the ultimate truth of life, in the form of the Law of *Nam-myoho-renge-kyo*. This phrase incorporates the two essential aspects of Buddhism: one is the truth itself, and the other is the practice to develop the wisdom to realize that truth. The Daishonin taught his followers to believe in the truth expressed by the phrase *Nam-myoho-renge-kyo*, and to chant it. *Nam-myoho-renge-kyo* thus represents the goal of our practice – and the goal of Shakyamuni and all the other Buddhas as well – and at the same time it is our means of achieving that goal. This dual nature of the phrase also typifies the simultaneity of cause and effect. The cause is our practice; the effect, the goal of Buddhahood. Looked at another way, the cause implies the Nine Worlds or the life of the common mortal before he or she attains Buddhahood, while the effect implies Buddhahood itself, the highest of the Ten Worlds. Thus the effect of Buddhahood lies latent and undeveloped in the cause of the Nine Worlds. So, when people in an unenlightened state practise the teaching of *Nam-myoho-renge-kyo* with faith, they are simultaneously manifesting the condition of Buddhahood. As their faith deepens and their practice strengthens, so their enlightenment is developed to a greater extent.

It is not my purpose in this book to explain the differences between the teachings of Shakyamuni Buddha and Nichiren Daishonin. Indeed, my basic premise is that both were enlightened to the same truth, and that their teachings differed only because of the differences in the times in which they lived, their audiences, the cultures in which they operated, and other elements. Their enlightenment is truly universal in that all of humanity can share in it through carrying out the correct practice of Buddhism. Suffice it to say that the teachings of Nichiren Daishonin contain the essence of all of the teachings of Buddhism; however, these various teachings were first expounded by Shakyamuni and later expanded upon by his successors. It is for this reason that in this book I refer to the teachings of Shakyamuni, Nichiren Daishonin, Nagarjuna, T'ien-t'ai and other Buddhist scholars.

My overall hope, however, is that, through examining the true nature of life from the viewpoint of Buddhism, I can shed light on the fundamental problems of existence and the path to their solution.

References

[1] *The Major Writings of Nichiren Daishonin*, vol. 1, page 52.
[2] Ibid., pages 52-3.
[3] *Nichiren Daishonin Gosho Zenshu*, page 740.

1

The Beauty of Birth:
The Promise It Holds

In this chapter we shall look at how Buddhism views birth.

The nineteenth chapter of the Lotus Sutra contains the statement, "In comfort they shall bear a happy child", indicating that devout believers will, in answer to their prayers, be blessed with a child who possesses a pure, immaculate life and good fortune. Indeed, among all the different peoples of the world, the successful birth of a child is usually an occasion for celebration. In some cultures the baby is bathed immediately after its birth and then placed briefly on the ground before being picked up again. This probably symbolizes the widespread belief that new lives well forth from the Earth, for the idea of Mother Earth is prevalent in both East and West. An old tale traditionally told to children in the West has it that storks are qualified to deliver human babies because they treat their own young with the tenderest affection. This tale, although of course very few people believe in it any longer, is still widely treasured, signifying that every parent powerfully desires a healthy and beautiful child.

In 1271 Shijo Kingo, one of Nichiren Daishonin's leading lay followers, and his wife had their first child, and immediately reported this news to the Daishonin. In his response, the Daishonin congratulated the couple and said: "The fulfilment of your wish [to have a child] is now complete, just like the tide at the high water mark or the blossoming of flowers in a spring meadow."[1] In one of the Daishonin's treatises we find: "When springtime comes, awakened by its winds and rains, the grasses and trees, though they have no mind, send forth buds, then blossom and flourish, thus gratifying the world."[2] As this passage suggests, "birth" may be understood as a much anticipated

17

event in which life wells forth vigorously, refreshing us with the vibrant pulse and rhythm of newly born existence. In another writing, the Daishonin considers the subject of birth from a more profound standpoint. Regarding the Bodhisattvas Emerging from the Earth he teaches, " 'From the Earth' denotes the place in which the seed of Buddhahood of the living beings of the Ten Worlds is born. 'Emerging' refers to the living beings of the Ten Worlds coming out from the mother's womb."[3]

However, the ultimate source of the life of all living beings is what we can call the "Earth of life", or the life of the Cosmos. When the necessary conditions are satisfied, through the workings of various internal and external causes, the "seed" for an individual life emerges from the life of the Cosmos; it then gestates within its mother's womb, is born, and grows to be an independent living being.

Buddhism teaches that there is no fixed boundary between an individual life and its environment, and the phenomenon of birth provides a good example. Being the result of a combination of causes, birth will not occur if any of its prerequisites are out of kilter. More and more, the world's scientific community is coming to accept this view, as research findings indicate strong connections between reproduction and such apparently unrelated phenomena as planetary movements, sunlight, the progression of the seasons, and other natural expressions of the workings of the Cosmos.

Seeking confirmation of this relationship between the Cosmos and conception, the Swedish scientist Svante Arrhenius (1859-1927) studied data gathered from more than ten thousand women and concluded that conception takes place more often at high tide than at any other time. He was unable to clarify any causal connection between the two phenomena, but he did find that there was a definite correlation between high tide and ovulation. Since the lifespan of the unfertilized ovum is as short as a few hours, we can assume that the probability of fertilization must be higher at this time than at others.

Taking a slightly different tack, two American scientists,

Drs W. and A. Menaker, have pointed out an apparent connection between childbirth and the cycle of the lunar phases, noting that more childbirths occur at full Moon than during any other phase. And the French-American bacteriologist Rēné Dubos has hinted at this same connection between human reproduction and the phases of the Moon:

> While the influence of the Moon on human physiology and behaviour has been part of folklore since the most ancient times, it is still poorly documented by scientific observations. Only during recent years has statistical evidence been obtained suggesting that human reproduction exhibits a lunar periodicity.[4]

Aside from the Moon and the tides, sunlight too is apparently crucial to the correct functioning of reproductive activities. On this subject, Dubos has the following to say:

> In all animal species, gonadal activity is increased by light rays reaching the retina; this effect is mediated through the anterior lobe of the pituitary. As is well known, egg production by hens can be maintained throughout the year by nocturnal illumination of the hen house ... Light plays a role in the hormonal activities of the human species just as it does in plants and animals. For example, Eskimo women are said neither to menstruate nor conceive during the long polar night; and similar statements have been made concerning Patagonian women of the Antarctic.[5]

The Oneness of Life and Environment

How many human beings can our globe accommodate? According to the latest figures obtained by Assistant Professor Naomichi Ishige of the National Museum of Ethnology, Osaka, Japan, the number is approximately three to four times the current world population of five billion – in other words, up to twenty billion. But the problems of overpopulation are already extremely serious. They must be seen in the context of various other problems, including those stemming from the individual egoistic desires of many members of humanity; but the matter of overpopulation is one of the most crucial facing us today, and the solution to it can come about only if mankind pools its collective wisdom.

Buddhism explains the relationship between human life and its environment using the concept of *esho funi*, or the oneness of life and its environment. The word *esho* is formed from the first syllables of two other words, the latter, *shoho*, denoting a living being, and the former, *eho*, denoting the environment upon which that living being depends for its life activities and for its survival. Neither *eho* nor *shoho* can exist apart from the other. Since *funi* means "two in manifestation but not two in essence", *esho funi* signifies the principle that life and its environment are simultaneously independent phenomena, on the one hand, and, on the other, fundamentally identified. In short, humanity and its environment are inseparable.

All problems concerning population and the environment must be approached from the premise that it is mankind's duty to maintain a certain harmony on our planet such that the world's natural rhythms are not disturbed. The relatively young science of ecology is likewise based on the understanding that all forms of life on Earth exist in an intricate relationship with each other, and that Man, far from being a unique creature, is an inseparable part of the overall ecosystem – the entirety of terrestrial life.

The implication of this view must be that the Earth itself is really a single, huge living organism. More than thirty years ago Josei Toda (1900-1958), the second president of the Soka Gakkai and my lifelong teacher, remarked: "The Earth itself is one living entity. And, if the necessary conditions are satisfied, individual forms of life are born from it." He considered that human life and the Earth together constituted a single living entity, to be set against the immeasurable vastness of the Cosmos. In this context, the birth of a new life is not just a matter of a baby emerging from its mother's womb: it is an event coextensive with our planet and even with the Cosmos as a whole.

That this is a fact is something which modern science has begun to confirm. Jim E. Lovelock of the UK and Lynn Margulis of the US have propounded a theory that is fairly close to Toda's idea. This theory, widely respected by scientists, has it that the Earth constitutes what may be termed a "life sphere", or biosphere. These two scientists claim that our planet, of its own accord, does its best to maintain a balance – to make necessary adjustments in such things as the chemical composition of the atmosphere and the Earth's surface temperature. Basing their argument on their own wide-ranging researches, Lovelock and Margulis have concluded that such phenomena can be explained only by regarding the entire Earth as a single living entity. They have called their hypothesis the Gaia Hypothesis, Gaia being the Greek goddess who personified the Earth.

I have spoken with several astronauts, and all of them said that observing the Earth from outer space was a dramatic spiritual experience, one that profoundly altered their perspectives. Perhaps nothing in the history of our species has altered our consciousness so radically as the first photographs of the Earth from space. Of course, by now we have seen such photographs so often that we are no longer quite as impressed, but those first photographs marked a turning-point for mankind: future historians will almost certainly regard them as symbolic of the twentieth century. Those photographs, widely used by the proponents of the abolition of nuclear weapons and the conservation of the environment, drive home to us the aptness of the term "Spaceship Earth".

We now realize how completely humanity is a part of the living entity that is the Earth; we are interdependent with the Earth to the extent that we could be regarded as symbiotic with it. Soon, humanity will realize how completely the Earth itself is part of the living entity that is the Cosmos. This conceptual leap cannot and must not be thwarted, for no one can realistically deny that the Cosmos, the Earth and living beings are intricately interrelated and, if allowed to work together, do so in perfect harmony.

Heredity and Environment
All parents want their children to be healthy and whole of limb, but of course some children are, unfortunately, born handicapped or deformed. Sadly, the incidence of

handicapped newborns is reported to be on the increase, and in many cases babies born normal develop abnormalities as they grow, so that the number of physically handicapped children in any group of newborns may double by the time the babies are one year old. In only about twenty per cent of the cases can the disability be traced to specific causes, split roughly 50:50 between hereditary problems (abnormal genes or chromosomes) and inadequacy or outright harmfulness of the environment. The remaining eighty per cent of cases are thought to result from a combination of these factors and others, but no one is as yet quite sure of the details.

Human beings normally have forty-six chromosomes arranged in twenty-three pairs. Lack of a chromosome (monosomy) or excess of a chromosome (trisomy) in one of these pairs causes physical or mental abnormality. Monosomy is linked to disorders such as Turner's syndrome, a female sexual anomaly: affected individuals are female in appearance but have no ovaries, and hence do not menstruate and cannot become pregnant. Trisomy is responsible for such disorders as Down's syndrome and Klinefelter's syndrome; in the latter disorder the person is apparently male but develops breasts, lacks bodily hair, and in general shows many female characteristics.

While *in utero* the unborn child is at the mercy of a number of factors. Viral diseases contracted by the expectant mother, especially rubella (German measles) and influenza, can cause the child to be born with cataracts, deafness and heart malformation. Diabetic mothers are prone to miscarriages or premature births, and their foetuses often have abnormally large bodies, so that delivery is difficult. Drugs taken by the mother are another danger: this first entered public awareness when it was found that the soporific drug thalidomide adversely affected the development of the foetus. Other medicaments, such as the anti-malarial drug quinine and the antibiotic streptomycin, not to mention injections of the hormones progesterone and testosterone, have been shown to create great risks for the developing foetus. Overexposure to X-rays can adversely affect the foetus's genes, as can overexposure to radioactivity. Research carried out on pregnant women who were close to the epicentres of the atomic bombs dropped on Hiroshima and Nagasaki has shown that about fifty per cent had either a stillbirth or a miscarriage. Of eleven babies in the study who were born alive, seven had abnormally small heads and proved to be mentally handicapped.

Even in its final stages of emergence into this world a foetus may encounter difficulties. As it passes through the birth canal, its neck may become entangled with the umbilical cord or its head may be compressed, so that it is born with cerebral palsy due to a deficiency of oxygen. Of fertilized ova, only about one-third grow successfully and are delivered. About one-half are miscarried due to natural causes before they can implant themselves in the uterine wall. The remaining fifty per cent are successfully implanted, but of these about one-third are miscarried before they become embryos. So fertilized ova undergo a natural selection process, with only those that survive the rigours of the pre-birth ordeal developing successfully.

Thanks to modern medicine, many foetuses that until quite recently would have certainly miscarried are nowadays able to come successfully to term. Some people say that this is the reason that the percentage of children born handicapped is on the increase; but in many cases medical science is simply baffled as to the reasons. Some of the causes probably lie far beyond the realm of medicine, in the area identified by Buddhism as karma. We shall return to this point later in this chapter.

Congenital abnormalities may be divided into two categories: those that are hereditary and those that are a result of the foetus's experience during its time in the womb – such as the abnormalities caused by rubella, which are not passed on to the next generation. Among the hereditary ailments is phenylketonuria, a congenital and recessive hereditary disease associated with a variety of mental disorders. In phenylketonuria the child's metabolism suffers from a lack of the enzyme phenylalanine, hydroxylase so that the brain fails to develop properly and/or there is a deficiency of pigment production in the skin, resulting in albinism. Today, however, many potential congenital mental disorders can be detected by examining the baby's urine and blood as soon as possible after birth, and appropriate action can be taken to prevent the potential disorder ever being realized.

Before we continue, we should briefly state precisely what we mean by the word "heredity". Heredity is the transmission of certain qualities from parents to child through genes, which are contained in chromosomes. This process occurs at the time of fertilization, or the union of the male and female gametes to form the zygote.

Birth, as we have noted, is the first of the four universal sufferings described in Buddhism. Birth is regarded in Buddhism as the beginning of everything. One of Nichiren Daishonin's writings on this subject reads: "When we trace our existence to its ultimate origin, we find that, of our father's and mother's pure blood, two drops, one white and the other red, become united to make our body."[6] It is at this moment, as the genetic material of both our parents commingles, that the basic potentials of our life are brought into being. Another of the Daishonin's writings states, "Among those who are born, there are good children and bad children, beautiful children and ugly children, tall children and short children, boys and girls."[7] No two people are born with exactly the same physical and mental characteristics or in precisely identical circumstances. However, for all of us, conception is the moment when the basic trends of our lives are established (to be reinforced during the early years of our upbringing). How exactly this comes about is one of the mysteries of life; Buddhism regards it as the inescapable working of karma.

It is worth considering whether or not our constitution, physique and character are hereditary.

Constitutional qualities – such as colour blindness (a sex-linked inheritance), the epicanthic fold, and some allergic diseases – are mainly inherited. The nature of one's earwax, too, is a matter of heredity. It is a race-linked characteristic: while the earwax of most Mongolian peoples, such as the Japanese, is dry, that of the Caucasian and

Negroid people is predominantly wet. Our tolerance to heat and cold is likewise largely a matter of heredity, although it is often influenced also by the environment in which we are raised.

It is rather harder to say if our height, weight and intelligence are determined by hereditary or environmental factors because these characteristics are the result of poly-genic inheritance; that is, they are traits determined by the workings of a combination of a great number of genes. Also, they are influenced by the childhood environment. Looking solely at the example of height, we find that our stature derives roughly thirty-five per cent from the genes of our father, thirty-five per cent from those of our mother, and thirty per cent from factors relating to our environment, such as food and exercise. Whether we become fat or not depends both on our inherited constitutional ability to metabolize fats and sugars and on environmental factors such as the type of food we eat and how much.

Is our character the result of heredity or of environment? This is an even more difficult question, and the whole subject is shrouded in controversy. Perhaps it is something that cannot really be decided one way or the other. Today, however, many people tend towards the deterministic view that an individual's nature is largely dictated by his or her genes; obviously, though, a person's character is such a complex thing that it cannot be entirely determined by hereditary factors.

There are two major schools of thought concerning the shaping of character: the "inborn" theory, which empha-sizes hereditary factors, and the "empirical" theory, which stresses environmental influences. The most reasonable assumption is probably that one's character is formed by the interaction of both. Moreover, human beings – unlike animals, whose behaviour is governed largely by instinct – are able to initiate action, another character-shaping factor which must be taken into account. Although we may wish to ascribe everything to causes such as heredity and environment that are not of our own making, it is important that we, as human beings, constantly try to change and

25

improve ourselves and to reach beyond our innate limitations. Only when we assume such a serious, positive attitude towards our own lives will we be able to enjoy the full range of our abilities as human beings, and to achieve things which otherwise we could hardly even conceive.

However much we take our own efforts into account, though, the fact still remains that our parents' characters greatly influence our own in terms of both heredity and environment. Since we inherit half of our genes from each parent, the hereditary part of our character would be a blending of those of our father and our mother. However, since so many genes are involved in transmitting information from parent to child, it would be virtually impossible to calculate which combinations were associated with which character traits. It is often said that boys take after their mothers and girls take after their fathers, but science fails to support this. In constitutional terms, however, there are some sex-linked recessive characteristics, of which the most notable is colour blindness. The daughter of a normal man and a colour-blind woman is extremely unlikely to be detectably colour-blind, but the son of such a union would almost certainly be. However, if the father is colour-blind and the mother is not, there is a 50:50 chance of each of their children, whether male or female, being colour-blind. This type of sex-linked heredity is, however, the exception rather than the rule.

And there are definitely no rules when it comes to similarity of character among siblings. Since the parents' genes are transmitted to the children, one would naturally expect there to be some points of resemblance between the children's characters. However, because of the mind-bogglingly huge number of potential gene combinations, it is likely there would be more difference than similarity in the characters of siblings.

One question often asked in connection with heredity and environment is this: What is it that makes a person a genius? Thomas Edison's response was that "genius is one per cent inspiration and ninety-nine per cent perspiration". Nevertheless, there is no denying that inborn tendencies and talents play a part in the emergence of an individual's genius. Yet these, on their own, are not sufficient to make a person a genius or to enable him or her to accomplish great feats. Rather, as Edison implied, concentration and persistence are far more important. As the old adage has it, "Persistence is power". Anyone can display immense ability if only they set themselves lofty goals and strive to attain them with a deep and lasting sense of mission.

Whatever the case, it is incontrovertible that, although we are all born into this world in similar fashion, no two of us develop in exactly the same way or in exactly the same circumstances. Some are born rich, others poor; some clever and others stupid. Why is it that people are born in such widely varying circumstances and with such equally diverse destinies? Buddhism gives a clear-cut answer, based firmly on the law of cause and effect. For example, the Sutra of Contemplation on the Ground of the Mind states:

> If you want to understand the causes that existed in the past, look at the results as they are manifested in the present. And if you want to understand what results will be manifested in the future, look at the causes that exist in the present.

As this passage implies, Buddhism does not limit its consideration of causality to the confines of this lifetime alone. Buddhism bases its view on the fact that life continues to exist eternally throughout past, present and future, and so through Buddhism we are able to perceive the profound meaning of all realities and phenomena, thereby gaining greater insight into human destiny and karma. Moreover, Buddhism gives us a guide as to how to overcome our individual destinies by changing our karma (as we shall see later on).

No one would dispute that humanity has benefited greatly from the discoveries of medical science. However, medicine tends to examine and treat only the superficial causes of life's miseries. By contrast, Buddhism devotes itself to the pursuit of profound, or ultimate, causes, so that a secure and happy future can be assured. In other words, while medical science pursues health, Buddhism seeks the purpose for which a person is born into this world, thus enabling that person to lead a life of the highest possible value. The Lotus Sutra defines this world as the place where "the people ... are happy and at ease". To be born on this Earth and to be able to enjoy every instant of living, until the last possible moment – this is the purpose of practising Buddhism.

Medical science has clarified much about the process of birth, from the instant of fertilization onwards, but recently a number of scientists in the US and Europe have advanced the theory that birth may be preceded by something far more profound than the union of the male and female gametes. For instance, some people engaged in "New Age" sciences have propounded the theory of the "holon", which has it that each part of anything possesses all the characteristics of the whole. Other scientists advocate the concept of "fluctuation", that every living organism adapts positively to its environment. The very fact that these and other related ideas are emerging in Western science shows that there is an increasing interest in delving into the ultimate nature of life. As an example, in 1984 Japanese and French "New Age" scientists held a joint symposium at Tsukuba University, in Japan. A French scholar with a solid grasp of the oriental concepts of *ch'i* (generally translated as "material energy" or "vital matter") and *reisei* ("spirituality") lectured on the *rendosei*, or interconnectedness, of life. This pinpoints what is probably the most important facet of "New Age" science, whose proponents are becoming ever more numerous and whose arguments are becoming ever more forceful: all of their theories rest on a common basis, and that is the *interconnectedness* of life.

The Buddhist Concept of Transmigration
There is something about the birth of a new life that cannot be explained simply by the union of the spermatozoon and the ovum. The process of fertilization, followed by the zygote's development based on the genetic information it has received and the environmental influences it experiences, cannot be ascribed merely to chemical or mechanical reactions. There must be something much more profound which causes life to emerge and develop.

Ever since history began, people have sensed the presence of some kind of spiritual force, the continued existence of which lies at the core of all things. In India, the concept of transmigration has been accepted since very early times, and some of the ancient Greeks, too, believed that there was something which continued on after an individual's death, something which underwent a continual cycle of birth and death. Around the seventh century BC a religion called Orphism advocated purification of the soul achieved through a cycle of reincarnation, and later, around the fifth century BC, the Pythagorean school advanced the concept of metempsychosis, or the transmigration of the soul.

Buddhism's interests probe far beyond just this lifetime. It expounds the concept that there are four stages of life: existence during birth, existence during life, existence during death and the existence during the period between death and rebirth (the "intermediate existence"). Life is understood by Buddhism to repeat the cycle of these four stages eternally.

Buddhism, as we have seen, regards birth as one of the four sufferings. For instance, the Nirvana Sutra lists two aspects of the suffering of birth: one is the suffering that accompanies first coming into existence (that is, the moment of conception) and the other is the suffering experienced on emerging from the mother's womb. The Sutra of the Path of Practice further divides this latter suffering into two: the pain one undergoes as one struggles through the birth canal, and the pain one experiences on coming into contact for the first time with things outside the mother's body. Another early Buddhist scripture says that, because individuals have to suffer these terrible pains in order to be born, they lose all memories of their past existences.

The *Record of the Orally Transmitted Teachings* states that "the world of Treasure Purity refers to our mother's womb".[8] It elsewhere reads:

With regard to the Buddha in the world of Treasure Purity: When one sets aside the literal meaning of the sutra's words and interprets it from the viewpoint of inner enlightenment, then the world of Treasure Purity is one's mother's womb. One's parents are therefore the carpenters who build the Treasure Tower. The Treasure Tower refers to the five wheels or five elements that compose our bodies.... Because it is the world of Treasure Purity of the Mystic Law, the wombs of all living beings of the Ten Worlds are without exception the world of Treasure Purity.[9]

The "world of Treasure Purity", where the Buddha Taho is said to dwell, denotes neither some special land nor some idealistic world. No treasure is more valuable than life. Therefore the mother's womb, in which life takes form and from which it is born, is itself this most sacred world of Treasure Purity.

Buddhism teaches that everything born must inevitably die, and describes the phase of existence between birth and death as "temporary existence". It goes further, identifying the immortal core of life – which causes such phenomena as birth to take place – with each individual's eternally continuing existence. This continuing existence is called the "true existence", as distinct from the "temporary existence".

All forms of life enact the drama of birth. Mammals, including human beings, are born from their mothers' wombs. Birds, fishes and insects hatch from eggs. Stars appear in space, born from clouds of gas and dust. Fields turn barren in winter, but in spring they blossom into expanses of greenery textured by flowering plants. And, though their lifespans vary, all forms of life eventually die. What is it that directs this profound, mystic drama of life?

Before we can answer this question we must first consider the relationship between life on our planet and that of the myriad heavenly bodies that twinkle in the night sky. They are born of outer space, which means that the Universe itself was the womb to those stars. The Universe itself, then, possesses the power, ability and compassion to give birth to countless celestial bodies, including galaxies at one extreme and the planet upon which we live at the other. Buddhism teaches that this is the case, and identifies the dimension of the Universe that has life-giving ability as the "true existence".

Turning from the macrocosm to the microcosm, from the Universe as a whole to the individual human being, we can assert that, given the optimum environment of the mother's womb, the *individual's life itself* is ultimately responsible for the great accomplishment of birth.

Life, in all its forms and at all times, contains within itself the urge to create, is inherently active, and possesses the positive power of self-regeneration. Indeed, life has a grand and eternal pulse that constantly seeks to make itself felt throughout the entire Universe. The Great Teacher Miao-lo of the T'ien-t'ai school of Buddhism in China declared that "our life pervades the entire Universe both physically and spiritually". The power and functions that work within life to promote its self-manifestation can be called "internal causes". Buddhism tells us that internal causes interact and harmonize with various external causes – in this case, conception within the womb – in order to bring about birth. Western medical science generally considers that the spermatozoon and the ovum are the sole essentials for conception, maintaining that only the fertilization of the female gamete is a necessary prerequisite. By contrast, the Buddhist view is that not only the spermatozoon and ovum but also life itself, in the state of "intermediate existence", are each necessary for human life to come into being and develop. Conception is the result of the union of all three.

Concerning birth, the Sutra of the Great Cluster of Jewels contains the following:

> I will next tell you, Ananda, how a new life is able to enter the mother's womb. If the father and mother have an urge to make love, the menstrual cycle is regular, and life in the state of intermediate existence is present, and provided the above-mentioned numerous troubles are absent and there is a correspondence between karma [internal cause] and external cause, then a new life is able to enter the mother's womb.[10]

This passage may need some explanation. It lists three conditions as essential if conception is to occur: first, that the father and mother wish to make love; second, that the menstrual cycle is regular; and, third, that life – in the state of intermediate existence – is present. Furthermore, if these three are to come together properly, it is necessary that there be no diseases or deficiencies that might impede conception, and that a correspondence exists between the karma, which is stored in the *alaya*-consciousness (see page 161) of life in the state of intermediate existence, and the external cause, provided by the father and the mother. On this subject the *Great Commentary on the Abhidharma* notes: "The union of the three factors means the coming together of father, mother and life in the stage of intermediate existence." Nichiren Daishonin, in his "Letter from Sado", states, "My body, while outwardly human, is fundamentally that of an animal, which once subsisted on fish and fowl and was conceived of the male and female fluids. My spirit dwells in this body ..."[11]

These two passages can be explained in terms of modern biology. The "male fluid" denotes the spermatozoon and the "female fluid" the ovum. The "three factors" are the spermatozoon, ovum, and life in the intermediate-existence stage. To turn this around, we can say that it is life in the intermediate-existence stage that plays the central role in conception, while the male and female gametes, which carry the genetic coding, have only an auxiliary role.

Changing Karma
A 1984 US news article related the heartrending tale of an elderly couple in Connecticut who finally came to the conclusion that their forty-two-year-old daughter, who had been on a life-support system for decades, should be allowed to die. At only seventeen she had contracted an incurable disease, multiple cerebrospinal sclerosis, and ever since then she had been bedridden. About three months before her parents made their sad decision, she had fallen into a coma, and a group of medical experts had pronounced that she could never recover. Her parents went to court to plead that their daughter be given the "right to die", and were given permission to instruct that the life-support system be switched off. In this way, they felt they had enabled their daughter, for whom they had cared for a quarter of a century, to die with dignity.

What excruciating grief and agony the parents must have suffered as they came to their decision. As I read this story, I felt as though I were a witness to the karmic suffering of the whole of humanity – something medicine cannot cure nor law redress. In Buddhist terms, the daughter's incurable disease would be classified as an "illness resulting from karma formed in previous existences".

"Karma" means action; it is also the generic term for the effects that result from our actions: the deeds we perform, the words we utter and the thoughts we have. Each of these physical, verbal and mental actions produces a latent effect on our lives: each is a cause that can produce some effect or other at a later date. Thus karma simultaneously denotes both the effect and the cause of the variety of things we think and speak about and do in our everyday lives – good and evil, light and heavy, shallow and profound. Buddhism considers karma to have diverse aspects, and accordingly divides it into a number of categories. Chief among these are good karma, evil karma, present karma, past karma, mutable karma, immutable karma, karma to be manifested in the present life, karma to be manifested in the next life, and karma to be manifested upon rebirth sometime in the remote future. Let us look briefly at each of these different types.

The term "good karma" indicates actions born from good intentions, kindness and compassion. When we talk of "evil karma" we refer to actions induced by earthly desires such as greed, anger and stupidity. *A Treasury of Analyses of the Law* and other treatises in the Buddhist tradition divide the causes of evil karma into ten evil acts: the three physical evils of killing, stealing, and unlawful sexual intercourse; the four verbal evils of lying, flattery (or random and irresponsible speech), defamation, and duplicity; and the three mental evils of greed, anger, and stupidity (or the holding of mistaken views). "Present karma" is karma that one has made and whose effects will appear in the present life. "Past karma" is karma formed in previous existences. "Immutable karma" is karma that produces a fixed result, whereas, by contrast, "mutable karma" is karma whose result is not absolutely fixed, and whose effect is not set to appear at a predetermined time.

Moreover, karma formed in this lifetime is further classified into three types according to the period required for the manifestation of karmic retribution. As you might expect, "karma to be manifested in the present life" is karma whose results appear during this lifetime. "Karma to be manifested in the next life" is karma whose result will be realized in our next existence. "Karma to be manifested upon rebirth sometime in the remote future" is karma whose effect will appear in a lifetime beyond the next.

As we have noted, Buddhism considers all our actions in terms of the cause-and-effect relationship. For example, some people study hard and, as a result, successfully pass difficult examinations. Others do things that benefit the local community and as a result are given awards or decorations. By contrast, other people indulge in an unwholesome way of living and so ruin their health. In all of these examples one can see the causal law at work; they are all categorized as present karma – karma that is relatively light and shallow.

By contrast, it is almost impossible for us human beings to perceive those karmic causes that are engraved in the depths of our lives – in our *alaya*-consciousnesses. However, Buddhism, working from the standpoint that life continues to exist eternally throughout past, present and future, is able clearly to pinpoint the strictness of the law of causality that governs the karmic causes and effects that are stored in the depths of our lives.

There will be no major problems if the karma one forms is good, or even if one's bad karma is light or shallow, but some karma is so heavy, so profoundly imprinted in the depths of one's life (*alaya*-consciousness), that one cannot easily alter it. For instance, suppose someone deliberately makes another person extremely unhappy or even causes his or her death. The guilty party may manage to escape apparent accountability or, conversely, may be arrested and dealt with according to the law. Either way, the person has created heavy evil karma. This evil karma will surely lead, according to the strict law of causality, to a karmic suffering

34

of extreme misery that is far beyond our ordinary powers to eradicate.

We have said several times that Buddhism teaches that life exists eternally – through past, present and future. This accounts for the existence of past karma – karma amassed in prior lifetimes. Past karma resides within our *alaya*-consciousness and, when activated by the moment-to-moment realities of this lifetime, moulds and shapes our lives strictly according to its dictates.

Buddhist scriptures explain the law of causality as it works in the lives of human beings from a variety of viewpoints. For example, as we noted earlier, the Sutra of Contemplation on the Ground of the Mind states:

> If you want to understand the causes that existed in the past, look at the results as they are manifested in the present. And if you want to understand what results will be manifested in the future, look at the causes that exist in the present.

In similar vein, the Parinirvana Sutra reads:

> Men of devout faith, because you have committed countless sins and accumulated much evil karma in the past, you must expect to suffer retribution for everything you have done. You may be reviled, cursed with an ugly appearance, be poorly clad and poorly fed, seek wealth in vain, be born to an impoverished or heretical family, or be persecuted by your sovereign.[12]

In light of the doctrine of karmic causality the view that a person's happiness or unhappiness is determined either by other people or by the person's environment is superficial. Some people believe that our individual destinies are predetermined by a transcendent being, but this notion negates the individual's independence. Buddhism, by contrast, teaches that the fundamental cause of one's happiness or unhappiness is to be found nowhere else but within that person.

Character traits are often shared by parent and child or between siblings. These resemblances can be considered as representative of the Buddhist concept of *kenzoku* – which translates literally as "relatives and followers". There are several aspects to this concept, and all of them are profound. T'ien-t'ai's *Profound Meaning of the Lotus Sutra* tells us why *kenzoku* has its name: "They are called relatives because they are by nature affectionate towards one another, and they are also called followers because they follow and obey one another." To say that they are "by nature affectionate" is to indicate that they are inherently similar in their basic tendencies; to say that they "follow and obey one another" means that they are connected to and associate with each other. However, although these resemblances obviously exist, siblings never have exactly the same character as each other or as their parents.

Why does a child on the one hand take after its parents and on the other differ in both character and appearance from all the other members of his or her family? Gregor Mendel gave a partial answer to this question when his experiments in cross-breeding dwarf pea plants led him to propose the basic laws of heredity in papers published in the 1860s (which were then widely ignored). Further studies in the field of genetics, especially since de Vries "discovered" Mendel's papers in the early part of this century, have led scientists to believe that genes play the central role in the manifestation of inherited characteristics, enabling hereditary information to be passed on from parent to child at the moment of fertilization, as male and female gametes fuse.

So far so good, but what exactly is the mechanism whereby a particular set is selected from among the millions of possible genetic codes, and then transmitted from parent to child? Modern geneticists have little to say on this subject: their only response is that random chance determines the exact selection of a person's genes. But Buddhism offers an answer to the question. Life in the stage of intermediate existence "selects" parents compatible with the karma stored in that life's own *alaya*-consciousness; moreover, it even participates in the selection and transmission of genetic codes so that they may be suited to its own karma. To put it another way, karma stored in the *alaya*-consciousness of life in the intermediate existence acts as the internal cause, while the parents' genetic codes, carried by their gametes, act as external causes. It is the combination of the internal and the external causes that initiates a new human life. Therefore, siblings of the same parents inherit different sets of genetic codes according to the karma stored in their lives in the intermediate existence phase. We see differences of character, predisposition, constitution and all sorts of other qualities among brothers and sisters, and a viable explanation for this is that the children have already accumulated differing karma in their prior lives.

As we have seen, Buddhism teaches that the karma we have accumulated in the past helps mould our present. This might lead us to ask a fairly fundamental question: Is it, therefore, meaningless for us to strive to accomplish something worthwhile or to improve ourselves? The answer, fortunately, is "no", for our deeds in the present will in turn shape our future. The concept of karma is nothing like the Western philosophical notion of determinism. On the contrary, Buddhism clarifies the Law which enables us to perceive the meaning of our own individual karma and, using the sufferings and anguish derived from that karma as a springboard, to change not only ourselves but also society and the world as a whole for the better.

Generally speaking, animals are not creative, but human beings are – indeed, this is an important distinction between humanity and most of the rest of the animal kingdom. So the very fact that we have been born as human beings indicates that we have the potential to alter the course of our lives, no matter how tainted by evil karma, so that they are filled with good karma. This, I think, is the essence of individual human independence.

Buddhism states that humanity's grief and distress, which even the greatest effort on the individual's part cannot relieve, are due to karmic suffering – that is, suffering derived from karmic causes, which themselves are a product of the workings of earthly desires. But Buddhism, in addition, clearly expounds how a person's life is endowed with a pure and powerful "self", which channels earthly desires to work towards the person's good and happiness.

This principle is one of the many teachings derived from the Lotus Sutra, but it is only in Nichiren Daishonin's teaching, which embodies the essence of Buddhism, that a practical approach to this doctrine is revealed. Thus it is by practising the Daishonin's Buddhism that we are able to actualize such Buddhist principles as "earthly desires are enlightenment" and "fundamental darkness is fundamental enlightenment", and thereby to change our karma for the better.

References

[1] *The Major Writings of Nichiren Daishonin*, vol. 3, page 39.
[2] *Nichiren Daishonin Gosho Zenshu*, page 574.
[3] Ibid., page 799.
[4] René Dubos, *Man Adapting*, page 47.
[5] Ibid., pages 49-51.
[6] *Nichiren Daishonin Gosho Zenshu*, page 983.
[7] Ibid., page 841.
[8] Ibid., page 740.
[9] Ibid., page 797.
[10] *Taisho Shinshu Daizokyo*, vol. 11, page 322.
[11] *The Major Writings of Nichiren Daishonin*, vol. 1, page 37.
[12] *Taisho Shinshu Daizokyo*, vol. 16, page 231.

2

Longevity: A Life of Value

All of us endure the trauma of birth. If we are fortunate, we develop to maturity, but then we experience the myriad of changes that together constitute the process of ageing. Our physical energy gradually ebbs.

In the past the elderly, with their wealth of experience, were the people chiefly responsible for imparting knowledge and tradition to the community, and so they were treated with great respect. But today, now that speed and efficiency are valued above tradition and time-honoured ways, the elderly are to a great extent excluded from the mainstream of society, their presence often being viewed more as a burden than an asset.

In these terms, it is hardly surprising that the vast majority of us resent the fact that we must grow old, and do everything in our power to forestall the ageing process. Whereas, formerly, people used simply to accept the inevitability of ageing, today many of us simply refuse to reconcile ourselves to the fact that we are growing older, every single second. Our body weakens, our skin wrinkles and sags, our senses dull, our desire to live may wane ... the catalogue is endless. Worse still, we may suffer from degenerative diseases such as cancer, atherosclerosis, high blood pressure and senile dementia. Even if we remain healthy, the longer we live the closer we approach the moment of death.

The problem of ageing requires more attention now than it used to, simply because the percentage of elderly people in most societies is higher than ever before – a trend which is expected to continue. Even as recently as the year 1900, common people in the developed countries were regarded as fortunate if they lived to be 50: the elderly were few, and were treated with respect. But things have changed radically. In Japan, for example, according to estimates produced by the Population Research Institute of Nihon University, by the year 2021 one-quarter of the population will be over 65 years old. Moreover, the percentage of elderly people in their late seventies and eighties will be significantly higher than it is today, as will be the number of elderly widows, the number of bedridden, and the number of senile people. The same picture can be extrapolated to other developed countries. Unless something is done *now*, this demographic change is going to create serious problems.

"In spite of the vast body of knowledge in gerontology," writes Diana S. Woodruff of the Ethel Percy Andrus Gerontology Center, University of Southern California, "we as investigators feel that we are only beginning to scratch the surface in understanding ageing. This feeling is most painfully apparent when we look at the plight of a large percentage of the old people in our society."[1]

The problems of ageing can be properly understood only if we approach them from a multiplicity of angles – biological, psychological and sociological. Biologists and physicians work to counter or even eliminate the degenerative diseases, their target being the extension of the healthy human lifespan to 110 years or even more. Psychologists attempt to alleviate the wide variety of depressive illnesses that commonly afflict the elderly. Social gerontologists work to make people's old age as comfortable and pleasant as possible. However, all of these endeavours are less than fully effective if they are not carried out in conjunction with each other. Although the various symptoms of ageing appear separately in terms of the biological, psychological and social well-being of the individual, there is generally an interaction among these various components. Therefore, if we are to find solutions to the many problems of ageing, we need the cooperation of scientists from a number of different disciplines.

Theories of Ageing
The process which we describe as "ageing" continues throughout the entire adult lifespan, and is really a combination of a number of different progressive changes

that occur over time. The primary goal of research into ageing – the science of gerontology – is to identify the factors that influence the changes which occur in our bodies between our attainment of maturity and our eventual death. Application of the discoveries of the gerontologists will, it is hoped, help medical science ameliorate or even obviate many of the disabilities currently associated with the ageing process.

Theories of ageing fall into two basic categories: genetic and nongenetic.

Genetic theories suggest that the ageing of the individual is really a sort of "planned obsolescence". Ageing, according to this type of theory, involves "ageing clocks", which cause a genetically determined sequence of alterations and shutdowns in various body systems, with the result that there is an overall physiological decline. Nongenetic theories suggest rather that there are "ageing events", which may be characterized as random or accidental; these random ageing events contribute to cumulative damage.

One of the genetic theories assumes that the lifespan of a cell or organism is genetically determined – that the genes of an animal contain some sort of a "programme" which determines its lifespan. Longevity is, therefore, recognized as a familial characteristic. Selective breeding of animals can produce long-lived (or, for that matter, short-lived) strains, which would seem to support this theory. Another of the genetic theories, although it has yet to receive adequate experimental underpinning, has it that cell death results from the introduction of errors during the chemical formation of certain key proteins, such as the enzymes that make possible the vital metabolic functions. The instructions necessary if enzymic molecules are to form correctly come from the DNA of the chromosomes, *via* RNA; this theory holds that slight, accidental distortions of the correct genetic information lead to the formation of malfunctioning enzymic molecules. A third genetic theory – the somatic mutation theory – assumes that ageing is the result of a gradual accumulation of mutated cells that fail to perform normally.

Nongenetic theories of ageing focus on factors that can

41

influence the expression of a genetically determined programme. For example, what we can loosely call the "wear and tear" theory suggests that animals and cells, like machines, simply wear out through frequent use over protracted periods of time. This theory assumes that waste products accumulate within cells and interfere with their functioning. The accumulation of highly insoluble material – "age pigment" – has in fact been observed in the muscle and nerve cells of human beings and other animals.

Another nongenetic theory concerns cross-linking. As we grow older, our tendons, skin and blood vessels lose their elasticity. This is due to the formation of cross-links between the long molecules of collagen (a fibrous protein) that give these tissues their elasticity: the linkages formed between the molecules inhibit their ability to stretch and contract. That this happens is beyond doubt; what the "cross-linking theory" proposes is that similar linkages are formed between or within other biologically important molecules, such as the body's enzymes. This could alter their shape – they would, in effect, tie themselves up in knots – so that they become unable to perform their functions within the cell.

Yet another nongenetic theory concentrates on the autoimmune system. It suggests that immune reactions, normally directed by the body against disease-producing organisms and foreign proteins and tissues (hence the difficulties of rejection experienced by transplant patients), begin to malfunction, attacking the healthy cells of the individual's own body. In other words, the autoimmune system, as the person ages, loses its ability to distinguish between "self" and foreign intruders.

All of these theories describe different aspects of the ageing process but, as in the famous tale of the blind men and the elephant, do so only in a piecemeal fashion. However, thanks to recent advances in gerontological research, theories are currently emerging that can account for whole spectra of ageing changes. One such is the free-radical theory put forward by Denham Harman of the University of Nebraska College of Medicine. Free radicals are extremely reactive molecules, present in vast numbers in the atmosphere, created by high-energy radiation; they can also be formed in our bodies by chemical reactions. These molecules – some of which are necessary participants in certain metabolic processes – are controlled by our enzymes. If our bodies were not equipped with protective mechanisms, the free radicals would soon kill us: in order to survive, all life-forms must be able to produce the requisite enzymes in order to control the activities of the free radicals. However, free radicals are present almost everywhere and so, despite our bodies' ability to control them, a few escape detection and cause damage. This damage, obviously, accumulates over the years. For example, DNA mutation brought on by free radicals is thought to be a major cause of cancer. If free radicals destroy the body's ability to produce the anticlot hormone found in healthy, youthful arteries, we suffer from the formation of clots (thromboses) in the arteries; for similar reasons, it seems that free radicals play a large part in arthritis. And it is known that free radicals are a major perpetrator of cross-linking, and produce accumulations of age pigment that slowly choke brain cells to death and cause the brownish liver-spots so often seen on the skin of elderly people.

All of these theories, even the ones that explain a diversity of aspects of the ageing process, cannot account for the syndrome as a whole. And, however much people may claim that youth can be prolonged using strategies based on one theory or another, there is in reality no proven way to completely hold off the ageing process. It seems, in fact, that ageing is to a large degree a predetermined process.

As we grow older our internal organs slowly atrophy and our joints become less supple, but these are not serious problems in themselves: even in old age we possess the inherent life force to repair the injured parts of our bodies, and there is no reason, even in old age, why we should not continue to exercise in order to maintain our physical well-being. If we suffer from a serious disease in our later years, we may be tempted to avoid using our bodies and minds quite so actively as before, even after we have recovered our health; but this in fact only weakens us. We should not have to restrict our activities simply because the years are ticking by.

One reason why this is true is that there are many differences among people at any particular age – especially when they are older. Indeed, people are far more alike when they are seven months old than when they are in their seventies: some look younger than their age and others look older. In 1970 I formed a group with some friends who were all born in the same year as myself. Every time I attend a meeting of this group I notice afresh that the people whose eyes shine look younger than they really are. This observation tells me two things. First, the calendar is not the ultimate measure of a person's age: physiological, psychological and spiritual factors all play their parts. Second, the shining eyes of an elderly person indicate his or her spiritual strength and, consequentially, physical strength. To sum up, although ageing is a real and inescapable process, the rate of ageing varies widely from one person to the next.

Old Age and the Development of Intelligence
In 1984 the *New York Times* published an article about research findings by a group of scientists under the headline: THE AGING MIND PROVES CAPABLE OF LIFE-LONG GROWTH. My curiosity was aroused by this, because my own motto is "Be ever youthful". The article concluded that, in terms of the mind, ageing brings about development in some areas and decline in others. While "fluid intelligence" decreases, "crystallized intelligence" gradually rises. "Fluid intelligence" is defined as "a set of abilities involved in seeing and using abstract relationships and patterns": this flexibility of thinking is used, for example, in playing chess. "Crystallized intelligence", on the other hand, means

> the ability to use an accumulated body of general information to make judgements and solve problems. In practical terms, crystallized intelligence comes into play in understanding the arguments made in newspaper editorials, or dealing with problems for which there are no clear answers, but only better and worse options.[2]

In order to explain the deterioration of certain of our mental capacities, some scientists have hypothesized that, after we reach the age of 20, every day about one hundred thousand of our brain cells die. However, Marian Diamond, a neuroanatomist at the University of California at Berkeley, tried to track down the facts underlying this hypothesis and was startled to find that she was unsuccessful. Her research, one of the few studies ever made directly to assess cell-loss rates as the brain ages, came to the conclusion that "while there is some cell loss, the greatest decrease is early in life and subsequent losses are not significant, even late into life".

It would appear that there is no scientific basis for the supposition that our grip on intelligence decreases significantly with age. Martha Storandt, at Washington University in St Louis, was quoted in the *New York Times* article as saying, "The fluid intelligence drop has some impact, but people learn to compensate, even in later life. You can still learn what you want to; it just takes a little longer." Warner Schaie, an eminent US researcher into ageing, added, in the same article:

> For some mental capacities, there begin to be slight declines in the sixties, and, for most people, there are meaningful declines by the eighties. But some mental capacities decline very little, or can even improve in old age. Some of our people have shown no declines that interfere with daily living into their eighties.

It may sometimes seem that our aptitude for learning is at its best when we are aged about 20 and thereafter declines as we grow older; that our memory, too, declines with age; and that our senses become less acute in later life. Whether or not this is true, we should not ignore other aspects of intelligence: as discussed in the case of crystallized intelligence, these may actually improve as we grow older. Even our memory does not decline if the things we are remembering concern our own speciality or are matters of great general interest. It would be reasonable to conclude that, as we age, the kind of work that requires speed, constant attention, good memory and abstract thinking is likely to cause us difficulties; similarly, adapting ourselves to a new way of life or to a new environment might present us with something of a challenge. Nevertheless, elderly people can almost always find things to do that are suited to their abilities and experience, and are rarely forced to adopt a new lifestyle.

Two significant factors account for much of what we describe loosely as the ageing process. On the one hand there are biological changes related to the ageing of the brain and other parts of the body – for example, the autonomic nervous system, the endocrine system and the circulatory system. On the other hand there are social customs and institutions, such as the mandatory retirement age, which may change the lifestyle and mental set of the elderly. As we have seen, the biological changes can be coped with. Now let us consider the problems of old age from a social viewpoint, concentrating especially on what we can do for the elderly and on what they can do for themselves.

Every society has both a bright and a dark side. Throughout most of recorded history, women, children and the aged have been forced to play their part on the shadowy outer edges of society rather than in the central limelight. Recognizing this, Nichiren Daishonin, in one of his letters,[3] refers appreciatively to King Wen of ancient China's Chou dynasty, whose attitude to the way things ought to be was quite different. A wise monarch, Wen was aware of the difficulties the elderly people of his country faced, and he determined to provide them with as much support as possible, establishing a kind of welfare state. The Daishonin states that, because of the king's widespread benevolence, the dynasty which Wen founded continued to prosper for thirty-seven successive generations, representing a period of some eight hundred years.

To digress, it is worth looking at another letter written by the Daishonin, this one to an elderly couple in 1275. About three years before he wrote it he had been exiled to Sado Island in the Sea of Japan, as a result of trumped-up charges. While he was in exile, the couple – called Ko Nyudo and

Ko-no-ama – became followers of his: converted during the most difficult period of his life, they provided him with food, clothing and other necessities. Even after he had been pardoned, and had moved to live at Mount Minobu (to the southwest of Mount Fuji), the elderly couple travelled all the way from Sado to make offerings to their teacher.

Ko Nyudo and his wife had no children and, being of advanced age, doubtless felt very lonely at times. In order to comfort them, Nichiren Daishonin wrote a letter saying, in part:

> Since you have no children, you live alone as husband and wife. The [Lotus] sutra states, "The living beings there [in the threefold world] are all my children." If this is so, then the Lord Shakyamuni must be the merciful father to the two of you. I, Nichiren, am your child, but, wishing to save the people of Japan, for the time being I am far off in the centre of the country. The good causes which you have accumulated from previous existences are truly great. At the time when Mongols invade Japan, you should make your way here in all haste. Because you have no children, when you draw near the end of your lives, consider coming to stay with me. There is nowhere on this Earth you can settle yourselves permanently. Be assured that Buddhahood is where you will at last reside in peace.[4]

These words express the Daishonin's deep compassion for this aged, childless couple, but they also reveal his penetrating insight into the nature of human life. Above all, he says to the couple: "I, Nichiren, am your child." Then, sensing their concern about where they can safely spend their later years, he assures them that Buddhahood is where they can dwell in peace. Every time I read this letter I find myself deeply moved; I can imagine how the Daishonin's concern must have touched Ko Nyudo and his wife.

Returning to our theme of longevity, a relevant statement appeared in 1939 in the US journal, *Annals of Internal Medicine*: "The society which fosters research to save human life cannot escape responsibility for the life thus extended. It is for science not only to add years to life, but more important to add life to the years."[5] The French surgeon Alexis Carrel, who won the Nobel Prize for

Physiology or Medicine in 1912, wrote in a similar vein in 1935: "Longevity is only desirable if it increases the duration of youth, and not that of old age. The lengthening of the senescent period would be a calamity."[6] What Carrel was pointing out is a dilemma faced not just by medical scientists but also by society as a whole. Were we to be stripped of our social responsibilities while we were still in the prime of life we should feel somehow robbed: having a sense of "mission", of a role to fulfil, is what makes our lives worthwhile. This is true for everyone – the elderly included. It is terrible when the aged feel that they have been cut off from society: their frequent response is to close their minds and to isolate themselves. It is our duty, therefore, to create a society in which the elderly can experience complete fulfilment by rounding off their lives just as they would wish. This, indeed, should be the ideal of the science of gerontology.

A psychologist once defined the three evils of old age as anxiety, loneliness and a sense of uselessness. A sociologist once said that they were poverty, sickness and loneliness. We can hope that some day society will be able to eliminate poverty and disease, but loneliness, the sense of uselessness and feelings of anxiety are much more difficult to tackle. From the time of birth to the time of death, what we all desire are somewhere comfortable to live, financial stability, good relations with other people, robust health and a meaningful purpose to our lives. Of course, we should strive to prepare so that these conditions prevail in our own old age, but that is not enough: we should also consider what we can do *now* for our elders.

In 1986 I spoke with Henry Kissinger, and we discussed the topic of ageing. He remarked:

> Old age is not for weaklings. In Japan I have the impression that at least there is a traditional respect for old age. In America, where there is such an exaltation of youth, it is a very difficult problem because, if you exalt youth, then you must accept that your best period is at the beginning of your life. Much of life is then anticlimactic and you have very little to look forward to. In societies in which old age is respected, the psychological strain

48

is less. But how to find a purpose to life when you are older is a very difficult problem for all modern societies.[7]

What, then, can old people do to maintain their sense of purpose and their usefulness of mind? The *New York Times* feature I mentioned lists the key factors as follows:

Staying socially involved. Among those who decline, deterioration is more rapid in old people who withdraw from society.

Being mentally active. Well-educated people who continue their intellectual interests actually tend to increase their verbal intelligence through old age.

Having a flexible personality. A longitudinal study found that those people most able to tolerate ambiguity and enjoy new experiences in middle age maintained their mental alertness best through old age.

People who, through their efforts in their earlier years, have accumulated great wisdom and experience inspire our confidence, and their degree of insight becomes even more profound with old age. It is, therefore, extremely important that, before old age is upon us, we consider the kind of life we are leading, for this will affect the nature of our own old age.

In respect to the value of old age, we find two seemingly contradictory passages in the teachings of Nichiren Daishonin. In one writing he states, "Life is the most precious of all treasures. Even one extra day of life is worth more than ten million *ryo* of gold."[8] (One *ryo* equals about 37 grams.) Elsewhere, though, he says, "Life as a human being is hard to sustain – as hard as it is for the dew to remain on the grass. But it is better to live a single day with honour than to live to one hundred and twenty and die in disgrace."[9] The lessons to be drawn from these statements are that we should make each day meaningful and that we should be more concerned with how *much* we live, rather than how long we live. If a single extra day of life is worth a fortune, it is important that we should recognize the sanctity of life: once a life is lost, it can never be recovered. However, this is not just a question of clinging to life as long as possible; rather, we should try to make every single day of our lives count. For this purpose, I believe it is essential for us to recognize our greatest inherent treasure – the Buddha nature. This is what can make our daily existence shine.

Another remark of the Daishonin's is apposite here: "If one considers the power of the Lotus Sutra, he will find perpetual youth and eternal life before his eyes."[10] Our bodies cannot remain forever youthful, and neither can they be immortal, and this makes it all the more important that we lead a meaningful and satisfying life; that is, that we make each day count. Buddhist doctrine has it that eternity is an endless series of moments, and that each single moment contains eternity. Furthermore, both eternity and the moment exist in our own lives. The purpose of Buddhism is to enable us to realize the eternity of our own lives and live them to the fullest.

Of course, no one is so foolish as not to know that at the end of old age lies death but, even when they are old, people tend to think that they will somehow continue to live on ... for at least a few more years. Most of us refuse, at a fundamental level, to recognize the fact that we could die at any moment. Rather than fear the approach of death itself, we are more horrified by the thought that we might be paralyzed by an accident or a stroke, and die in misery. But really we should bear in mind that understanding the full meaning of death is probably our greatest challenge in life. If we do not fully understand death, we can neither live meaningfully nor die in peace.

Old age is the period in which we can, as it were, put the final touches to our lives. Perpetual youth is ours, albeit in spirit alone. In this state we can contribute to life, each in his own different way, for as long as we live. Nevertheless, death is inevitable, and so it makes sense for us to view death positively as the point of departure for a new life. First, however, we have to accept the truth that life itself is eternal. Usually, though, society does not allow us leisure for meditation on questions of life and death; instead, it occupies most of our time with worldly affairs.

Perhaps the chief purpose of philosophy and religion is to

present us with the opportunity to understand the meaning of death and why we are alive. Without a full understanding of birth and death – of where we have come from and where we are going – we cannot establish our own identity, in the fullest sense of the word. Such matters are inseparable from the questions of what death really means and how we can prepare for it.

References

[1] *Ageing*, D. Van Nostrand Company, New York, 1975, page 3.
[2] *New York Times*, 21 February 1984.
[3] *Nichiren Daishonin Gosho Zenshu*, page 1250.
[4] Ibid., page 1323.
[5] *Annals of Internal Medicine*, vol. 12 (1939), page 976.
[6] *Man the Unknown*, Harper and Brothers, New York, 1935, page 180.
[7] Conversation held in Tokyo on 3 and 4 September 1986.
[8] *The Major Writings of Nichiren Daishonin*, vol. 1, page 230.
[9] Ibid., vol. 2, page 279.
[10] Ibid., vol. 1, page 120.

3

Health and the Conquest of Sickness

People often seem to think that religious faith and medicine are in some sense mutually incompatible. However, in the Buddhist view, they combine harmoniously, each in its own way helping us enjoy a more fruitful existence. After all, they have a common concern: the solution to human suffering.

Religion and science were combined in Buddhist medicine, which absorbed Vedic and Brahmanistic medical traditions and, later, Chinese medicine as well, when Buddhism spread to China. However, even though Buddhist medicine has borrowed from other traditions, it is distinguished by its unique views of disease and health. Although the Buddha himself was steeped in the medicine of his day – so much so that he is often referred to as "the great medicine king" – his was a system of medicine quite distinct from all the others. Through contemplation he was led to conclude that enlightenment, or Buddhahood, is the best of medicaments, because through its virtues we are enabled to draw forth the innate wisdom and life force necessary to cure our own physical and mental ills. Therefore, Buddhist medicine's chief aim is to help individuals develop their natural self-healing powers by cultivating enlightenment through their Buddhist practice. Buddhist practice for attaining liberation includes various methods of controlling one's physical and mental condition – methods that may well have produced the additional benefit of promoting health.

Buddhism explains our physical and mental functions in terms of the theories of the four elements (earth, water, fire and wind) and the five components (form, perception, conception, volition and consciousness). Next, Buddhist medicine concerns itself with the causes of our various ailments. The learned Indian scholar Nagarjuna (c. 150-250)

52

said that there were two categories of illness: those whose causes are to be found in this lifetime, and those whose causes can be traced to previous existences. He further subdivided the former category into illnesses of the body and illnesses of the mind. The former category was still further subdivided into illnesses caused by external factors (such as cold, heat, drought, war and accident) and those caused by internal factors related to, for example, immoderate eating and drinking and irregularities in the rhythm of life.

Later, in China, T'ien-t'ai listed six categories of the causes of illness: irregularities in the four elements, immoderate eating and drinking, bad posture, attack by demons from outside the person, attack by devils from within the person, and, finally, by the workings of karma.

In general, then, we can say that Buddhist medicine focuses on three aspects: (1) developing the condition of Buddhahood, (2) achieving and maintaining harmony of the four elements within our bodies as well as balance between this internal harmony and the four elements as they manifest themselves in our external environment, and (3) achieving and maintaining harmony among the five components. In the course of this chapter we shall elaborate on these basic aspects of Buddhist medicine.

The Age of Sickness
It is estimated that there are about fifty thousand different diseases in the world today; however, for practical purposes, the World Health Organization (WHO) identifies 7,129 categories of disease (most modern medical scientists follow this system of classification). Also, surveys made in industrially developed countries have shown that the percentage of sick people in those countries is rising. For example, in Japan in 1955, 38 out of every 1,000 people suffered from some kind of illness, yet for the year 1982 this figure had risen to 138 out of every 1,000 – in other words, the figure had nearly quadrupled in less than thirty years. Commenting on this social phenomenon, the Japanese newspaper *Asahi Shimbun* made the point that most people living in urban areas today seem to have lost a measure of

either mental or physical stability and that there are now as many diseases as there are people. The increasing incidence of disease has led people to be much more concerned about their own health. People are much more likely to think about the foods they eat, to exercise, to abstain from smoking and to take vitamin pills than they were only a few years ago.

However, the borderline between good health and disease is still rather blurred. Even though most people require medical attention only rarely, at any particular moment there are a lot of people worrying or feeling insecure about their health, or suffering from languor, a sense of fatigue or chronic pain. Surveys in Japan have shown that 60 per cent of all people are worried about their health and that 40 per cent regularly take some kind of medication. Moreover, increasing numbers of people are in a condition such that, while they are not out-and-out ill, neither can they be described as being in full health.

People living in modern industrialized societies face a great deal of pressure in their daily lives. Computerization, efficiency-oriented management, the sheer pace of everyday life and the complex rules and regulations of modern society – all of these intricate, elaborate elements of modern society may bring us many benefits, but at the same time they are responsible for dehumanization and they put pressure on us. So health in our society is not something that can be regarded any longer as an individual concern: it is a problem which society as a whole must solve.

People often think that if they are not ill then they are in good health. This is not the case. The WHO puts its collective finger on the truth of the matter in the preamble to its charter: "Health is a state of complete physical, mental, and social well-being and not merely the absence of disease or infirmity."

Ancient Medicine
Ever since humanity first appeared, health and disease have been primary concerns. Our prehistoric ancestors must have been troubled by sudden fevers, diarrhoea, coughing,

internal bleeding and many of the other symptoms of disease that we know today. People in those days were probably terrified by these symptoms, partially because they may have been unclear as to their causes. However, as the millennia rolled by, people saw how maladies progressed and how the victims reacted, and thereby gradually learned empirically a great deal about what to do at the onset of an illness and how to tend the ailing. Although this was a somewhat primitive medicine, it was based on reason, and it was scientific to the extent that it sought to identify the latent healing properties of the substances to be found in primitive peoples' environments. Archaeological studies have shown that primitive peoples often made use of vegetables and herbs, animal substances and even minerals in the remedies they concocted. Such remedies were useful for many of the milder diseases, but it seems that our ancestors regarded the more serious diseases, against which their concoctions were powerless, as having a supernatural origin – and therefore requiring treatment by magic or religious ritual rather than by herbal medicines. The role of religion in early medicine was therefore an important one, with the duties of priest and physician often being assumed by the same person, the shaman.

In ancient Mesopotamia, Egypt, India and China primitive medicine was remarkably similar, all the different systems displaying the characteristics just described. In ancient Greece, too, medicine arose from a confluence of empirical and mystical traditions. Ancient Greek civilization was strongly influenced by the earlier civilizations in Babylonia and Egypt and, to a lesser extent, those of India and China. According to the Greeks, "supernatural" cures occurred because of the activities of Asclepius, the god of medicine, whose origin has been tentatively traced to a real-life Asclepius who was honoured for his medical skills and who apparently lived about 1200 BC. Temples dedicated to the god Asclepius were constructed throughout ancient Greece, and in them, during what was known as "incubation", or "temple sleep", the healing ritual for sick people was conducted. People went to the temple to pray for a cure and to receive oracles from Asclepius as they slept. The temple priests served as interpreters of the oracles: they based precise methods of treatment – usually a matter of diet, bathing and exercise – on the messages received by the patients during their dreams. When (and if) patients recovered they would offer a tribute to the god along with a gift that symbolized the part of their bodies that had been cured. Many of these artefacts survive at the sites of the ancient temples, and from them we can deduce a rough picture of the diseases common in ancient Greece, and of the treatments prescribed.

Although the cult of Asclepius persisted well into the Christian era, the status of priest-physicians (shamans under another name) was increasingly threatened as a result of the rise of the Greek philosophers, starting with the scientist and mystic Pythagoras, who probably lived around 580-500 BC. Pythagoras and many of the Greek philosophers who followed him took a great interest in medicine, and thanks to their influence the subject passed from the priest-physicians to the people who actively sought the organic causes of illness, rejecting the supernatural and concentrating instead on the physical.

Hippocrates of Cos (c.460-c.377 BC), often called the "Father of Medicine", was born in a time notable for an increasing interest in logic and reason. While teaching and practising medicine in Athens and elsewhere in Greece, Hippocrates stressed the importance of clinical observation and of rational study of the body and its various functions. An excellent physician and a man widely reputed to have been of superb character, he and his followers left the ancient world the Hippocratic Collection, a compilation of writings which represents an attitude towards life, disease and the sick person which is becoming ever more widely appreciated today. Hippocrates agreed with his contemporaries that the human body – like the rest of the Cosmos – was composed of the four elements, earth, air, fire and water, and that bodily functions occurred as a result of an imbalance among the four humours – blood, phlegm, choler (or yellow bile) and melancholy (or black bile). To simplify a little, Hippocrates believed that a human being is healthy when all four of the humours are in harmony: by contrast, when the humours fall into disharmony, the person becomes ill. Another aspect of Hippocrates' ideas was his keen awareness of the body's own innate native healing power.

Hippocrates' attitude towards medicine is summarized in the Hippocratic Oath. The sentiments expressed in this oath, which is still recited on graduation by students at medical schools all over the world, have been adopted by physicians throughout the ages.

Buddhist Medicine
In Buddhism's eighty-four thousand teachings there are many references to illness, describing causes and the appropriate treatments. The range of disorders covered are today the concern of such disciplines as physiology, pathology and clinical medicine. Taken as a whole, the teachings present a unique system of medicine.

Buddhism itself can be viewed as a means of healing the ailing human spirit, or for solving the fundamental problems of human suffering: many Buddhist sutras liken people's sufferings to illness, Shakyamuni to a great physician, and his teachings to good medicine. As the prince of a small Indian kingdom, Shakyamuni himself was traditionally said to have studied medicine and thus to have acquired knowledge about the medical techniques taught and prac- tised in his day. His teachings about illness are, therefore, representative of the standard of medical knowledge in ancient India. They are, moreover, based on his enlighten- ment to the true nature of life, and incorporate three important principles: the oneness of body and mind, the oneness of life and its environment, and the eternity of life.

Here I would like to introduce some actual cases of medical treatment and health care as described in the sutras. In Shakyamuni's day there were many casualties from snake- bites. Once, while the Buddha was staying in Shravasti, a monk was collecting firewood in preparation for a hot bath. As he rummaged about near a dead tree, a venomous snake suddenly bit him on the finger. Afraid that the poison would enter the rest of his body, the monk promptly lopped off the finger. When the Buddha heard about the incident he suggested that, if the same thing should happen again, the finger should instead be tied up and only the injured part excised in order to expel the poisonous substance. The Buddha, therefore, said that, in order to protect the victim, the finger could be cut, even though Buddhist precepts prohibit damaging the body.

In a different sutra, the Buddha proposed that another way of dealing with snake-bites was by preventing them through the development of a more compassionate attitude. He taught that profound mercy for all living things – even lowly life-forms such as snakes, spiders and centipedes – and unfailing life force from within the individual are important elements in the prevention of such adversities as venomous snake-bites. This focus on attitude is characteristically Buddhist; nevertheless, Buddhism allows commonsense solutions to practical problems, as the tale of the monk in Shravasti shows.

Whitlows (felons) – acute suppurative inflammations of the deeper tissues of the fingers or toes – were another common affliction. These inflammations caused acute pain but, more importantly, when not properly cared for, could spread even deeper, resulting in damage to tendons, bones and joints. Ajatashatru, a king of Magadha in Shakyamuni's day, at one time suffered from deep inflammation of the tissues. Regarding this, his mother told him:

> When you were small, you once had a felon on your finger. It was so painful that you could sleep neither day nor night. Your father took you into his lap and placed your ailing finger in his mouth. Thus comforted by your father, you were able to sleep, and the warmth of his mouth matured the felon, finally rupturing the abscess. The Great King wondered if he should draw his mouth away from the finger to spit out the pus. But thinking that this would again cause you great pain, he instead swallowed the pus. This is what your father did for you.

Ajatashatru's father, Bimbisara, was treating the finger using his mouth to much the same effect as a hot compress.

Continuing to cover the finger with his saliva after the rupture was especially useful, because of saliva's sterilizing effect. But far more important than any physiological considerations contained in this episode is the emphasis it places on compassion – which Buddhism teaches should underlie all medical treatment.

Shakyamuni as a matter of principle forbade all use of the surgeon's knife, especially in the case of haemorrhoids and other ailments in the anal region. Because of the difficulty of maintaining proper hygiene, he instead employed dietary and ointment therapy for afflictions in this area. But this precept was not absolute: if it was absolutely essential that an incision be made, Shakyamuni would, for example, permit a suppurating abscess to be pricked using a lotus-flower stem in order to let the pus drain out. Nevertheless, it was only as a last resort that he would permit the use of the knife. Considering the difficulties of hygiene in those days, Shakyamuni's position seems entirely reasonable.

In talking about Buddhist medicine, we must not forget Jivaka. He was a disciple of Shakyamuni, and is described in the sutras as the "medicine king". The accounts of his origin to be found in the sutras differ, but it is generally believed that he was the son of a courtesan and an aristocrat – supposedly King Bimbisara – and that he was abandoned by his parents while still an infant. As an adult, he studied medicine under a master physician. He was able to cure migraines, treat diahrroea, heal injuries of the toes and fingers, cure blindness, heal boils, operate on anal fistulas, etc.

A wealthy man in Rajagriha suffered from terrible headaches. He tried one physician after another, but none of them could help him – indeed, their prognoses for his survival were far from optimistic: one predicted that he had only seven years left to live, another said five years, another seven months, and yet another as little as a month or even just a few days. In desperation, the wealthy man visited Jivaka and asked him to cure his ailment. It seems likely that Jivaka knew that the treatment would not be an easy one, because at first he refused. However, partly as a result of a petition from the king, he eventually agreed to at least investigate the possibility of treating the man. He faced the patient, asked questions about his condition, examined him, and came to the conclusion that the treatment had a good chance of success.

First, Jivaka gave the man some extremely salty food to make him very thirsty. Next he had him drink some liquor, to make him sleepy and anaesthetize him. He tied the patient's body to the bed and called his (the patient's) next of kin to the bedside. With a knife Jivaka cut open a hole in the man's skull and showed the hole to the relatives, saying: "Worms fill the entire cavity. This causes the disease. If things are left the way they are, the worms will devour the brain entirely and bring on his death within seven days." Jivaka then cut out the affected part and cleaned the region, put ghee mixed with honey into the man's head, fixed the hole in the skull, replaced the skin, stitched up the cut, and finished off the operation by applying salve to the lacerated area. The man's illness was immediately cured, and in due course the skin and hair on his head grew back so well that it was impossible to tell where the operation had been performed.

The description we have does not tell us how Jivaka cut through the skull; however, in view of what we know about the development of surgical instruments at that time, we can assume that an appropriate tool was available. The very fact that the operation was successful tells us a lot about Jivaka's skill and the high standard of Indian surgery in those days. It was only from the middle of the nineteenth century, with the advent of anaesthesia and more effective sterilization techniques, that Western surgeons began to undertake brain surgery, and even then they had many difficulties; in fact, it is only in the last few decades that we have been able to regard brain surgery as fairly safe.

Since the earliest times Buddhism has been noted for its observance of monastic precepts regulating daily activities. Certain of these are related to the maintenance of sanitary conditions. For example, it was taught that robes stained by dirt were a violation of the Law, and various ways were stipulated by which robes could be washed and kept clean – there are sutras teaching that hot water, ashes, bean powder, earth and cow dung can be used as a detergent. Bathing is frequently mentioned in the sutras, and several types are discussed: cold-water, hot-water, sauna and hot-spring bathing, the hot-water and hot-spring baths being used mostly in the treatment of illness. Incidental details – such as when to bathe, how to wash the body, what to use as soap – were precisely stipulated in the form of precepts.

The value of physical exercise was recognized: it was known to aid good digestion, freedom from illness, ease of concentration and clear thinking. Rinsing one's nose, washing one's eyes and brushing one's teeth were regarded as important parts of daily health care; condensed milk, oils and fats were used for cleansing. These practices were regarded as important also in the treatment of headaches, eye diseases and other ailments. According to one source, Nagarjuna, a Mahayana scholar, is said to have lived an extremely long life partly as a result of his habit of rinsing his nose every day. Shakyamuni taught that it was important to get sufficient sleep and to eat moderately.

In sum, then, we should note the *practicality* of Buddhist medicine in the way that it concerned itself with the maintenance of good health and the healing of the body. Shakyamuni never resorted to religious healing, nor did he ever instruct the sick to perform magic rituals of any kind. Instead, he gave people scientific, rational ways of dealing with their injuries and diseases; this exemplifies the fundamental Buddhist attitude towards life. At the same time, if patients were suffering from ailments that medicine was unable to cure, Shakyamuni told them not to despair, but to strive to develop their native healing power by bringing forth the Buddhahood inherent in their lives.

Buddhist medicine had its origins in Buddhism itself. It prospered with the rise of Buddhism and, as Buddhism declined in India, likewise Buddhist medicine fell into disrepute. As the vigorous Buddhist drive to save the people disappeared, so did the religion's living power: Buddhists instead focused their attention on formality and doctrinal studies. The great role Buddhist medicine played in people's daily lives, now glimpsed only dimly in the sutras, is today overshadowed by the glories of modern Western allopathic medicine. Yet recently some aspects of Chinese medicine, notably acupuncture and moxa cautery, have attracted the attention of the West, and have brought to light people's misgivings about the limits and deficiencies of Western medicine. I hope that, in the same way, greater understanding of Buddhist medicine will broaden the horizons of Western physicians – not through advances in technology but through the adoption of a new philosophy, or attitude, towards health and life that may serve as the backbone of a truly modern medicine. Such a fusion of the wisdom of East and West will definitely make a large contribution to the prosperity and happiness of the existence of every human being on this planet.

The Buddhist View of Health
As a proverb has it, health is better than wealth. Nichiren Daishonin amplifies upon this point: "More valuable than treasures in a storehouse are the treasures of the body, and the treasures of the heart are the most valuable of all."[1] It is usually only when we lose our health that we really begin to appreciate it. Even if we enjoy excellent health, though, from time to time we may experience physical disorders of one kind or another. Sickness, like old age, is an integral part of human life. It is reasonable to state that health and sickness coexist in our own bodies. For example, according to Western medicine, cancer cells born in our bodies are likewise eliminated by our bodies, thanks to the actions of our immune system – assuming it is functioning effectively.

Josei Toda used to say: "A person is healthy as long as he or she can eat and sleep enough." What he meant was that, as long as we are eating and sleeping sufficiently, we should stop worrying about our health and instead concentrate on other matters. Toda's statement may sound simplistic, but it has definite relevance in an age when many people have become highly sensitive about – or even morbidly afraid of –

illness. According to Jean-Jacques Rousseau, "Temperance and industry are man's true remedies",[2] and the French philosopher Henri Bergson, in his *Les Deux Sources de la Religion et de la Morale* (1932), defined health as the desire to act and the will to participate in the creation of history while adjusting flexibly to everyday life in one's society.

From the viewpoint of the Mahayana teachings, promoting good health can be identified with the state of Bodhisattva, a condition of compassion acquired through performing selfless, altruistic activities for the benefit of humanity as a whole. To illustrate this, we can look at a story from the Vimalakirti Sutra. Vimalakirti, who lived in Vaishali during Shakyamuni's time, was a wealthy lay believer. He had mastered the profound doctrines of the Mahayana and had skilfully instructed other people in its ways. According to the Vimalakirti Sutra, at one stage he became ill. Shakyamuni sent Bodhisattva Manjushri to inquire about Vimalakirti's health. Manjushri asked about the man's condition: "Man of Great Virtue, what is the cause of your illness? Is it long since your illness emerged? How are you going to cure it?" To this Vimalakirti answered:

> Because all beings are ill, I am ill. If the illnesses of all beings are eradicated, my illness will also be eradicated. The Bodhisattva enters the path of birth and death for the sake of all other beings. On the path of birth and death there naturally is illness. If the beings are free from illness, the Bodhisattva will also be free from illness. It is like the relationship between parents and their only child. If the child is ill, the parents will also become ill, and if the child recovers, the parents will also recover. The Bodhisattva is exactly like this. When the beings are ill, the Bodhisattva is ill, and when the beings recover from illness, the Bodhisattva recovers as well.

Manjushri asked a further question: "From where does your illness originate?" To this Vimalakirti answered: "The sickness of the Bodhisattva arises from his great compassion."

The Buddhist concept of good health, as illustrated by these extracts, is not just a question of the absence of disease: it is a matter of the presence of tremendous compassion for all human beings, based on an inexhaustible life force that equips us to face and cope with every possible difficulty. The attainment of the Bodhisattva state means the embodiment of such great inner strength, and this is also, according to Buddhism, the epitome of good health.

Shijo Kingo, one of Nichiren Daishonin's samurai followers, was a physician. When the Daishonin was ill at Mount Minobu he was treated by Shijo Kingo, and later he wrote gratefully: "I survived this time only because Shakyamuni Buddha sent you to assist me."[3] One gathers from this comment that Shijo Kingo treated his Buddhist master with great compassion – indeed, the Daishonin also went so far as to say that he would entrust his life to this disciple. Compassion is certainly the most important human quality of all, and the one we need most if we are to survive in the midst of a world fraught with sufferings, where we are subjected to physical, chemical, biological and psychological stress. According to Buddhism, health is not a state set apart from negative influences but is instead an especially positive, active state in which we face up to and try to solve various problems – not just our own but those of other people, too. Rather than merely escaping from negative influences, then, as Buddhists we hold ourselves responsible for them.

The very word "disease" implies a lack of ease, or comfort. It is all too tempting to interpret the state of comfort as being simply freedom from difficulties. More profoundly, though, comfort implies the strength to meet and overcome any problem. During his lifetime Nichiren Daishonin suffered many persecutions. Even after retiring to Mount Minobu he endured great hardship because of the harsh winters. In one of the letters he wrote at the time he says: "For the past eight years I have become weaker year by year because of sickness and old age."[4] Yet it was at Mount Minobu that he fulfilled the purpose of his entire lifetime's work – that is, the embodiment of the Mystic Law in the form of a mandala.

Dengyo, a great Buddhist teacher in Japan in the late eighth and early ninth centuries, once wrote: "The shallow is easy to embrace, but the profound is difficult. To discard the shallow and seek the profound requires courage."[5] In context, "the shallow" means all Buddhist teachings other than the Lotus Sutra, while "the profound" means the Lotus Sutra itself or, in the ultimate sense, the Mystic Law which is the essence of that sutra. We can interpret this more broadly to mean that we should courageously seek the most profound way of living so that we can achieve something equally profound in our own lives. If we follow such a way of life, we shall have the strength to overcome any difficulties we may encounter.

A similar vision of the nature of health is to be found today among the works of occidental scientists. René Dubos says in his *Mirage of Health* (1959) that

> While it may be comforting to imagine a life free of stresses and strains in a carefree world, this will remain an idle dream.... Man has elected to fight, not necessarily for himself but for a process of emotional, intellectual and ethical growth that goes on forever. To grow in the midst of dangers is the fate of the human race, because it is the law of the spirit.

And the Austrian-Canadian biologist Ludwig von Bertalanffy states in his *General System Theory* (1971):

> Life is not a comfortable settling down in preordained grooves of being; at its best, it is *élan vital*, inexorably driven towards a higher form of existence. Admittedly, this is metaphysics and poetic simile; but so, after all, is any image we try to form of the driving forces in the Universe.

Regarding the purpose of disease in the drive towards perfection, the Swiss philosopher Karl Hilti (1833-1909) said:

> Just as the flooding of a river digs up the soil and nourishes the fields, illnesses serve to nourish our own hearts. A person who understands his illness correctly and perseveres through it will achieve a greater depth, strength and greatness in life.

Buddhism views illness as an opportunity for us to attain a higher, nobler state of life. It teaches that, instead of agonizing about a serious disease, or despairing of ever

65

overcoming it, we should use illness as a means to build a strong, compassionate self, which in turn will make it possible for our lives in this world to be truly fulfilling. This is what Nichiren Daishonin means when he states: "Illness awakens a great seeking spirit."[6]

Components of Life

Buddhism views human beings as the temporary union of the five components – form, perception, conception, volition and consciousness.

By "form" we mean life's physical aspect, which was said to be composed of the four elements: earth, water, fire and wind. (Sometimes space is added to the list of elements, bringing them up to five.) "Form" includes the five sense organs – eyes, ears, nose, tongue and skin – as well as their respective objects in the external world. "Perception" is the function of receiving information through the sense organs and through the mind, which integrates the impressions of the senses. "Conception" refers to the way whereby we create ideas or concepts about what we have perceived. "Volition" is the will to act based on the conception of what we have perceived. Finally, "consciousness" is the function of discernment, which in itself gives rise to and integrates the other spiritual functions – perception, conception and volition. Taken together, then, "form" represents life's physical aspect, while the other four components represent its spiritual aspect.

"Form", as we said, means both the body and the external world. "Form" is subject to change and destruction, and occupies a certain amount of space. According to Buddhism, "form" can be broken down into infinitesimally small particles – ultimate particles that cannot be divided further. Each of these ultimate particles is held together by six other particles: four are distributed about its horizontal plane, while there is one each above and below. This combination of seven particles makes up one microspeck; likewise, seven microspecks make up a larger particle. According to Buddhist thought, the whole of matter is made up of such multiples of basic particles. This view of the microcosm is startlingly like the ideas of modern physics, which describes the existence of elementary particles – from quarks through atoms to molecules.

The four elements – earth, water, fire and wind – can also be understood in terms of their natures or functions. Each of them corresponds to a quality of matter: earth to hardness, water to wetness, fire to heat or warmth, and wind to movement or fluidity. In his "Heritage of the Ultimate Law of Life" Nichiren Daishonin states:

> The function of fire is to burn and give light. The function of water is to wash away filth. The winds blow away dust and breathe life into plants, animals and human beings. The earth nourishes the grasses and trees, and heaven provides nourishing moisture.[7]

The four elements represent four intrinsic forces that are inherent in the Universe itself. The confluence of their fundamental energies was thought, in traditional Buddhism, to underlie all the material changes in the world.

The element earth is represented in the external world by things like mountains, rocks, sand and pebbles; in the internal world of the body it is represented by the skin, hair, nails, teeth and bones – that is, all the hard bodily parts. The element water manifests itself in the world as rivers and seas, while in terms of the body it is manifest as blood and the other bodily fluids. Fire is found in our planet's crust in the form of volcanoes and igneous intrusions, but it is felt, too, in the temperature of the body and in the process of digestion. Wind is apparent externally in the fluidity of the air and, internally, in the body's respiration and metabolism.

Buddhism, therefore, teaches that the individual body and the Universe are connected, in that both of them share the same four elements. It follows that disharmony among the external elements affects the harmony of the internal elements and that, if the body's internal *status quo* cannot bear the burden of the external disharmony, there will arise a state of internal disharmony – that is, disease. If our health is to be good, then, we must have the flexibility and endurance to withstand the effects of external influences. To use a biological term, we must have homeostasis.

In Buddhism the term "consciousness" derives from the Sanskrit word *vijnana*, meaning the act of discerning, recognizing or understanding. By "consciousness" we refer to the mind as a whole, including the vast realm of the unconscious – which, at its deepest, is identical to the life of the Cosmos itself. The whole matter of consciousness is explored in greater detail, in terms of the nine consciousnesses, in chapter Six; for now we can simply say that Buddhism developed theories of the unconscious centuries before Freud, Jung and Adler came on the scene.

Through the doctrine of the four elements Buddhism points to the oneness or inseparability of the individual life and its environment; likewise, through the doctrine of the five components, Buddhism reveals the inseparability of body and mind – mind extending from the innermost realm of life to the furthest reaches of the Universe, transcending the framework of space-time. At the core of all life lies latent and undeveloped the Buddha nature. The Chinese Buddhist master Miao-lo writes:

> You should realize that our life and its environment are the entity of *ichinen sanzen* [i.e., of universal, ultimate reality]. When we attain Buddhahood, according to this principle, our life pervades the entire Universe both physically and spiritually.

The manifestation of the Buddha nature in one's way of living blocks out the appearance of the negative and destructive tendencies that originate in earthly desires and enables one to harmoniously unify the four spiritual functions of perception, conception, volition and consciousness. Further, manifesting the Buddha nature in one's own life creates harmony on the plane of form and, through the correct balance of the four elements, one's life is able to attain vibrancy and strength. This is the Buddhist ideal of good health.

Causes of Illness
In Buddhism, illnesses are classified in many different ways.

Some sutras categorize them according to the element whose imbalance is thought to be the cause, whereas other sutras classify them according to the part of the body that is affected, and yet others classify them according to the time they were caused – that is, they differentiate between diseases whose causes have occurred in this lifetime and those whose causes are to be found in previous lifetimes. For example, according to Nagarjuna's *Treatise on the Sutra of the Perfection of Wisdom*, diseases are divided into "karmic diseases" and "present diseases", the latter category being subdivided into diseases of the body and diseases of the mind. Diseases of the body are yet further subdivided into "internal diseases" (illnesses arising from internal causes) and "external diseases" (those whose causes are external to the body). T'ien-t'ai's *Great Concentration and Insight* gives six causes of illness. These may in turn be organised into three categories: those arising from disharmony of the four elements (diseases of the body), those caused by "devils" (diseases of the mind), and those that result from karma. The diseases of the body can be further categorized in three groups: those caused by excessive eating and drinking, those caused by bad posture, and those caused by external "demons".

The classification of diseases in modern occidental medicine is, of course, far more systematic and thorough than the various systems presented in the Buddhist scriptures and treatises. However, the Buddhist approach to medicine is nevertheless scientific, in that it takes into account cause-and-effect relationships. And, while modern medicine tends to view the ailing part of the body in isolation from the rest, treating it alone as if one were fixing a malfunctioning part of a machine, Buddhist medicine views disease as a reflection of the total body system, or life itself, and seeks to cure it not only through medical treatment but also through adjustments in the person's lifestyle and outlook.

The most systematic presentation of the Buddhist view of disease and its causes is probably T'ien-t'ai's classification, referred to above, upon which Nichiren Daishonin based his own teachings concerning illness. In a writing called "Curing Karmic Disease" the Daishonin quotes a passage from *Great Concentration and Insight*:

> There are six causes of illness: (1) disharmony of the four elements, (2) immoderate eating or drinking, (3) poor posture, (4) an attack by demons from without, (5) the work of devils from within, and (6) the effects of karma.[8]

In T'ien-t'ai's classification, the first four of those causes correspond to illnesses of the body, the fifth to illnesses of the mind, and the sixth to karmic disease.

With regard to illnesses of the body, the Daishonin says in a letter entitled "The Treatment of Illness":

> Physical diseases comprise 101 disorders of the earth element, 101 imbalances of the water element, 101 disturbances of the fire element and 101 disharmonies of the wind element, a total of 404 maladies. These illnesses do not require a Buddha to cure them. Skilled physicians such as Jisui, Rusui, Jivaka and Pien Ch'üeh prescribed medicines which never failed to heal physical sickness.[9]

"Disorders of the earth element" are illnesses in such places as the internal organs, skin, bones, muscles, teeth, hair and nails; "imbalances of the water element" are ailments of the blood or other bodily fluids (e.g., the lymph system); "disturbances of the fire element" are maladies affecting those bodily systems that regulate temperature; and "disharmonies of the wind element" are illnesses of the respiratory and metabolic systems. T'ien-t'ai is quite specific in his description of diseases arising from disturbances of the four different elements:

> If the body becomes heavy, stiff and painful all over or if it becomes weak, thin and numb, these are the symptoms of disturbances of the earth element. If the body swells, that is a symptom of disturbances of the water element. If the entire body is feverish and suffers from pains in the bones and joints and [the patient] has difficulty in breathing, this is a matter of

disturbance of the fire element. If one becomes absentminded, depressed and easily forgets things, this is an aspect of disturbances of the wind element.

As to the causes of an excess of one or more of the elements – or, conversely, their insufficiency – T'ien-t'ai has this to say in *Great Concentration and Insight*:

> The disharmony of the four elements occurs when one overworks oneself and one's body becomes exhausted. When a body in this condition is placed in a hot environment, the external heat reinforces the body's internal fire element, and this consequently destroys the water element. This is the way disease arises from excess of the fire element. When external coldness strengthens the water element, the water element begins to destroy the fire element. This is the cause of diseases produced by the water element. When external wind strengthens the internal energy, the energy augments the fire element and adversely affects the water element. This is the way the diseases arising from the wind element are caused.

Therefore it is not just the physical condition of the body but also the natural environment that affects the internal harmony of the elements, any disruption of which will cause physical disease. No one is free from external – environmental – influences. Even were we to lock ourselves away in a concrete room, in an attempt to shut ourselves off entirely from the outside world, we would still be affected by the earth on which the room stood and the air that we breathed, as well as by the diurnal and annual movements of the Earth as it rotated on its axis and revolved around the Sun. If the environment is damaged in any way, people's physical and mental health will likewise suffer, and so protecting the environment is in itself an important way of preserving the health of human beings. The various conservationist movements all over the world are therefore, from a Buddhist standpoint, both important and meaningful.

So far we have been for the most part discussing the diseases that result from disharmonies of the four elements in terms of the interaction between the physical body and the external environment. But such disharmonies, and their corresponding maladies, also result from causes included in T'ien-t'ai's next three categories: immoderate eating or drinking, poor posture, and attack by "demons" from outside the body.

Great Concentration and Insight informs us: "If there is no moderation in one's eating and drinking, it will cause illness." The book gives various instances; for example, that too great an intake of sweet substances like sugar and honey will create an imbalance by increasing the water element, too much bitter food will overbalance the fire element, too many pears will overbalance the wind element, and too much oily food will overbalance the earth element. The work has a few words to say also on the relationship between foods and the functionings of the five main internal organs:

> A sour taste will assist the functioning of the liver and impede that of the spleen; bitterness will strengthen the heart and weaken the lungs; spiciness will intensify the working of the lungs and reduce that of the liver; saltiness will increase the kidney function and decrease the heart function; sweetness will enhance the spleen and weaken the kidney.

From the viewpoint of modern medicine, T'ien-t'ai's comments are of course a little wide of the mark, but they do show that at least he tried to establish relationships between the excessive intake of certain foods and drinks and the resulting diseases. This is very much a concern of modern preventive medicine, in that relationships like these almost certainly have a bearing on the degenerative diseases that are nowadays frequently responsible for death.

Poor posture, too, affects the four elements. Here "posture" means not just the way the body is held but also the rhythm of daily living. In Buddhism, the word was originally applied to the way of sitting for meditation (including a suggested method of breathing), but today we may interpret it as referring to the daily rhythm of activities, from the moment we rise in the morning until the moment we go to sleep at night. In modern society there are all sorts of intrusive elements that can disrupt the rhythm of our daily lives. We have constantly to be aware of and adjust ourselves to our surroundings if we are to have any chance of keeping the four elements harmonized and of staving off physical ailments.

T'ien-t'ai's third cause of bodily illness – that is, disturbance of the harmony of the four elements – is attack by "demons" from outside the body. We have used the words "demon" and "devil" several times already in this book, and it might seem that we are calling upon old-fashioned bogies as a way of explaining illness. This is not in fact the case. The concepts referred to by these terms are actually far from old-fashioned (although they are old): they are strikingly modern. In *Great Concentration and Insight* T'ien-t'ai states:

> When demons enter the four elements and the five internal organs and cause a disease, such a disease is called demonic disease.... However, demons do not plague human beings without reason. Demons are activated when people harbour evil thoughts [i.e., earthly desires and illusions] in their minds.

In other words, when evil thoughts and desires arise, "demons" are attracted from outside. They enter the body and cause illness.

The concept of "demons" implies any of the many external forces or influences that can cause physical suffering or even death. It corresponds, for example, to invasive pathogenic bacteria or viruses, or even to the modern notion of stress, now widely recognized as a cause of many diseases. According to the cover story of the 6th June, 1983, issue of *Time* magazine, before the 1930s stress had always been regarded as something too intangible to be taken into account by medical science, but then the Austrian-born physician Hans Selye began to research the subject. An early understanding of the nature of stress was gained through studying the condition known as "soldier's heart" – that is, the palpitations which soldiers suffered on the battlefield. Strange as it may seem, these were originally believed to be caused by the vibrations from exploding artillery shells affecting the blood vessels of the brain. It was only later that scientists showed that hormonal changes and the subsequent physiological symptoms associated with "soldier's heart" were in fact the direct products of psychological stress. There are other examples of this sort of thing at work. The abnormal increase in the number of ulcer patients in London hospitals during World War II was a result of the stress caused by the Blitz. And the British medical journal *Lancet* a few years ago contained a report on the sharp increase in the incidence of heart attacks in Athens in the immediate aftermath of the 1981 earthquake.

Investigations of the effects of stress on the human body have been wide-ranging, even revealing the extent to which the foetus is affected by the condition of its mother and by the external world. According to research carried out by Canadian psychologists, one can actually quantify the stress effects on the foetus of events in the mother's life. For example:

mother's high blood pressure	1.10
mother's anaemia	1.12
mother having argument with neighbour	2.00
mother in conflict with relatives	4.00
mother in fight with her husband	6.00

Such findings lend force to the arguments for prenatal training; they also correspond with the idea of the inseparability of life and its environment, as propounded in Buddhism.

So, even though the term "demons" may sound a bit alien to our modern scientific world, it is notable that this ancient Buddhist concept is very similar indeed to the scientific notion of stress as a factor causing illness. The afore-mentioned *Time* article pointed up the similarity of the two concepts perfectly:

The saber-toothed tiger is long gone, but the modern jungle is no less perilous. The sense of panic over a deadline, a tight plane connection, a reckless driver on one's tail are the new beasts that can set the heart racing, the teeth on edge, the sweat streaming.

Illnesses of the Mind

The fifth cause of disease, according to T'ien-t'ai's classification, is the working of "devils" from within. This manifests itself in the form of mental illness. Of mental diseases Nichiren Daishonin writes:

> The second category is illnesses of the mind. These illnesses arise from the three poisons of greed, anger and stupidity and are of eighty-four thousand kinds. They are beyond the healing powers of the two Brahman deities, the three ascetics, or the six non-Buddhist teachers. Medicines prescribed by Shen Nung and Huang Ti are even less effective.[10]

"Devils" – in Sanskrit the word is *mara*, often translated as "the destroyer" or "robber of life" – are the personification of the evil functions inherent in life; that is, they are the earthly desires that hinder people in their pursuit of truth and work to prevent people from cultivating a strong, positive life force from within. T'ien-t'ai states in *Great Concentration and Insight*:

> Devils destroy the meditations on the mind and the wisdom of the Dharma body. Devils are different from demons in that the former cause people to have ill thoughts and rob them of their benefits while the latter cause people to suffer illness and physical death.

So, when we talk of "devils", we are really using another name for those aspects of our lives that hamper our Buddhist practice. To this we can add that "devils" represent the fundamental tendency of the individual's own life towards disharmony of body and mind. Unlike the other four causes of illness, this one affects the realm of the mind, and it has its source not in external influences but in the individual, so that the person's life is robbed of its brilliance: the result is the emergence of life's fundamental darkness or delusion.

Buddhist medicine regards mental illness as the result of uncountable earthly desires, represented collectively by the three poisons of greed, anger and stupidity. These three are understood as the source of all earthly desires and illusions. Let us look at them in turn.

The poison of greed lets loose an unlimited burst of earthly desires, thereby draining us of our innate life force. It sets all five of the sense organs off in search of wealth, love, food, fame, idleness, and so on. When our lives are dominated by greed, all our life energy is directed towards the object of our desire, so that we are weakened – just as we would be if blood were draining from our bodies. The fresh green land of our lives is transformed into the desolate, parched land of Hunger. Anger disturbs the harmonious relationship between the depths of our beings and the surface of our minds, and this disturbance can assume colossal proportions and eventually destroy our lives. The sense of suffering and helplessness which accompanies it places us in the world of Hell. Stupidity emasculates us, leaving only our instinctive desires active; these lowly desires do not create any impetus for growth or positive change. We can think of stupidity as being like dark, gloomy, stagnant clouds squatting over our internal skies. The idle state induced by stupidity is characteristic of the world of Animality.

These three poisons, plus arrogance, doubt and incorrect views, together comprise the six fundamental earthly desires. Each of these is accompanied by a number of derivative earthly desires. Greed, for example, brings in its train miserliness, self-indulgence, guilt, deceit and adulation; while anger is associated with resentment, hatred, irritation, jealousy and the urge to harm other living beings.

Twenty such derivative earthly desires are identified in Buddhism, and they in turn give rise to an even greater variety of earthly desires. Their effects exacerbated by external influences or the effects of karma, these can interrupt and disrupt the harmony of life to such an extent that we are unable to reverse the process. The varied ways in which mental illnesses manifest themselves and the complexity of the workings of all these earthly desires account for the fact that there are said to be 84,000 different types of mental illnesses as opposed to a mere 404 types of physiological illnesses.

Another way of looking at earthly desires is in terms of the three categories of illusions: illusions of thought and desire, illusions as uncountable as particles of dust and sand, and illusions about the true nature of existence.

Of the illusions of thought and desire, illusions of thought are primarily mental and acquired, while the illusions of desire are chiefly emotional and inherent. By "illusions of thought" we mean false perceptions of the truth. These can take several forms; for example, mistakenly regarding our existence as absolute, even though our bodies are formed as a result of a temporary union of the five components; the mistaken belief that we own what does not in fact belong to us forever; the erroneous notions that either, on the one hand, life ends at the moment of death or, on the other, that life persists after death in some eternally unchanging form; lack of recognition of the law of cause and effect; and adherence to misconceptions with such closed-mindedness that we regard inferior things as superior. Illusions of desire can be summarized much more briefly: they include base emotions such as greed, anger, stupidity and arrogance arising in connection with specific objects or events.

The illusions as uncountable as particles of dust and sand are those that prevent bodhisattvas from saving other people. In order to save other people, bodhisattvas have to be well versed in innumerable religious and secular teachings. This second category of illusions constitutes those that arise when bodhisattvas try to master these teachings. These illusions, which emerge in response to acts of compassion for others, originate deep within the unconscious – from a level even deeper than that where illusions of thought and desire reside.

Illusions about the true nature of existence prevent bodhisattvas from attaining Buddhahood. They lie in the deepest reaches of the unconscious, and they have the devastating potential to cast our lives into total darkness, by depriving us of the illumination of compassion and wisdom. These are the most fundamental of all: they lead to self-destruction. The other two categories can be thought of as merely derivatives of illusions about the true nature of existence. In practical terms, they manifest themselves as the impulse to kill and destroy, or as the still more primitive urge to sacrifice others and even delight in doing so. Buddhism teaches that living on the basis of such impulses is in itself a mental illness. Just as our physical condition has an effect on our mental state, our bodily health is to a great extent affected by the beliefs we hold and our attitude towards life – factors that have their origins in the mind. The mind, we can therefore conclude, is on one hand supremely powerful in terms of our health, and yet at the same time especially subtle and susceptible to external influences.

Karmic Disease

The first five causes of illness have their origins in our present lifetimes, but the sixth, the effects of karma, is very different because its origins lie in our previous existences. In "Curing Karmic Disease" Nichiren Daishonin said: "Illnesses of the sixth [kind], which result from karma, are the most difficult to cure. They vary in severity and one cannot make any fixed pronouncements."[11] Karmic disease can manifest itself in the form of either mental or physical illness.

People who do not believe in the Buddhist concept of karma may say that the underlying cause of a fatal disease is destiny, or the will of some transcendent being, or simply chance. But are any of us willing to submit to the blind force of destiny without trying to do something to counter it? Do we really want to obey the dictates of a cruel god, or give ourselves up entirely to the vagaries of chance?

The concept of karma was not developed in order to persuade us to resign ourselves to hopeless suffering. If we understand the notion of karma correctly we automatically come to recognize that we are responsible for whatever problems we might face in life and that we, ourselves, must strive to overcome those problems. This recognition enables us to establish true independence. In the case of karmic diseases, then, we can act to eradicate the negative karma

78

that is causing the illness, and by so doing we can cause the illness to disappear.

Karmic disease is characterized by the degree of physical, spiritual and social suffering it causes, and so the specific diseases involved have changed over the course of history, and presumably will continue to do so. For example, the sutras often refer to leprosy as a karmic disease, because in Shakyamuni's time it was incurable and the victims had to suffer not only the realization that disfigurement and death were almost certainly fairly imminent but also the loathing of and ostracism by their fellow citizens. In other words, to the physical torment was added very considerable mental anguish. However, today leprosy can be controlled and the individual can lead a reasonably normal life. Many other diseases have been virtually eradicated thanks to modern medicine – smallpox is a prime example. Still, there are many diseases that are incurable and new ones – such as AIDS – appear continually. Some are born from the development of society, some even arise from medical treatment itself. It is unlikely that medical science will ever be able to eliminate all diseases: it is more probable that some will always remain a mystery, and that it is our destiny to have to cope with incurable diseases and be faced by the fear of death. Karmic disease is thus, from the secular perspective anyway, an unavoidable enigma – but Buddhism offers us the clues as to its solution.

We can no longer regard karmic disease and its cure as matters just for the individual. Mankind as a whole has accumulated a horrific amount of evil karma, symbolized by our obscene stockpile of nuclear weapons, use of a small fraction of which would spell the end of all land-based life on the planet. Our lives are marred by the deadly influence of poisonous man-made substances, from food additives to industrial wastes. Another problem is the degradation of the human spirit, resulting in upward-spiralling violence and the ever-increasing search to gratify egoistic desires. All of these negative aspects of our lives – and we could list many others – can in a broad sense be considered symptoms of humanity's collective accumulation of evil karma.

We can go a little further, and say that the collective karma of human society as a whole interacts with the karma of each individual in that society, and that living in such a society can in itself lead the individual to experience greater karmic suffering. This is a reflection of the principle of the oneness of life and its environment. Dealing with a karmic disease is, therefore, not just a matter involving the individual: it is something that demands the efforts of society as a whole. However, it is only through transforming our individual karma that we can transform that of society.

Native Healing Power
No one could deny the contributions modern medicine has made to the curing of disease – myself least of all, because my physical condition was poor during my youth, and I owe a lot to medical science. Yet, for all its impressive technology, effective medicaments and elaborate diagnostic techniques, modern medical science is not omnipotent. Moreover, its treatments often tend too much towards a materialistic or mechanistic view of the human organism, neglecting the view of life as an entity composed of both body and mind.

Whereas modern medicine inclines to dependence on the use of drugs and technology, Buddhist medicine instead concentrates on what the patient can do to cure his or her own sickness. The development of wisdom for self-control is thought by Buddhism to be especially important.

Buddhism regards disease as an external manifestation of internal disharmony. Furthermore, Buddhist medicine maintains that the quality of human life or health is determined by the balance of an indescribably vast number of factors, each of which is in a state of constant flux. Establishing a state of equilibrium among these factors is little short of miraculous, and so it is hardly any wonder that the perfect balance is from time to time disturbed, with the result that we suffer illness. Most people live with a number of diseases or detrimental agents constantly at work in their lives, although the ailments are so minor that we seldom even notice their onset and disappearance. In this context the Buddhist belief in the inseparability, or oneness, of health and disease becomes especially significant: according to the Lotus Sutra, even a Buddha who embodies the ideal state of life will never be completely free of ailments.

If we agree that disease is a natural expression of one's state of life, whether it be caused by internal disharmony, earthly desires or karma, what ultimately matter are our attitude and our ability to mobilize life's innate healing power. The cultivation of this healing power depends on our individual will: the role of will in curing a person's illness is becoming ever more apparent as medical research continues. If we are shocked and weakened when we discover we have a serious disease we are much more likely to succumb to it than if we refuse to accept the news as a death sentence and elect to fight the disease. Our willpower affects also our body's ability to produce natural "medicines", in the form of hormones, enzymes and antibodies, which the body marshals to combat negative influences and preserve life. Willpower thus has a major part to play in helping us take full advantage of our own native healing abilities.

"Willpower" in this sense refers to the depth with which we can grasp the true aspect of our lives, which are, in the world-view of Buddhism, entities of infinite potential and cosmic scale. This type of willpower derives from our absolute confidence in the vastness of our existence, our irreplaceable mission and our responsibility to this world.

The strength of Buddhist medicine lies in the key it provides to the activation and utilization of the unlimited potentials and energies inherent in the individual human life, brought about through the development of the Buddha nature from within. Nichiren Daishonin gives an explicit explanation in "The Daimoku of the Lotus Sutra", in which he clarifies the three aspects of *myo*, or mystic. *Myo* is a syllable taken from *Myoho*, which means the Mystic Law, or *Nam-myoho-renge-kyo*. This Law pervades the entire Universe and exists as the Buddha nature in all things, whether sentient or insentient. According to the Daishonin, *myo* means three things simultaneously: to revive, to be fully endowed and to open.

Regarding the first of these three aspects of *myo*, we find two noteworthy passages in the Daishonin's explanation: "*Myo* means to revive, that is, to return to life,"[12] and "The Lotus Sutra ... can cure the dead as well as the living."[13] When the Mystic Law – or Buddha nature – is activated in our lives it can bring us back to life even if we teeter on the brink of death. In a broader sense, this implies that we have the power to change a sickly person into a healthy and happy one.

Going on to the second aspect of *myo* we find another relevant passage:

> *Myo* means "fully endowed", which in turn has the meaning of "perfection".... To illustrate, one drop of the great ocean contains within it the waters of all the various rivers that flow into the ocean, and the wish-granting jewel, though no bigger than a mustard seed, is capable of showering down all the treasures that one could wish for.[14]

Each of our individual lives is fully endowed with all of the potentials that exist in the Cosmos: when the Mystic Law is brought into play it orchestrates our spiritual and physical functions in a superb harmony, thereby vitalizing all of our vast innate potentials. As a result, the greatest healing influence of all – our own unhampered life force – rises to the occasion and enables us to overcome even the most virulent of diseases.

The third meaning of *myo* is explained in the same text:

> The Lotus Sutra says, "This sutra opens the door of expedient teachings and reveals the true aspect of reality." The Great Teacher Chang-an comments on this as follows: "*Myo* means to reveal the depths of the secret storehouse." And the Great Teacher Miao-lo says of this: "To reveal means to open." Hence the character *myo* means to open.[15]

If we examine this passage in the context of health we can see that the Mystic Law enables us to reveal "the depths of the secret storehouse", which is the Buddha nature, and "open" our existence to the environment. In other words, we can establish a basis from which we will always be able actively and positively to interact with our environment, transmuting all of its influences so that they benefit us.

In short, then, these three functions of the Mystic Law are: to activate our inherent life force, to harmonize our spiritual and physical functions, and to equip us with the resources to influence our environment for the better while responding to its myriad changes with wisdom and maintaining a balance between it and ourselves. When we base our lives on this Law we can tap the limitless power inside ourselves, so that disease is rendered no longer a matter for despair. In fact, the opposite is true: empowered by the Mystic Law we can transform disease into a source of joy and true fulfilment.

So far as modern medicine is concerned, it seems sensible for it to abandon its current defensive posture and adopt a more aggressive one – that is, it should see its primary role as preventing, rather than curing, disease. Every effort should be made to obviate disease *before* it causes illness, not after it has done so.

References

[1] *The Major Writings of Nichiren Daishonin*, vol. 2, page 279.
[2] *Émile*, translated by Barbara Foley, London, Dent, 1911, page 23.
[3] *The Major Writings of Nichiren Daishonin*, vol. 1, page 226.
[4] *Nichiren Daishonin Gosho Zenshu*, page 1583.
[5] *Hokke Shuku*, cited in *The Major Writings of Nichiren Daishonin*, vol. 1, page 117.
[6] *Nichiren Daishonin Gosho Zenshu*, page 1480.
[7] *The Major Writings of Nichiren Daishonin*, vol. 1, page 24.
[8] Ibid., vol. 2, pages 247-8.
[9] Ibid., vol. 3, pages 273-4.
[10] Ibid., vol. 3, page 274.
[11] Ibid., vol. 2, page 249.
[12] Ibid., vol. 3, page 23.
[13] Ibid., vol. 3, page 24.
[14] Ibid., vol. 3, page 15.
[15] Ibid., vol. 3, pages 12-13.

4

Death: One Facet of Eternal Life

According to the Buddhist view, life is eternal. It is believed to undergo successive incarnations, so that death is thought to be not so much the cessation of an existence as the beginning of a new one. For Buddhists the phenomenon of transmigration is self-evident – as, indeed, it was to the ancient Indians, who gave it the Sanskrit name *samsara*. In a brief essay called "Philosophy of Life", the second Soka Gakkai president, Josei Toda (1900-1958), puts forward his ideas on the eternity of life. He vividly describes his experiences while being held as a prisoner of conscience during World War II, and tells of the way in which he awakened to many of life's truths:

> While detained in a cold prison on ungrounded accusations, living a life of loneliness and isolation, I meditated day after day and month after month on the ultimate nature of life. What is life? Is life eternal? Does it exist in this world alone? Wise men and holy men throughout the ages have pondered these great riddles, each attempting to solve them in his own way.
>
> In the filth of prison, lice breed prolifically. One day, as if invited by the balmy spring sunshine, several lice strolled out lightheartedly ... I crushed one of them with my fingernail, but the others were still nonchalantly moving. Where did the life that had animated the creature go? Did it disappear forever from this world?

Next in the essay he describes his first encounter with Nichiren Daishonin's Buddhism, after he had researched various other spiritual teachings. He tells us about a great moment of insight he achieved as a result of chanting two million *daimoku* (*Nam-myoho-renge-kyo*) and continually contemplating the Lotus Sutra. Through this awakening he acquired a direct understanding of the truth that life is indeed eternal.

Such writings [which assume life is eternal] are innumerable. Without this conception, there is no Buddhism. This is what life really is and the first gate for sages' enlightenment. Many intellectuals may scoff at the Buddhist idea of life, denying it as superstition, but I am afraid that, in taking this attitude, they only reveal their own thoughtless and basically unscientific approach. The law of causality is essential to science. All phenomena in the Universe are governed by the law of cause and effect; therefore, to ignore this law by stating that life is no more than the result of the union of spermatozoon and ovum is superficial because it only explains appearances, failing to take into account a certain original cause. If one is prepared to conclude that life occurs fortuitously and disappears like a bubble, while assuming that every phenomenon is ruled by cause and effect, it must be said that one's attitude is amazingly insensitive to the nature of life itself.

Some people are brilliant by birth, others not. Some are beautiful, others not. Some are healthy, others not. There are many distinctions. Some are poor despite their efforts to be successful. Some suffer from earthly desires, like greed or jealousy, which cannot be alleviated by means of science or social institutions. These differences must have fundamental causes; therefore, man's problems cannot be solved without a thorough investigation into the nature of life.[1]

The fundamental premise of Buddhism is that life is eternal and that individual living beings undergo a continuing cycle of birth and death. Some of the findings of recent scientific research in the fields of both medicine and parapsychology tend to support this view. These researches include studies of "near-death experiences" and "past-life experiences".

Research into near-death experiences concerns itself primarily with the impressions of people who, having been pronounced clinically dead, have later "come back to life", and with documenting the process whereby people adjust to the reality of imminent death. For some decades now researchers have been compiling accounts of near-death experiences and studying the details in order to try to find some sort of coherent pattern. A patient interviewed in one of these studies described his experience:

I was in an utterly black, dark void. It is very difficult to explain, but I felt as if I were moving in a vacuum, just through blackness. Yet, I was quite conscious. It was like being in a cylinder which had no air in it. It was a feeling of limbo, of being half-way here, and half-way somewhere else.[2]

This is only one among many similar accounts. Together they can be taken as offering evidence that, despite all appearances to the contrary, life, as subjective experience, is not in fact extinguished at the moment of death.

The other way of approaching the matter of transmigration is to investigate past-life experiences, and here a most useful tool has been hypnotic regression. Using hypnosis, scientists have been able to evoke from their subjects what appear to be memories of past lifetimes and so have provided serious evidence in favour of the idea of transmigration. Years ago, when only a handful of parapsychologists were concerning themselves with the phenomenon of reincarnation, most scientists were sceptical about what they regarded as a highly unscientific realm of inquiry. However, during the 1950s, when new techniques of hypnosis were developed which facilitate the regression of the hypnotic subject back through time, enabling people to recall their experiences not just in infancy but while they were still *in utero*, a few subjects were discovered who were apparently able to remember experiences they had had even before the moment of conception. A number of scientists tried to match up these accounts with historical fact and, although they unearthed a number of "unconscious hoaxers", there were several cases in which the recollections seemed to accord sufficiently with historical fact to provide very strong evidence for transmigration.

At this stage, though, many scientists contended that the correlation between the subjects' recollections and historical fact had nothing to do with reincarnation: instead, they said, it was simply that the subjects were (quite honestly) recalling histories and biographies they had read and were merely repeating these as if they themselves had been the protagonists. So the scientists rejected the evidence, saying that in fact these cases provided no proof one way or the other about reincarnation.

In 1966, however, Dr Ian Stevenson, a professor of psychiatry at the University of Virginia, in the US, published the results of his researches into past-life memories and thereby created something of a controversy. In his book *Twenty Cases Suggestive of Reincarnation* he not only produced good evidence of the accuracy of people's memories of their previous existences but also established similarities of behaviour, preferences, habits, constitution, talents and physical features between the subjects as they were in their current lifetimes and the people they believed they had been in earlier ones. This additional step Stevenson took in a deliberate attempt to provide the guidelines for further research into the question of the existence of past lives.

Buddhism is based on intuitive wisdom while modern science is based largely on empirical proof, yet both systems of knowledge concern themselves with human affairs and recognize the law of causality. Thus they have very similar intellectual origins, and so it is hardly surprising if their conclusions are often identical. Already studies in the fields of medicine and parapsychology seem to substantiate the concept of transmigration. In this sense, science is approaching the view of life expounded by Buddhism, while at the same time offering strong evidence in its favour.

Stages in Death
Dr Elisabeth Kübler-Ross is widely regarded as a pioneer in the field of the clinical study of death. She contends that terminally ill patients generally pass through five stages as they approach death. At the first news that they are terminally ill most patients respond with shock and a refusal to believe that the diagnosis is correct; they often change their doctors many times, hoping to be reassured that their condition is not in fact fatal. The second stage involves anger: patients accept the fact that they will die, but then become angry with the people around them and perhaps also with their god for letting their prayers for recovery go

unheeded. In the third stage patients start to try to bargain with god or fate in an effort to prolong their lives: this phase might be seen as a sort of time of truce. The fourth stage is characterized by depression: patients are convinced that death is imminent, and gradually sink into a deep depression known technically as "preparatory grief". After these four stages the patient enters the fifth and final one: acceptance. If patients lack moral support or care during the crucial period before acceptance, or if they are isolated in hospital, they will almost certainly slump into a depression. On the other hand, patients who have accepted their fate will prepare themselves to die with peace and dignity. Patients who have genuine faith – whatever the religion, including those that do not give credence to the idea of an afterlife – tend to die more calmly than those who have no religious beliefs.

Many people, Kübler-Ross says, approach death with feelings of anger or depression. People who resist death to the very last moment may create for themselves just that much extra agony; while people who have accepted the fact of their dying only at a superficial level, merely resigning themselves to their fate, are likely to pass away far less peacefully than those who have genuinely accepted that this life is soon to end – that is, right up until the last moment they may despairingly cling to a faint hope that they might be given a reprieve.[3]

Conversely, coming face to face with death can give rise to positive feelings of compassion or benevolence. At the end of our lives both positive and negative energies gush forth from our unconscious – or what in Buddhism is termed the "*alaya-consciousness*". Often the negative emotions overwhelm positive ones; in order to control this negativity we have to transform it – that is, we have to strengthen the positive energy. It is here that we find the necessity of fully understanding the teachings of Buddhism if we are correctly to prepare ourselves for death. In one of Nichiren Daishonin's writings we find the following passage:

Nagarjuna explains the character *myo* of *myoho*, or Mystic Law, saying, "It is like a great physician who can turn poison into medicine ..." Poison means the three paths of earthly

88

desires, karma, and sufferings of life. Medicine means the three virtues of the Law: the Dharma nature, wisdom, and emancipation or freedom. To turn poison into medicine means to change the three paths into the three virtues.[4]

This passage implies that the ultimate Law of the Universe can change the negative aspects of life, as represented by the three paths, into positive aspects, as characterized by the three virtues. The Mystic Law can transform the sphere of the *alaya*-consciousness, where all of our karma – both negative and positive – is stored: it is identified with the sphere of the *amala*-consciousness, or ninth consciousness, which transcends the other, shallower consciousnesses and is free of all karmic impurity. Through acceptance of and belief in the ultimate Law, the potential life force of Buddhahood dormant in our *amala*-consciousness is activated, so that the other levels of consciousness are bathed in the vigorous stream of this life force.

The life force of Buddhahood, then, turns the three paths into the three virtues, strengthening all the positive elements on the level of the *alaya*-consciousness, affecting the upper consciousnesses, and thereby totally changing the individual's life. This is the spiritual dynamic of the attainment of Buddhahood.

The Process of Dying
When we pass through the portal of death – the gateway between this life and the next – both our physical conditions and our psychological states are profoundly affected. The manner in which we do so also has a crucial impact on the conditions into which our life is reborn.

As we saw in chapter one, numerous Buddhist scriptures, such as *A Treasury of the Analyses of the Law*, identify four stages of existence to which all forms of life are subject: existence during birth, existence during life, existence during death, and existence between death and rebirth (the "intermediate existence"). Existence during death is therefore considered in Buddhism as quite distinct from existence during life, implying that the phase of death is

89

completely different from that of living. In the process of passing through death to the intermediate existence we experience a transformation of our being. During this phase, life's various functions become dormant, and are stored in the *alaya*-consciousness. These functions include those of the five sensory consciousnesses, the mind-consciousness and the *mano*-consciousness, which is the centre of self-consciousness. When the mind- and *mano*-consciousnesses become dormant, all psychological activities, including mental functions and emotional desires, are converted into dormant seeds and deposited in the karmic storehouse of the *alaya*-consciousness. At the same time, our physical being begins to disintegrate, and its energy, too, is absorbed into the *alaya*-consciousness.

In the general turmoil of this process, it is natural that our experience should be very different from that of normal life. If we become frightened and confused because of all the unaccustomed sensations, allowing earthly desires and illusions to permeate our lives in a final frantic struggle at the moment of death, all the efforts we may have made to elevate ourselves, if not based on the Mystic Law, may be nullified in a single instant. The way in which we face the moment of death determines whether or not we crown our lives with complete fulfilment.

From the Buddhist perspective, our ability successfully to pass through the dying process depends upon our steady efforts during life to accumulate good causes and to strengthen the foundation of goodness in the depths of our lives. We can enter the intermediate existence peacefully and without losing our presence of mind if, at the time of death, we are able to manifest an enlightened life-condition based on faith in the Mystic Law. Nichiren Daishonin encourages this attitude: "Be resolved to summon forth the great power of your faith, and chant *Nam-myoho-renge-kyo* with the prayer that your faith will be steadfast and correct at the moment of your death."[5]

In order to prepare for a tranquil death we must refrain from speech and conduct that will have an adverse effect on the lives of other people. Any speech or behaviour that harms others will create causes whereby we may enter the three evil paths. Negative behaviour of this sort is caused by derivative earthly desires (see Glossary) stemming from anger, one of the fundamental earthly desires inherent in humanity; these derivative desires include indignation, grudge-bearing, distress, jealousy and personal antipathy. The recurrence of such desires etches evil causes deeper and deeper into the individual's life, and this accumulation of evil causes is stored as karma in the person's *alaya*-consciousness: at the moment of death this karma is released and activated, to the torment of the dying person. In short, negative desires or evil acts that we perpetrate during life may cause us agony at the time of our death.

The other side of the coin is that, of course, all of one's altruistic and compassionate acts during life are likewise recorded as karma and imprinted in the *alaya*-consciousness. The accumulation of good karma serves to protect us from experiencing agony at the time of death by offsetting our karmic "liabilities" with "assets".

The balance of karma at the time of our death is important, but far more so is our ability to maintain unshakable faith in the Mystic Law. This is what fundamentally transforms the terminal suffering of the three evil paths into the joyful experience of an elevated state of life. Thus Nichiren Daishonin recommends that, as Buddhists, we uphold throughout life the habit of chanting *Nam-myoho-renge-kyo* with the deep conviction that our life is in essence identical with the life of Buddhahood. To quote the Daishonin:

> If one attains full awakening to the truth that the mind of common mortals and the mind of the Buddha are one, neither will evil karma obstruct his dying in peace nor will distracting thoughts bind him to the cycle of birth and death.[6]

If a person can eradicate evil karma and overpower distracting thoughts in his or her daily life through the practice of chanting *Nam-myoho-renge-kyo* he or she will certainly enjoy a peaceful death, untrammelled by illusions or distracting impulses. With the strong life force acquired through Buddhist practice, which creates good karma and a positive attitude, we can experience an elevated and joyous life-condition while passing through that gate between life and death. This enlightened state, filled with goodness and compassion, is at death reflected in the body, the individual's physical aspect.

The effects accumulated through chanting *Nam-myoho-renge-kyo* far transcend the dimension of ordinary good or evil karma. Thus, irrespective of any sufferings or calamities one may encounter in life, if a person believes in the Mystic Law and chants *Nam-myoho-renge-kyo* he or she will inevitably enjoy peace of mind at the moment of death, as his or her life fuses with the life of Buddhahood in the Universe. Furthermore, if family members practise Buddhism together and attain Buddhahood they will, regardless of their individual times of death, be able to be together in the next existence. On this issue Nichiren Daishonin comments, in a letter to one of his followers:

> Those who practise this sutra [the Lotus Sutra] ... will betake themselves to the same place, Eagle Peak. Moreover, as your deceased father believed in the Lotus Sutra along with you, he will definitely be reborn in the same place with you in the next life. [7]

Caring for the Terminally Ill
In technologically advanced countries today about half the people die in hospital, and a great many of these do so in an intensive care unit, in isolation from their loved ones. It used to be the case that most people spent the last stage of their lives surrounded by their relatives and friends but now, despite all the advances in medical technology, the appropriate comfort and care often cannot be given to the terminally ill.

Most people involved in medical care today are well versed in the physiological processes of death but they seem to have very little knowledge of its emotional and psychological aspects – that is, the internal experiences of the dying person. It is perfectly understandable, therefore, that some people reject the idea of being taken into hospital, preferring instead to die at home in a serene, loving environment. The only trouble is that, almost always, family members too do not know how to care compassionately for the dying person.

Clinical death is thought to occur at the moment when death becomes irrevocable, a moment signalled by physiological symptoms such as the death of the brain stem and the cessation of breathing and the heartbeat. It is at this moment that the individual is believed to be experiencing death. If relatives and friends continue to chant *Nam-myoho-renge-kyo* after this, the dying person is helped to pass peacefully through the process of death. At this moment the individual's mental and physical energies, such as the five components of life – form, perception, conception, volition and consciousness – all become dormant and are subsumed into the sphere of the *alaya*-consciousness. Hearing the chant, the life of the deceased in the intermediate existence, if not already on its way, begins the journey towards the pure land of Eagle Peak – which represents the life of Buddhahood in the Universe.

According to Mahayana scriptures, life after death fuses with and is incorporated into the larger cosmic life in the state of "non-substantiality", or *ku*. Nevertheless, although it has become fused with the Universe, one's individuality is preserved in the form of seeds of karma stored after death in the *alaya*-consciousness. These seeds affect the condition of one's life in the intermediate existence in that one experiences pleasure or suffering in accordance with the karma one has accumulated during life.

In *A Treasury of the Analyses of the Law* the noted Indian Buddhist theoretician Vasubandhu tells us that the karma accumulated during past lifetimes cannot be changed during intermediate existence, but Nichiren Daishonin teaches that prayers offered by the living can in fact alter the karma of the deceased and affect the conditions of his or her next rebirth. This, according to the Daishonin, is because if the prayers are offered based on the state of Buddhahood they are transmitted to the dead person's *alaya*-consciousness.

So, even if a person has created causes in the three evil paths, he or she can be enabled to enter a joyful state as a result of the effects of prayer on his or her behalf.

A person who has continued chanting *Nam-myoho-renge-kyo* until the moment of death, and who has thereby attained Buddhahood, the highest state of life, fuses with the life of Buddhahood inherent in the Universe. The Daishonin describes the state of such a person at the moment of death in his "Heritage of the Ultimate Law of Life":

> For one who summons up his faith and chants *Nam-myoho-renge-kyo* with the profound insight that now is the last moment of his life, the sutra [i.e., the Lotus Sutra] proclaims: "After his death, a thousand Buddhas will extend their hands to free him from all fear and keep him from falling into the evil paths." How can we possibly hold back our tears at the inexpressible joy of knowing that not just one or two, nor only one or two hundred, but as many as a thousand Buddhas will come to greet us with open arms![8]

In "On Practising the Buddha's Teachings" the Daishonin expands:

> Even if someone were to cut off our heads with a saw, impale us with lances, or shackle our feet and bore them through with a gimlet, as long as we are alive, we must keep chanting *Nam-myoho-renge-kyo*, *Nam-myoho-renge-kyo*. Then, if we chant until the very moment of death, Shakyamuni, Taho and all other Buddhas in the Universe will come to us instantly, exactly as they promised during the ceremony at Eagle Peak. Taking our hands and bearing us upon their shoulders, they will carry us to Eagle Peak. The two saints, the two heavenly gods and the Ten Goddesses will guard us, while all the Buddhist gods raise a canopy over our heads and unfurl banners on high. They will escort us under their protection to the Buddha land. How can such joy possibly be described![9]

In both of these passages the Daishonin refers to the countless Buddhas who will greet us at the moment of our death. His intention in mentioning these Buddhas was to convince his contemporaries – who deeply respected the

Buddhas – of the greatness of his teaching. However, if we analyse the texts more carefully we realize that what he meant by phrases such as "a thousand Buddhas" and "Shakyamuni, Taho and all other Buddhas in the Universe" was in fact the Buddhahood inherent in our own individual lives and also in the cosmic life. So what he was actually saying was that people who believe in and chant *Nam-myoho-renge-kyo* will, immediately upon their death, merge with the Buddhahood of the life of the Universe.

In a letter to a believer the Daishonin elaborates on this theme:

> And when you are happy, you should remember that your happiness in this life is nothing but a dream within a dream, and that the only true happiness is that found in the pure land of Eagle Peak, and with that thought in mind, chant *Nam-myoho-renge-kyo*. Continue your practice without wavering up until the final moment of your life, and when that time comes, look carefully! When you climb the mountain of wondrous enlightenment and gaze around you in all directions, then to your amazement you will see that the entire Universe is the Land of Tranquil Light. The ground will be of lapis lazuli, and the eight paths will be set apart by golden ropes. Four kinds of flowers will fall from the heavens, and music will resound in the air. All Buddhas and Bodhisattvas will be present in complete joy, caressed by the breezes of eternity, happiness, true self and purity. The time is fast approaching when we too will count ourselves among their number. But if we are weak in faith, we will never reach that wonderful place.[10]

The Daishonin, when he uses images and concepts of an ideal world, such as the pure land of Eagle Peak or the Land of Tranquil Light, is in fact referring to the life force of Buddhahood in the Universe. In Hinayana Buddhism, the attainment of nirvana implies the cessation of transmigration among the Six Paths and the end of life itself. According to Mahayana Buddhism, however, even after achieving Buddhahood one will, very soon after death, reappear in the terrestrial world, taking the form of an ordinary mortal, in order to work for the salvation of others. The time that it takes for a life to pass through the intermediate stage between death and rebirth depends upon the condition of that individual's life. If, on dying, a life enters the world of Buddhahood in the Universe, it takes very little time before subsequently being reborn into this world. If, on the other hand, it fuses with the life of Hell in the Universe it does so almost immediately, but may have to stay there for aeons. However, when we talk about the time required before an individual life is reborn, this is a rather different "time" from that which we experience in this world: it is time as sensed by that particular life, and its duration, as sensed, will vary according to the individual's spiritual state. To use an analogy, if you are extremely happy time flies by, so that an hour may seem like little more than a minute; conversely, if you are suffering, time drags its feet so that a minute seems like an hour.

However, we should note that in Buddhism there is no such thing as an eternal Hell. Even if we descend into Hell (more precisely, if our life in the intermediate existence merges with the life of Hell in the Universe), we will eventually be reborn out of Hell and back into this world. And our rebirth will be into a better spiritual state, because we will have received adequate retribution for our extremely bad karma.

Conditions for Rebirth

Modern medical science regards the fertilization of the ovum by the spermatozoon as the sole necessary prerequisite for the generation of a new life, but Buddhist medical concepts add another requirement: the presence of the intermediate existence.

According to Buddhism, all causal relationships involve four interrelated elements: internal cause, external cause, latent effect and manifest effect. We must define these four terms with respect to rebirth.

Internal cause is life's inherent ability to produce an effect of the same nature as itself; for example, an acorn has the inherent ability to produce an oak tree. So this internal cause – i.e., the acorn's genetic information – simultaneously contains a latent effect, the potential oak tree.

External causes are the outside stimuli that help internal causes produce their manifest effects. External causes do not comprise the environment as a whole, only those parts of it that relate life to its environment. To continue with the example of the acorn and the oak tree, the external causes are the provision of the soil, water, sunlight and so on needed for the acorn to grow into a tree. This combination of external and internal causes is necessary if any manifest effect – i.e., the oak tree – is to occur.

Modern medicine suggests that the precise details of the selection of genetic information contained in the chromosomes is a matter determined by pure chance, but the Buddhist view is that these details are instead determined by the individual's karma. It is internal cause – in this case the karma stored in the *alaya*-consciousness and carried over into the next lifetime – that accounts for the fact that every individual is unique. Character differences between siblings – even identical twins – are thereby understood to be a result of the fact that every individual has different karma. The internal cause for the generation of life is, therefore, the karma possessed by life in the intermediate existence, while the external cause is the genetic information provided by the father's spermatozoon and the mother's ovum. Only when these two factors coincide can the generation of new life occur.

After death the individual life, in the condition of non-substantiality (*ku*), fuses with the greater life of the Universe. Nevertheless, the *alaya*-consciousness, which stores the records of a person's karma, continues to exist. When the external cause – the genetic information provided by the prospective parents – exactly matches the internal cause stored in the *alaya*-consciousness, life in the intermediate existence can immediately manifest itself in this world, regardless of the parents' location, because life in the state of *ku* transcends the spatial/temporal framework. To align this with the ideas of modern biology and psychology, we can say that at the time of conception the internal cause and latent effect stored in the *alaya*-consciousness of an individual life in the intermediate existence are manifested as a result of the activating force of the parents' genes.

Nichiren Daishonin writes on the subject of people who attain Buddhahood during a previous lifetime – manifesting the Buddha nature and realizing the oneness of their own lives and the Universe – and then are reborn into this world:

> One cherishes and profoundly awakens to the truth [of life], and is in accordance with the will of all Buddhas throughout time. He receives the protection of the two saints, the two heavenly gods and the Ten Goddesses, and without impediment attains rebirth in the supreme Land of Tranquil Light. In a moment he returns to the realm of dreams in which he repeats the cycle of birth and death in the Nine Worlds. His body [of the Law] pervades the lands in the ten directions, and his mind enters the lives of all sentient beings. He urges from within and induces from without, appropriately combining the two [to lead people to enlightenment]. Harmonizing internal and external causes, he employs his infinite power of compassion in order to widely benefit living beings.[11]

In this passage the Daishonin reveals his views about the ultimate nature of life and death. If we attain Buddhahood during our lifetime and pass through the stage of death in the most elevated of spiritual states we will attain the state of life referred to by the phrase "the supreme Land of Tranquil Light". We shall swiftly be reborn into this world so that we can share our wisdom with others, leading them to enlightenment and, in so doing, physically and spiritually affecting all sentient beings. Thus a person who attains Buddhahood is continually reborn into this world to help other people become Buddhas.

Nichiren Daishonin teaches that, as a person escapes from the vicious circle of birth and death in the Six Paths, he or she will simultaneously commence the Bodhisattva's work of leading others to salvation, in the process undergoing innumerable cycles of birth and death. Therefore, to the Bodhisattva, birth and death are the cause of enlightenment, not of suffering, and the means whereby he or she works for the benefit of others.

Accidental Death

Some people die young due to accidental causes, while others die naturally in extreme old age. Nowadays cases of accidental or violent death are so frequently reported in the media that we are numbed: we insulate ourselves from the reality of death, and tend to see it in terms of remote statistics rather than as a matter of individual human beings. At the same time, the experience of people dying has been taken out of our lives: as we saw, most people in the technologically advanced countries die in hospital, separated from their families. Their survivors are thereby deprived of the opportunity to learn about this stage of life.

On 12 August 1985 a Japan Air Lines jumbo jet crashed in the mountains north of Tokyo, and 520 people lost their lives. I heard the news with great sadness, and prayed for the victims, recalling a passage from the Lotus Sutra: "Now this threefold world is all my domain. The living beings in it are all my children. Yet this world has many cares and troubles from which I alone can save them."[12] The husband and parents of one of the crash victims, all of whom practise Nichiren Daishonin's Buddhism, have written to me and reported that, while originally they bitterly regretted the tragedy, they have since become able to confront the situation face-to-face and use it to strengthen their faith in the Mystic Law. They have been able to do this because they have increased their understanding of what Buddhism teaches about how one can lessen the retribution of one's negative karma through experiencing such tragedies.

For the 4 February 1958 issue of the *Seikyo Shimbun*, the Soka Gakkai's newspaper, Josei Toda wrote an article on the subject of Buddhists who, despite their efforts to achieve happiness through faith, nevertheless suffer tragic deaths. To highlight the principle of lessening karmic retribution he cites a passage in the Daishonin's "Letter from Sado":

The *Hatsunaion* [Parinirvana] Sutra reads [as we saw on page 35], "Men of devout faith, because you committed countless sins and accumulated much evil karma in the past, you must expect to suffer retribution for everything you have done. You may be reviled, cursed with an ugly appearance, be poorly clad and poorly fed, seek wealth in vain, be born to an impoverished or heretical family, or be persecuted by your sovereign." It further states, "It is due to the blessings obtained by protecting the Law that one can diminish in this lifetime his suffering and retribution."[13]

Toda refers also to a passage in the "Letter to the Brothers":

The Nirvana Sutra reads, "By suffering sudden death, torture, slander or humiliation, beatings with a whip or rod, imprisonment, starvation, adversity or other relatively minor hardships in this lifetime, he will not have to fall into hell."
This means that we, who now believe in the True Law, once committed the sins of persecuting its votary in the past, and should therefore be destined to fall into a terrible hell in the future. However, the blessings gained by practising the True Law are so great that we can change our karma to suffer terribly in the future by meeting relatively minor sufferings in this life.[14]

According to Toda in this essay, a person's untimely death can be regarded as one of the "relatively minor hardships" whereby that person can expiate negative karma and be spared having to fall into the state of Hell.

Nichijun Shonin (1898-1959), the sixty-fifth high priest of Nichiren Shoshu, writes in January 1922 that

It cannot unequivocally be said that a believer in the Mystic Law will necessarily be able to live a long life and will not have to experience disaster ... However, for us who bask in the compassion of the Buddha, a disaster is not a disaster in the ordinary sense of the word. In our case, even a short life can be as fruitful as a long life. Misfortune by no means ends in misfortune. We should accept all phenomena that we encounter as manifestations of the Buddha's compassion ... Because there is nothing which surpasses the power and blessings of the Mystic Law, the only thing which we have to do is to pray wholeheartedly to the Buddha, confident that it is impossible that the prayer of a believer would go unanswered. Faith and practice are concerned with existence in the real world. Therefore, benefit is also concerned with reality.

100

However, many people tend to misunderstand this truth. It is no exaggeration to say that almost all the believers in other Nichiren schools mistakenly believe the benefit of Buddhist practice to consist in the termination of calamities or disasters so that everything goes smoothly ... Faith is concerned with the revitalization of life itself. Whether what is happening is good or bad, only with faith can one find infinite meaning in each event.[15]

I have quoted these passages at some length because they delineate very clearly the Buddhist belief in the importance of life's adversities in the eradication of the individual's negative karma. In this connection we should note the brutal disaster that Shakyamuni Buddha himself suffered during the later years of his life when King Virudhaka of Kosala commanded the massacre of the Shakya tribe. Although historical accounts differ, it seems that the Shakya tribe was virtually annihilated at Virudhaka's behest. The massacre is counted as one of the nine great ordeals experienced by the Buddha. Several of Shakyamuni's most eminent disciples also suffered greatly in the course of their Buddhist practice. During the Buddha's life Utpalavarna, a Buddhist nun, was beaten to death by Devadatta when she reproached him for attempting to kill the Buddha by dropping a boulder onto him from the top of Eagle Peak, and Maudgalyayana, reputed to be the foremost Buddhist disciple in the sphere of occult powers, was murdered by what was essentially a lynch mob while he was practising religious mendicancy in Rajagriha. Nevertheless, even though Shakyamuni Buddha personally suffered considerable ordeals and even though his followers were persecuted, he continued to teach people the way in which they could free themselves from suffering, so that they would be gradually led along the path to enlightenment. It is thanks to Shakyamuni's determination to spread his teachings that Buddhism was for a time widely revered in India and China and eventually became a world religion.

The Nirvana Sutra says:

Bodhisattvas, have no fear in your hearts because of such things as wild elephants. But evil friends – they are what you should

101

fear! If you are killed by a wild elephant, you will not fall into any of the three evil paths. But if evil friends lead you to your death, you are certain to fall into one of them.[16]

The meaning of this passage is that, so long as we live in human society, we cannot avoid suffering. However, even if an unexpected accident – symbolized in the Nirvana Sutra by wild elephants – were to cause our death we would not fall into the evil paths. By contrast, if we are swayed by evil friends and give up our faith in Buddhism, thereby closing off the way to enlightenment, we shall, according to the sutra, fall into the three evil paths.

Buddhism thus distinguishes between the death of an individual's body and the death of that individual's mind seeking enlightenment. In terms of the Buddhist idea of eternal life physical death does not have a direct bearing on the individual's true happiness. Rather, so long as individuals maintain their Buddhist practices during their lifetimes, they will be able to minimize the duration of their intermediate existence and be very swiftly reborn into this world. To sum it all up in a few words, the ultimate frightful thing from the standpoint of Buddhism is not physical death but the death of the quest for the Law in people's hearts.

A Broad Perspective
Throughout our eternal lives we continuously undergo the natural cycle of birth and death. At death, our life merges back into the life of the Universe, much in the same way that the spray of waves dissolves back into the waters of the ocean. Buddhism gives us the eternal Law that permeates every living being and every phenomenon in the entire Universe. The birth and death of living beings, the occurrence and cessation of nonliving phenomena and the constant flux of the whole Universe are all manifestations of that Law. The Law enables our lives to continue eternally from one existence to the next.

Shakyamuni regarded his own death as a means to an end, because it assisted him in his primary aim, the salvation of the unenlightened. He explained to his followers that, were

102

he to remain forever in this world, people would come to rely on him rather than on their own mental perception for their enlightenment. Therefore, he taught, the Buddha would not remain in this world in perpetuity but would come and go at intervals. He therefore urged people instead to seek the Buddha's compassion, wisdom and mercy – in other words, he told them to strive towards enlightenment through his teachings and their own diligence.

Every individual's death is, likewise, a means to an end; that is, a means to our rebirth. As we grow older we become weak and sickly and eventually die. But we do not die for nothing: we die in order to start a new life. The fundamental purpose of death, then, is to allow us to be reborn in the next phase of our eternal life cycle.

The sixteenth chapter of the Lotus Sutra, "Lifespan of the Tathagata", tells us: "There is no ebb and flow of birth and death." In his *Record of the Orally Transmitted Teachings* Nichiren Daishonin interprets this sentence as follows:

> If birth and death are perceived to be immanent in eternal life, there is no birth and death. If there is no birth and death, neither is there appearance and disappearance. This is not to say simply that there is no birth and death. Regarding birth and death with abhorrence and trying to separate oneself from them is delusion and reflects the view that enlightenment is acquired at some specific time. To clearly perceive birth and death as alternating phenomena of eternal life is awakening, the realization that enlightenment is inherent eternally. Nichiren and his disciples who chant Nam-myoho-renge-kyo become aware that birth and death or appearance and disappearance are expressions of the intrinsic workings of eternal life.[17]

This passage expands the view that birth and death are immanent in eternal life – one of the most profound of all the Buddhist doctrines. The word "immanent" deserves a little explanation: it means that one's life was brought into being neither by some transcendent being (i.e., a god) nor by the actions of one's parents, but that it has always existed within the Universe. The term "eternal life" signifies that one's life has continued and will continue to exist eternally with the Universe; that is, it has neither beginning nor end, and its existence is not intermittent but continuous. Apart from birth and death, there can be no eternal life. Birth and death exist throughout eternity as necessary concomitants of life.

If we correctly perceive birth and death as intrinsic workings of eternal life, as Nichiren Daishonin teaches, we proceed from delusion to awakening or, to put it another way, from the superficial view that enlightenment is attained when we free ourselves from birth and death to the profound understanding that enlightenment is inherent within us always. We will then have no fear of the "sufferings" of birth and death, but can instead accumulate treasures of boundless value within our lives, based upon our eternal and indestructible Buddhahood, so that we eternally and joyously repeat the cycle of birth and death.

If we have faith in and practise the Mystic Law we naturally come to realize that our own lives are eternal. At the same time, whether we recognize it or not, we are able naturally to develop all the treasures of eternal life.

When we look at nature, society and our own daily affairs we can hardly fail to notice that all three are in a constant state of flux, never remaining in the same state and constantly repeating the cycle of birth and death. And, as soon as we perceive that life is coexistent with the Universe and that birth and death are alternating aspects of a life that is eternal, we come to understand our own lives and the lives of those around us – not to mention the world as a whole – with a truly profound insight. No longer do we experience fear at the thought of death. In the act of discovering our immutable self – the self unaffected by the concerns of human life or society – we are able to overcome our fears of death. It is my conviction that there is nothing more wonderful for a human being than to attain this state of life.

I believe that a completely new form of human society, based upon the concept of the eternity of life, will usher in a dawn more brilliant than any in all the millennia of human history, and that this dawn will represent the blossoming of eternal happiness. This will be the time when humanity will bring about the end of its history of misery and start its advance along the great road of eternal happiness. Of all humanity's undertakings, this will be the greatest.

References

[1] *Toda Josei Zenshu*, vol. 3, pages 5-12.
[2] Raymond A. Moody, Jr.: *Life After Death*, Mockingbird Books, Atlanta, 1975, pages 29-30.
[3] Elisabeth Kübler-Ross: *On Death and Dying*, Macmillan Publishing Company, New York, 1970, pages 38-137.
[4] *Nichiren Daishonin Gosho Zenshu*, page 984.
[5] *The Major Writings of Nichiren Daishonin*, vol. 1, page 25.
[6] *Nichiren Daishonin Gosho Zenshu*, pages 569-70.
[7] Ibid., pages 1508-9.
[8] *The Major Writings of Nichiren Daishonin*, vol. 1, page 22.
[9] Ibid., vol. 1, pages 106-7.
[10] Ibid., vol. 3, pages 216-7.
[11] *Nichiren Daishonin Gosho Zenshu*, page 574.
[12] *The Major Writings of Nichiren Daishonin*, vol. 4, page 76.
[13] Ibid., vol. 1, page 40.
[14] Ibid., vol. 1, pages 137-8.
[15] *Nichijun Shonin Zenshu*, vol. 2, page 683.
[16] *Taisho Shinshu Daizokyo*, vol. 12, page 497.
[17] *Nichiren Daishonin Gosho Zenshu*, pages 753-4.

5

Ichinen Sanzen:
Life's Unlimited Potential

The Buddhist tenet that life is sacred is of especial relevance today. If we are to solve the serious problems confronting mankind we have, first, to acknowledge the inherent dignity of human life. Buddhism sheds light on the inner sphere of human life and seeks the highest values therein. Mahayana Buddhism, in particular, stresses that life is sacred because it possesses, in latent form, the Buddha nature. As we have seen, Nichiren Daishonin teaches that all the treasures of the Universe are not worth as much as a single human life, and that people should respect both themselves and everyone else as beings endowed with the Buddha nature.

This reverence for life is not confined to human beings: Buddhism regards the lives of all the millions of species – plants as well as animals – as equally endowed with inherent dignity. To the Buddhist, even entities that are generally regarded as nonsentient – such as grass and trees, mountains and rivers – are all living and all possess their own unique functions and qualities. For example, in the Buddhist sutras – which were written down nearly two thousand years ago – we find many different types of plants mentioned, a fact which reflects the typical Buddhist awareness of both sentient and nonsentient forms of life. A comparison of Chinese recensions with the original Sanskrit and Pali texts reveals that no fewer than 498 different types of plants were mentioned in the sutras. Among the twenty-eight chapters of the Lotus Sutra is one called "The Parable of Medicinal Herbs". The parable explains that, just as the rain falls equally on all sorts of trees, shrubs and medicinal herbs, enabling each to benefit according to its nature, so does the Buddha's compassion extend equally to all beings. It was a common practice of Buddhist scriptures to use parables or metaphors of this kind in order to convey some profound truth. This parable shows us that the Buddha impartially expounded the Lotus Sutra to *all* beings, thereby offering every being enlightenment. This single teaching – described by Buddhists as the "excellent medicine" of the Mystic Law – can relieve all people equally of their sufferings and illusions, irrespective of race, nationality, social system and time.

An interesting digression on the subject of plants and Buddhism is that certain varieties of plants were in fact instrumental in the spread of Buddhism. When scholars began to record the teachings of Shakyamuni Buddha they selected their materials with some care, because they wished their records of the True Law to live on in perpetuity. They therefore chose to carve the teachings on the durable leaves and bark of the *tala* tree (a type of palm). Because they did so the Buddhist scriptures were preserved and transmitted through the many centuries before the art of papermaking developed.

Nichiren Daishonin uses various plants for metaphorical purposes in his writings. For example, in a letter to Oto Gozen, the daughter of his follower Lady Nichimyo, who lived in Kamakura, he writes that "wood is vulnerable to fire, but sandalwood cannot be burned",[1] using sandalwood as an analogue for the power of the Mystic Law. Elsewhere, in a letter to Myomitsu Shonin, another follower who lived in Kamakura, he writes: "He [the believer] will be like mugwort growing in a field of hemp or wood marked with a carpenter's line. Though the mugwort and the wood may not be straight to begin with, they will as a matter of course become so."[2] He is using the example of the ordinarily crooked mugwort growing straight among hemp plants to illustrate the fact that a life based on the Mystic Law will be naturally purified and corrected.

Throughout this modern age, the development of Western scientific civilization has been bolstered – perhaps even dominated – by humanism, a doctrine which stresses mankind's superior position as a rational being. However, the attitude of the proponents of humanism towards the dignity of mankind has not always been grounded in a comprehensive life-view, with the result that there has been a tendency to anthropocentrism – that is, a view based on the idea that Man is the centre of the Universe. This attitude, justified by reference to the human capacity for reason, proves, not surprisingly, to be narrow and egocentric when adopted as a life-view. We cannot deny that a sense of "self" or ego is necessary for a fulfilling life, but Buddhism firmly points out that there are considerable dangers in the attachment to the idea of "self" as the *whole* of all that exists. By contrast, Buddhism teaches that the road to liberation from the sufferings of birth and death lies in our awakening to the far broader life that lies beyond the confines of the finite self.

Our consciousness of "self" forms the framework whereby we support our world-view. Our perceived division of the Universe into two parts – "self" and "other", or internal and external – arises from our consciousness of "self". This consciousness likewise gives rise to other dualities: for example, the duality of mind and body (in which we somehow regard the mind as being our true self whereas the body is not), the duality of the material and the spiritual, or the duality of mankind and nature. Dualistic thinking like this has underlain the evolution of modern civilization, but it is also the root of many of modern civilization's present crises.

Buddhism points the way to the resolution of such crises by demonstrating the truth that our lives are not limited to the self alone but encompass other people, the world and even the Universe. Perhaps nowhere do we find a better exposition of this idea, that the individual and the Cosmos are inseparable, than in the principle of *ichinen sanzen*, which has it that a single moment of life possesses three thousand realms. In this chapter we shall discuss this profound Buddhist concept and the principles deriving from it – such as *shikishin funi* (the oneness of body and mind) and *esho funi* (the oneness of life and its environment).

The philosophical system of *ichinen sanzen* was developed in China by that outstanding Buddhist theoretician of the

108

sixth century, T'ien-t'ai (formally given the title Great Teacher by the Imperial Court in China). He based his ideas on the Lotus Sutra, which in eastern Asia gradually came to be, partly due to his efforts, revered as the highest teaching of Shakyamuni Buddha. *Ichinen sanzen* constitutes a world-view, explaining the mutually inclusive relationship of all phenomena and the ultimate reality of life.

A literal translation of the word *ichinen* is "one thought" or "one mind"; *ichinen* is therefore the true aspect or ultimate reality of life that arises at each moment in the existence of common mortals. *Sanzen*, meaning "three thousand", refers to the phenomena of the Cosmos. Of course, there are vastly more than three thousand phenomena in the Universe, but here the number is taken to indicate the multitude of invariable laws according to which the ultimate reality shows itself. The figure of three thousand is derived from a multiplication of *ichinen sanzen*'s component principles – we shall discuss these in some detail later. Here, though, we can note that those components consist of, first, the Ten Worlds, or states of life. Each of these possesses all ten within itself, so that one hundred worlds are constituted. Each of these hundred worlds is endowed with ten factors: simple multiplication gives us one thousand factors. Finally, each of these factors operates in three realms – and so we arrive at our total of three thousand realms.

So we see that the principle of *ichinen sanzen* reveals the moment-by-moment interaction between the phenomenal world and the ultimate reality of life. It teaches also that all phenomena, without exception, exist within each moment of an individual's life, and that every such moment therefore contains infinite potential. In "On Attaining Buddhahood" Nichiren Daishonin writes:

> Life at each moment encompasses both body and spirit and both self and environment of all sentient beings in every condition of life, as well as nonsentient beings – plants, sky and earth, on down to the most minute particles of dust. Life at each moment permeates the Universe and is revealed in all phenomena.[3]

His point is that the individual's *ichinen* – the individual's life at each moment – simultaneously both permeates the entire Universe and encompasses within itself all the laws and phenomena of the Universe. It is, therefore, literally coextensive with the Universe. This relationship between the microcosm of human life and the macrocosm of the Universe is mysterious – and marvellous.

If we look at the physical world we can easily see that even infinitesimally small things contain vast potential. All of the vast Universe had its origins in a "cosmic egg" that physicists believe to have been almost indescribably small – perhaps the size of a subatomic particle. The fusion of minuscule nuclei can produce the vast energies of the hydrogen bomb. Hundreds of millions of "bits" of information are stored in a gene too small to see through the microscope. The human brain is believed to contain about fourteen billion neurons, each of which spreads its dendrites to form a network with perhaps one thousand other neurons. The number of connections (synapses) in the brain's total network is of incomprehensible vastness – about ten to the power of three trillion. To gain some conception of the hugeness of this figure, consider the fact that the total number of subatomic particles in the Universe is "only" about ten to the power of one thousand. The potentials of the human brain are, therefore, virtually infinite.

From a temporal standpoint, life at each single moment might be thought of as a cross-section of an unbroken continuum stretching from the infinite past into the infinite future. In this respect, we can think of a person's *ichinen* as being rather like a television picture. In the space of a second, thirty successive images flash across the television screen, merging together to form a coherent moving picture. But the length of a moment, as explained in the Buddhist scriptures, is far shorter than the duration of one of these images. The *Great Commentary on the Abhidharma* says that there are "sixty-five moments in a single snap of the fingers". In fact, though, the Buddhist conception of a "moment" implies an almost inconceivably brief duration. Our lifetime is an accumulation of myriad such minuscule

110

moments, which flow without interruption from the past through the present to the future. Therefore, because eternity consists of moments, and because each moment is the condensation of an entire lifetime, the most important thing is our state of life at each moment. Our state of life from moment to moment determines the overall course our life takes.

One of the ten honorific titles given to the Buddha is "Thus Come One" (Sanskrit *Tathagata*), meaning a person who has arrived from the world of truth. "Thus Come One" also means to emerge from the truth moment by moment, and indicates that in every moment the Buddha manifests the ultimate truth. In yet a further sense "Thus Come One" or "Buddha" can be understood to mean the ultimate reality manifesting itself in every moment as the phenomenal world. Though the moment itself passes away inevitably with the flow of time, life at each moment transcends the temporal framework, in that it encompasses the ultimate reality – which remains unchanging throughout past, present and future. This is something far beyond the ordinary bounds of our comprehension.

Josei Toda, the second president of the Soka Gakkai, when discussing *ichinen*, often cites a passage of the Sutra of Infinite Meaning, a prologue to the Lotus Sutra. The passage in question is:

> The entity is neither existence nor nonexistence; neither cause nor circumstance; neither itself nor another; neither square nor round; neither short nor long; neither rising nor falling; neither birth nor death; neither creation nor appearance, nor artificial; ... neither blue nor yellow, nor red nor white; neither scarlet nor purple, nor any other colour.

This collection of negatives serves to show us that the ultimate reality of life is beyond not just our powers of description but also our conception. We can observe the physical and mental activities of our lives to a certain extent through such disciplines as biology, biochemistry, physiology and psychology; but the phenomena with which all these sciences are concerned are merely expressions of life,

111

not life itself. The ultimate reality of life is intangible and invisible, unconstrained by time and space. Nonetheless, in every single moment it manifests itself as the phenomenal world.

Our physical bodies are composed of many millions of cells which are constantly dying and being replaced. Our minds, too, change, as various emotions and thoughts occur. We are subject to change, then, both physically and mentally, and, as time flows by, we continually repeat the cycle of death and rebirth. The constantly changing circumstances of our bodies and minds are considered to be the inherent workings of a fundamentally unchanging reality. The Buddhist world-view extends beyond limited descriptions of birth and death, setting as its horizon a changeless and eternal truth that expresses itself in all things – "self" and "other", tangible and intangible, sentient and nonsentient – and alternately manifests itself as the active phase called life and recedes into the latent phase called death. Toda often illuminates the Buddhist view of life and death by quoting from "Lifespan of the *Tathagata*", the sixteenth chapter of the Lotus Sutra: "I [the Buddha] let the people witness my nirvana as a means to save them, but in truth I do not die; I am always here, teaching the Law." In other words, as a result of the Buddha's great compassion his death inspires people to seek enlightenment, yet the Buddha nature, or the ultimate reality that the Buddha has realized, is eternal and unchanging.

Another passage from this chapter goes yet further in helping us see beyond ideas of impermanence and change into the realm of the eternal. It runs: "The *Tathagata* perceives the true aspect of the threefold world exactly as it is. There is no ebb and flow of birth and death, nor life in this world and later extinction." However, Nichiren Daishonin teaches, conversely, that the "true aspect" actually encompasses both the eternal and the changing: birth and death, according to the Daishonin, are both inherent workings of life, which is eternal. Toda explains this view of death by applying the above quotation from the "Lifespan of the *Tathagata*" to our own individual lives. As he puts it,

112

Nirvana, that is, our death, is a means to our rebirth. With age, we are destined to become weak and sickly, and, eventually, to die. At death, our physical body will decay, but our life will merge back into the great life of the Universe. In this latent state, it recharges with energy, so to speak, for its next rebirth. In this way, we repeat the cycle of birth and death, based on the Law permeating all living beings and phenomena in the Universe. Death, then, can be likened to the function of sleep. It is an expedient means to dispel our fatigue and rejuvenate our lives for our next existence.

Birth and death are thus natural expressions of the eternal reality of life; this eternal reality is, in turn, the ever-changing phenomena of birth and death. Freedom from the suffering of change comes only at the moment when we waken to the timeless truth manifest in our *ichinen*. Then, as the Daishonin says, "we repeat the cycle of birth and death secure upon the earth of our inherent enlightened nature".[4]

Although the moments of our life appear to flit by we can see that, from a more profound viewpoint, together they encompass the ultimate reality. Every single moment transcends the bounds of space and time to be simultaneously one with the cosmic life force – the ultimate reality of the Universe. All forms of life interrelate endlessly in the vast totality of cosmic life, and yet none of them ever loses its uniqueness. Nichikan Shonin, the twenty-sixth high priest of Nichiren Shoshu, expresses this idea in his work "The Threefold Secret Teaching":

In light of the Lotus Sutra, the phrase "three thousand worlds in a single moment of life" has two meanings: to include and permeate. On the one hand, the entire Universe is included in each moment, and on the other, each moment permeates the entire Universe. Each moment is a particle of dust that possesses the elements of all lands in the Universe, or a drop of water whose essence differs in no way from the vast ocean itself.

Let us turn now to the relationships that exist between the component principles that comprise each moment, or *ichinen sanzen*. These are the Ten Worlds, their mutual

113

inclusion, the ten factors and the three realms. At the beginning of a treatise called "The True Object of Worship" Nichiren Daishonin quotes a passage from T'ien-t'ai's *Great Concentration and Insight*:

> Life at each moment is endowed with the Ten Worlds. At the same time, each of the Ten Worlds is endowed with all the others, so that an entity of life actually possesses one hundred worlds. Each of these worlds in turn possesses thirty realms, which means that in the one hundred worlds there are three thousand realms. The three thousand realms of existence are all possessed by a single entity of life. If there is no life, that is the end of the matter. But if there is the slightest bit of life, it contains all the three thousand realms.[5]

When T'ien-t'ai writes, "Life at each moment is endowed with the Ten Worlds," he means that in every single moment of life there exists the potential for ten conditions: Hell, Hunger, Animality, Anger, Humanity, Heaven, Learning, Realization, Bodhisattva and Buddhahood. None of the Ten Worlds is fixed. Life in any of the Ten Worlds has the Ten Worlds within it; in other words, it has the potential, in each moment, to manifest any one of the Ten Worlds. This concept is the mutual inclusion, or "mutual possession", of the Ten Worlds. As we saw a few pages ago, because each of the Ten Worlds has all Ten Worlds within it, we have a total of one hundred worlds.

T'ien-t'ai's expression that "each of these worlds in turn possesses thirty realms" is explained by understanding that each of the Ten Worlds includes the ten factors of life, each one of which in turn possesses the three realms of existence. On its own, this would mean that the Ten Worlds together had a total of three hundred realms; however, since each of the Ten Worlds contains the other nine in addition to itself, the true total is three thousand realms. The ten factors of life are: appearance, nature, entity, power, influence, internal cause, relation (or external cause), latent effect, manifest effect and, finally, their consistency from beginning to end. The three realms of existence are: the realm of the five components of life (form, perception, conception, volition and consciousness), the realm of living beings, and the realm of the environment. So the figure of three thousand was not chosen at random: rather, it reflects the immensity and diversification of life.

Throughout history there have been people who have realized that all natural phenomena are elusive and uncertain, and so they have set out to seek the eternal, unchanging truth of life. Different teachers have offered different explanations of the relationship between this absolute truth and the ephemeral world that we experience. Some have suggested that the ultimate truth governs this world from a higher plane; others that it lies beyond or behind phenomena, or that phenomena are in fact mere illusion and that the ultimate truth alone is real. A similar dualistic tendency is found in some of the Buddhist teachings predating the Lotus Sutra; these generally held that the mind is the basis of all phenomena, and that all phenomena arise from the mind. By contrast, the principle of *ichinen sanzen*, based on the Lotus Sutra, has it that the mind (or each moment of our lives) and the phenomena of the Universe are "two but not two". All phenomena are manifestations of the ultimate reality, and the ultimate reality exists only in changing phenomena: in other words, neither can exist independently of the other. Thus all of the events in the Universe, being manifestations of our *ichinen*, are integrated to form a single entity, so that every individual being is directly connected with everything else in the Universe. Every moment of every being's life pervades the three thousand realms, and the three thousand realms are encompassed in each and every one of those moments. It is as a result of their interrelation that all of the phenomena of the Universe derive their form.

From the viewpoint of the *ichinen sanzen* principle, every single person has the potential to become a Buddha, awakened to the eternity and boundlessness of life. However, what people actually experience is rather different from this potential. Recognizing this difference, T'ien-t'ai formulates two views of *ichinen sanzen* – the theoretical and the actual. By theoretical *ichinen sanzen* he means the life of

115

common mortals, or unenlightened people, through the Nine Worlds from Hell to Bodhisattva, in which Buddhahood remains dormant. By contrast, actual *ichinen sanzen* indicates the life of Buddhahood; that is, the life in which Buddhahood is fully active and manifest. The *ichinen sanzen* described in the second, "Means", chapter of the Lotus Sutra is identifiable as theoretical, because it explains Buddhahood as a potential inherent in people of the Nine Worlds. The *ichinen sanzen* indicated in the sixteenth chapter, "Lifespan of the *Tathagata*", is described as actual because it presents Buddhahood as a reality manifested in Shakyamuni's life. According to Nichiren Daishonin's Buddhism, however, even the version of *ichinen sanzen* described in the sixteenth chapter is incomplete, because it is explained only as an *effect* – that is, as the enlightenment Shakyamuni attained some time in the remote past. Since the description of *ichinen sanzen* in this sixteenth chapter fails to reveal the cause which enabled Shakyamuni to attain his original enlightenment, it falls short of a full clarification of the ultimate reality. Nichiren Daishonin was the person who identified the original cause of Shakyamuni's enlightenment – and, indeed, of the enlightenment of all Buddhas – as *Nam-myoho-renge-kyo*, or the Mystic Law. In "The Essence of the 'Lifespan of the *Tathagata*' Chapter" he writes: "*Nam-myoho-renge-kyo*, the heart of the 'Lifespan of the *Tathagata*' chapter, is the mother of all Buddhas throughout the ten directions and the three existences of past, present and future."[6]

The question we must ask is: How can common mortals of the Nine Worlds awaken to and manifest their latent Buddhahood? T'ien-t'ai's Buddhism was – and is – extremely difficult to understand, and the meditational practices it prescribed for "observing the mind", or perceiving the three thousand realms within oneself, were hardly feasible for the vast majority of people, being suited only to a small monastic elite. Furthermore, these practices focused solely on the inner workings of life, and had little relevance to the outer world – the life we all have to live in society. Nichiren Daishonin, on the other hand, sought to establish a way of realizing *ichinen sanzen* that would be open to all, a practice that would not only illumine the inner realm of life but would also transform the world we live in. Accordingly he embodied his enlightenment to the Law of *Nam-myoho-renge-kyo* in the form of a mandala called the Gohonzon which, in his teaching, is the fundamental object of worship. The Daishonin teaches that belief in the Gohonzon and the chanting of *Nam-myoho-renge-kyo* in themselves constitute the "observation of the mind", or the attainment of Buddhahood. So, through the inscription of the Gohonzon, he established a way whereby all people, equally, could realize *ichinen sanzen* and attain Buddhahood in their ordinary lives. To use an analogy, we may know nothing about electronics or the workings of a television set, but we can still enjoy watching television simply by turning on the set. Faith in the Gohonzon is analogous to the act of turning on the television and selecting the channel; the picture we then watch can be likened to the Buddhahood we enjoy as it manifests itself from within our lives. In this way the Daishonin gives concrete and practical expression to the Buddhist philosophy taught by Shakyamuni and later systematized by T'ien-t'ai.

The Ten Worlds
The Ten Worlds, the first of the component principles of *ichinen sanzen*, are the ten states or conditions of life that we experience. The Ten Worlds, taken together, comprise an analysis of the states or conditions a single life manifests over the course of time. The idea of the Ten Worlds describes the subjective sensations experienced by the self at the most fundamental level of life. As we have seen, the Ten Worlds are, working from the lowest to the highest, Hell, Hunger, Animality, Anger, Humanity, Heaven (or Rapture), Learning, Realization, Bodhisattva and Buddhahood.

The idea of the Ten Worlds had its origins in a cosmological theory; that is, it was thought that there were ten distinct and separate realms into which people were reborn, the particular realm being determined by the nature of the individual's accumulated karma. For example,

Humanity denoted the world of human beings, Animality the realm of beasts, Heaven the dwelling of the gods, and Hell an underground prison. However, in the doctrine of *ichinen sanzen*, the Ten Worlds are viewed not as physical locations but as states or conditions that are inherent in each of us and which we experience moment by moment through our interaction with the environment. Nichiren Daishonin, as we saw on page 10, discusses this view of the first six worlds in "The True Object of Worship":

> When we look from time to time at a person's face, we find him sometimes joyful, sometimes enraged, and sometimes calm. At times greed appears in the person's face, at times foolishness, and at times perversity. Rage is the world of Hell, greed is that of Hunger, foolishness is that of Animality, perversity is that of Anger, joy is that of Rapture, and calmness is that of Humanity.[7]

The four higher worlds are likewise inherent in life. According to Nichiren Daishonin's Buddhism, Hell, Heaven and even Buddhahood are potential conditions in life:

> As to the question of where exactly Hell and the Buddha exist, one sutra says that Hell exists underground and another sutra says that the Buddha is in the west. However, closer examination reveals that both exist in our five-foot body.[8]

So all of the Ten Worlds exist within our ordinary daily lives.

The Ten Worlds Considered Individually

The first world, Hell (Japanese *jigoku*), indicates a state utterly devoid of freedom, a condition of extreme suffering and despair in which one is spurred by rage to destroy oneself and others. Buddhist sutras describe various kinds of hells – such as the eight hot hells, the eight cold hells and the sixteen minor hells. Much in the same way as Dante described in his *Divine Comedy* the nine levels of Hell, the nine levels of Purgatory and the ten levels of Paradise – a scheme typical of mediaeval Christian cosmology – Nichikan Shonin likewise refers to traditional cosmology when he writes in his "Threefold Secret Teaching" that

Hell is a dwelling of red-hot iron, and Hunger, a place five hundred *yojana* beneath the human world. Those in Animality live in the water, on the land and in the air. Anger dwells at the oceanside or on the sea floor. Humanity is life on the Earth, and beings of Heaven reside in a palace.

However, as we have noted, the concept of the Ten Worlds can be viewed not only as a cosmological system but as a schema of the potentials inherent in all life. In this sense the statement that "Hell is a dwelling of red-hot iron" may be understood as describing the inescapable torment we suffer when we are in the state of Hell.

The second world is Hunger (Japanese *gaki*). In this state we are governed by constant cravings for objects or certain experiences, such as wealth, fame, power and pleasure. The causes of this state are to be found in such tendencies as greed, miserliness and jealousy. Originally the world of Hunger was viewed as a realm inhabited by the spirits of the dead, thought to be suffering from starvation as karmic retribution for the greed and selfishness they had displayed while alive: in art they are often depicted with distended bellies and needle-thin throats. In his *Treatise on Accordance with the Correct Doctrine* the Indian scholar Samghabhadra, who lived during the fifth century AD, describes three kinds of hungry spirits, each of which is further subdivided into three; the Sutra of Meditation on the True Law lists thirty-six kinds. The realm inhabited by these hungry spirits was said to be located five hundred *yojana* beneath the surface of the Earth. (A *yojana* was a unit of measurement used in ancient India: estimates as to its length vary from 9.6km to 24km.) The image of a dark narrow dwelling, deep underground, vividly conveys the restrictions of the state of Hunger, in which we are imprisoned by our insatiable desires.

The third world is that of Animality (Japanese *chikusho*). In this state we are like an animal driven by survival instincts and lack any restraining virtues such as reason or morality. People in this state observe only the law of the jungle. They take advantage of those weaker than themselves and toady to those who are stronger.

119

Fourth of the worlds is Anger (Japanese *shura*). The first three states – Hell, Hunger and Animality – are collectively known as the three evil paths; life in these states is dominated by instinctive desires and passions. In this next state, Anger, there is an awareness of ego – but it is a ravening, distorted ego, determined to succeed over others, whatever the cost, and seeing everything as a potential threat to its survival. This state was said to be characterized by *asuras*, contentious demons found in ancient Indian mythology. As we saw, Nichikan Shonin wrote that "Anger dwells at the oceanside": the crashing waves of the ocean and its fearsome potential to overwhelm anything in split seconds can be thought of as representing the belligerent and overbearing ego that is the hallmark of Anger. In this state we value only ourselves, holding everyone else in contempt. We believe that we are superior to everybody else, and cannot bear to be found inferior to anyone else in any respect. The three evil paths, taken together with Anger, are called the four evil paths, or the four lower worlds.

Fifth of the Ten Worlds is that of Humanity (Japanese *nin*). This world is symbolized by the stability of the vast, flat Earth. Humanity is a state in which we can use reason to control our instinctive desires, so that the more truly humane qualities such as love and benevolence can emerge. People in the state of Humanity exercise sound judgement, distinguish right from wrong and, in general, behave in a humane fashion.

The sixth of the worlds is that of Heaven (Japanese *ten*). This state can best be understood by thinking of the intense joy we experience when, for example, we have the satisfaction of attaining something we have long desired, or when long-term suffering has finally been relieved. Although it is intense, the joy experienced in this state is short-lived and extremely vulnerable to external influences.

These first six states, from Hell to Heaven, are collectively called the Six Paths, or the six lower worlds. All of them have in common one thing: they are brought about through either the fulfilment or the thwarting of various desires and impulses. Their appearance or disappearance is therefore governed by external circumstances. Buddhism points out that most people spend their lives shuttling back and forth among these six states without ever realizing that they are completely at the mercy of their reactions to their environment. Any happiness or satisfaction that we may gain in these states is entirely governed by circumstances, and is therefore transient. But when we are trapped in the six lower worlds we fail to realize this, instead basing our entire happiness – indeed, the whole of our identity – on external factors that are by definition beyond our control. However, when we recognize that everything experienced in the six lower worlds is impermanent, a recognition which prompts us to begin a search for lasting truth, we enter the next two states, Learning and Realization; these two states, along with the final two, Bodhisattva and Buddhahood, are named the Four Noble Worlds. Unlike the Six Paths, which in essence constitute our passive reactions to the environment, these four higher states are attained only through deliberate and continued effort on our part.

In the state of Learning we seek truth vicariously through the teachings or experiences of other people. The Japanese word for this state, *shomon*, can be translated as "voice hearer": originally it was used for those of the Buddha's disciples who had heard him preach in person. Beyond Learning is the eighth world, Realization (Japanese *engaku*). This state is rather similar to that of Learning, except that here we seek the truth not through other people's teachings but through our own direct perception. The Sanskrit word for this state, *pratyekabuddha*, means a person who arrives independently at an understanding of Buddhist truths. Learning and Realization are together described as the "two vehicles". In these states, having realized the impermanence of all things, we have won a measure of independence: no longer are we subject to our reactions to the environment, as we were when travelling in the six lower worlds. But things are far from perfect. People of the two vehicles have a tendency to be contemptuous towards those who have yet to reach this level of understanding – that is, who are still trudging along in the Six Paths. In addition, their pursuit of truth is largely a matter of self-interest, so that people in these two states may retain a measure of egotism.

Beyond them is the ninth world, that of Bodhisattva (Japanese *bosatsu*). This state, in contrast to the two vehicles, is characterized by compassion and altruistic behaviour. Bodhisattvas, although they aspire to achieve supreme enlightenment, at the same time are determined that all other human beings, too, should reach the same understanding. Conscious of the bonds that link us to everyone else, when we are in the Bodhisattva state we realize that any happiness that we enjoy solitarily is illusory and only partial, and so we devote ourselves to alleviating other people's suffering – even if it should cost us our lives. When we are in this state we find that our greatest satisfaction comes from altruistic behaviour. Nichiren Daishonin pinpoints the aim and spirit of the bodhisattva in one sentence of his *Record of the Orally Transmitted Teachings*: " 'Joy' means that both oneself and others rejoice."[9] Dr Hans Selye, in his book *The Stress of Life* (1956), emphasizes the importance of expanding one's personal horizons; he says in effect that transforming one's selfish impulses into altruistic deeds, thereby arousing a sense of gratitude in other people, is the path to true inner security. This concern for others is characteristic of the state of Bodhisattva.

The states from Hell to Bodhisattva are collectively known as the Nine Worlds. The term is often used to indicate the unenlightened condition of common mortals, as contrasted with the tenth of the Ten Worlds, Buddhahood (Japanese *butsu*). The state of Buddhahood implies a condition of perfect and absolute freedom, the supreme state in which we are awakened to the perfect and ultimate truth that is the reality of all things. The ten honorific titles of the Buddha, which appear in Nagarjuna's *Commentary on the Ten Stages*, are believed together to describe the great power, wisdom, virtue and competence unique to the state of Buddhahood. The ten titles are:

- "Thus Comes One." As we have seen, this means someone who has come from the world of truth. A Buddha embodies the fundamental truth of all phenomena, and grasps the law of causality that permeates past, present and future.
- "Worthy of Offerings." This means a person who is qualified to receive offerings from both human and heavenly beings.
- "Right and Universal Knowledge." This implies someone who comprehends all phenomena correctly and perfectly.
- "Perfect Clarity and Conduct." This title describes a person who understands the eternity of past, present and future, and who carries out good deeds to perfection.
- "Goodness Attained." This means a person who has gone to the world of enlightenment.
- "Understanding of the World." This implies a person who, through his or her grasp of the law of causality, understands all secular and religious affairs.
- "Unexcelled Worthy." A person who stands supreme among all other human beings.
- "Leader of People." This title describes someone who instructs and leads all people to enlightenment.
- "Teacher of Gods and Humans." In other words, a teacher who can guide all human and heavenly beings.
- "Buddha, the World-honoured One." This means a person endowed with perfect wisdom and virtue who can win the respect of all people. Buddhism constitutes a practical system of teachings which together provide a means for realizing this ideal state of Buddhahood.

When we look around us today we see evidence everywhere of the remarkable achievements of science and technology over the past few decades, and yet, ironically, these very advances often work to restrict our freedom, giving us the impression that we are just a cog in the huge machine of a bureaucratic society. Moreover, illnesses born from the nature of our modern civilization – such as the stress-related diseases and various emotional disorders – are endemic.

Despite our gains, then, we have yet to free ourselves from the sufferings of the six lower worlds. Arnold Toynbee once noted in a dialogue with me that

> The disparity between our knowledge and our ethics is greater today than it has ever been. This is not simply humiliating; it is mortally dangerous ... this sense of humility ought to spur us on to achieve the dignity without which our life has no value and without which our life cannot be happy.[10]

He also, at the same time, voiced his expectation that important keys to the solution of problems facing the modern world might be found in Eastern philosophy.

Yujiro Ikemi, Professor Emeritus at Kyushu University and an authority on psychosomatic medicine, has proposed a theory that categorizes human life into four phases, which he terms C (child), A (adult), P (parent) and S (self). We can find correlations between this theory and the concept of the Ten Worlds. C could be said to correspond to the four states of Hell, Hunger, Animality and Anger – conditions bound by suffering, desire or instinct, in which the breadth and quality of life are brutally impoverished, to the extent that one can only just survive. In the C state the workings of the brain stem and the hindbrain predominate. The A state can be thought of as corresponding to the worlds of Humanity and Heaven: it is characterized by reason and intelligence, both of which are products of the forebrain. The P state, parallelling the worlds of Learning, Realization and Bodhisattva, is typefied by conscience, responsibility and a sense of morality, and is supported by the workings of the entire cerebral cortex. Finally, the S state represents the true self, rooted in eternal life. It integrates C, A and P, and leads to a full awakening of our potential.

Should any of the C, A and P states gain exclusive dominance within us our characters will suffer from various distortions. Predominance of the C state manifests itself in the form of blind self-centred urges, corresponding to what Buddhism terms the "three poisons" of greed, anger and stupidity. Predominance of the A state may suppress intuitive functions, so that we are led to lean exclusively on our analytical and conceptual abilities. Excessive influence of the P state can cause us to become hypocritical or judgemental of others, or we may find ourselves the prisoners of a repressive conscience. In general, any imbalance among these states may work to suppress and thwart our life force, and in some cases may cause irreparable harm – hence the necessity of fostering the S state, which works to integrate and balance the others. If the S state is highly developed, the physical and mental energies of the C state are able to redirect instinctive desires and impulses positively, thereby maintaining the proper functioning of the body; the A state will allow us to pursue our self-development in a humane and balanced fashion, without placing exclusive emphasis on the intellect; and the P state's sense of morality will be tempered by compassion, so that we do not fall into the trap of hypocrisy and self-righteousness.

The S state is therefore analogous to the state of Buddhahood, which balances, integrates and elevates the workings of the Nine Worlds. Buddhahood entails the wisdom to recognize the ultimate reality of our lives, infinite compassion, a perfected eternal self, and a total, incorruptible purity of life. According to Buddhist teachings, it is only when we have established as our basis this highest state, Buddhahood, that we can bring about a reformation of our entire existence, directing all the physical and mental activities of our Nine Worlds towards altruistic and valuable goals.

The Mutual Possession of the Ten Worlds
Nichiren Daishonin, in his treatise "The Opening of the Eyes", writes: "The concept of *ichinen sanzen* begins with an understanding of the mutual possession of the Ten Worlds or states of existence."[11] Mutual possession, or mutual inclusion, means that each of the Ten Worlds encompasses all of the other worlds within itself. We can interpret this to mean that all ten states are inherent in every individual; a person experiencing the state of Humanity in one moment may, in the next, either remain in the state of

125

Humanity or manifest one of the other nine worlds. What this principle tells us, then, is first that life is not fixed in one of the ten conditions but at any moment can manifest any of the ten, and second that life in any one of the conditions possesses all of the other conditions latent within itself.

The idea of mutual possession explains the interrelationships of the Ten Worlds as one or another of them moves from dormancy to active manifestation or from active manifestation back to dormancy. For example, at one moment we may be experiencing the joy of Heaven, but in the next moment some factor in our surroundings may suddenly change, so that we plunge into the depths of Hell. But this does not mean that the state of Heaven in us has ceased to exist: it has simply shifted from a manifest state to a latent one and, with the appropriate external stimulus, will emerge again from dormancy. In such a way the ten states from Hell to Buddhahood are activated by our relationship with the external world, manifesting themselves in both the physical and spiritual aspects of our every activity. Within a single individual the Ten Worlds, although they are of course each different from the other, are at the same time unified in their potential to shift from dormancy to activation and back again.

We can see, then, that the idea of the mutual possession of the Ten Worlds is a concept that describes the dynamic structure of life in an all-embracing way. We have already mentioned (see page 10) Nichiren Daishonin's explanation of the concept, as contained in his "The True Object of Worship": "Even a heartless villain loves his wife and children. He too has a portion of the Bodhisattva world within him."[12] Thus the state of Bodhisattva – like all the other states – exists even in the world of Hell. Konrad Lorenz pointed out that, although animals normally act solely in accord with their instincts, there are some that will assist an ailing fellow creature. We can take this as an example of the world of Bodhisattva existing in the world of Animality.

Which of the Ten Worlds will manifest itself at a given moment depends not only on external influences but also on one's basic tendencies. A given external influence need not necessarily bring out the same world in two different people. Of course, our conditions fluctuate from one moment to the next but, looked at in a broader perspective, there is always one condition or set of conditions around which our activities centre and to which we are most likely to revert; for example, some people's lives revolve around the three evil paths, some shuttle back and forth among the six lower worlds, and some people's primary motivation is the quest for the truth which characterizes the two vehicles. The underpinning of the concept of the mutual possession of the Ten Worlds – which clarifies the fundamental equality and infinite potential of every human being – lies in its implication that every single individual possesses the potential to elevate his or her basic tendencies. In other words, through continuing effort in Buddhist practice we can gradually raise our basic tendencies until we eventually establish the supreme state of Buddhahood as our foundation. Although the state of Buddhahood is impossible to describe in words – impossible even to imagine – we can think of it as a condition of absolute joy and confidence experienced in the very depths of our being, and expressing itself through the Nine Worlds of everyday life.

During the process of raising our basic tendencies, our perceptions and values are certain to change. In a letter to his disciple Soya Kyoshin the Daishonin writes:

> Hungry spirits perceive the Ganges River as fire, human beings perceive it as water, and heavenly beings perceive it as *amrita* [divine nectar]. The water itself is the same, but it appears differently according to the karmic capacity of individuals.[13]

The Daishonin is saying that a life in the state of Hunger perceives the waters of the Ganges as if they were its own self-consuming flames of greed, whereas a life in a different state has a totally different perception. Although the passage refers only to perception in the states of Hunger, Humanity and Heaven, the same principle obviously applies to all the other states as well. In the final analysis, then, when we establish Buddhahood as our immutable foundation, so that our individual lives fuse with the Buddhahood of the Cosmos, we will be certain to be able to create a life of limitless joy and absolute freedom.

The Ten Factors of Life

We have already encountered the ten factors of life, which are set out in a passage from "Means", the second chapter of the Lotus Sutra:

> The true entity of all phenomena can only be understood and shared between Buddhas. This reality consists of appearance, nature, entity, power, influence, internal cause, relation [or external cause], latent effect, manifest effect, and their consistency from beginning to end.

The expression "all phenomena" can be taken to mean all ten of the Ten Worlds, from Hell to Buddhahood.

The principle of the ten factors of life is an analysis of those aspects of life that remain constant in all changing phenomena. While the Ten Worlds describe life's differing expressions, the ten factors clarify the various aspects of existence common to all life in any of these states, across the spectrum from Hell to Buddhahood. Life in any of the Ten Worlds equally possesses the same ten factors. The principle of the ten factors also enables us to understand how life shifts from one of the Ten Worlds to another.

In the Japanese text of the sutra the word *nyoze*, meaning literally "like this", prefixes the names of all the ten factors. This indicates that all ten manifest the ultimate entity of life. Let us look at the ten factors in turn.

The first is appearance (Japanese *nyozeso*), and it describes those aspects of things which can be perceived or discerned from the outside. In the factor of appearance are included such attributes as colour, form and behaviour; in terms of human beings, appearance refers to the physical side of our existence, including the body and its various functions. Second of the ten is nature (Japanese *nyozesho*). This describes inherent disposition, or those qualities that cannot be discerned from the outside. In terms of human existence, the factor of nature refers to the spiritual aspects of life, such as mind and consciousness. The third factor of life is entity (Japanese *nyozetai*), the entity of life that manifests itself as both external appearance and internal nature but is in itself neither. It is the entity of life in any of the Ten Worlds.

These first three factors describe life from a static viewpoint; that is, they describe what life *is*. The next six factors, by contrast, describe the dynamic functions of life: power and influence describe the workings of life in terms of space, while the others deal with causality and the explanation of life's functions in terms of time.

Power (Japanese *nyozeriki*), the fourth of the factors, is life's inherent capacity to act – its potential strength or energy to achieve something. To give a couple of examples, life in the state of Humanity has the power to uphold ethical standards, and life in the state of Bodhisattva has the power to relieve the sufferings of others. The fifth factor, influence (Japanese *nyozesa*) represents the action or movement produced when life's inherent power is activated. It is the exertion of influence, either good or evil, in thought, speech or action. These two factors – power and influence – presuppose the existence of some object towards which movement or action is directed. When accompanied by the dynamic factors of power and influence, entity can be thought of as an autonomous self that can act relative to other existences.

The next four factors explain how the actions of that self cause it to shift from one of the Ten Worlds to another.

Internal cause (Japanese *nyozein*) is the cause latent in life that simultaneously contains a latent effect of the same nature as itself; that is, a good cause produces a good effect and a bad cause produces a bad one. Relation, or external cause (Japanese *nyozeen*), is the function that relates life to its surroundings; it works as an auxiliary cause. An internal cause activated through the factor of relation undergoes a change, and simultaneously produces a new latent effect; also, it is through the factor of relation that latent effects become manifest. Relation, then, can be viewed as the

129

connection between life and outside influences; through it one is able both to make causes and experience their effects. When an internal cause is activated by the factor of relation there is an effect in the depths of our being. This effect, constituting the eighth of the ten factors, is latent effect (Japanese *nyozeka*). Since both internal cause and latent effect are inherent in life, they occur simultaneously. By contrast, there is often a time-lapse between an action and its manifest effect. Manifest effect (Japanese *nyozeho*) is the concrete, perceivable result that emerges over time as a consequence of internal cause and latent effect. Manifest effect also indicates the experience of results whose causes we made in our own past.

The tenth and final factor is consistency from beginning to end (Japanese *nyoze hommatsu kukyoto*). This is the integrating factor that unites the other nine in every moment of life. In other words, where there is one factor, all the other nine *must* be present.

As we have said, the first three factors – appearance, nature and entity – together constitute an analysis of what life is. However, these three factors are not all on the same plane. Appearance (life's physical aspect) and nature (life's spiritual aspect) cannot simply be combined to form entity: entity (the changeless reality or ultimate truth of life) actually gives rise to the phenomena of appearance and nature – that is, they are its manifestations.

Power, influence, internal cause, relation, latent effect and manifest effect all represent the functions of life, but these factors, too, exist on different planes from each other. For example, power is latent in life whereas influence is power's manifestation directed towards our surroundings. Similarly, internal cause and latent effect are both inherent in life, while manifest effect is the perceivable result of their activation, and relation (external cause) is the intermediary connecting the potential with the manifest.

Finally, consistency from beginning to end, in integrating all the others, demonstrates that, if we define the first three factors collectively as entity, or beginning, and the following six factors as function, or end, the entity of all phenomena and the functions of that entity – in other words, both beginning and end – are inseparable.

In his "On the Ten Factors of Life" Nichiren Daishonin relates the first three factors to various important Buddhist concepts, such as the three truths, the three properties and the three virtues:

> First, "appearance" signifies the physical aspect of our lives, which is interpreted as the Buddha's enlightened property of action, emancipation, or the truth of temporary existence. Second, "nature" means the spiritual aspect of our lives and corresponds to the Buddha's enlightened spiritual property, wisdom, or the truth of non-substantiality. Third, "entity" refers to the entity of our lives, and corresponds to the property of the Law, the truth of the Middle Way, the Dharma nature of the Law or enlightenment.[14]

What do we mean by "the three truths", "the three properties" and "the three virtues"?

The three truths are three integral aspects of the truth as expounded by T'ien-t'ai on the basis of the Lotus Sutra. They are: the truth of Emptiness or non-substantiality; the truth of temporary existence, and the truth of the Middle Way. The Buddha is enlightened to the perfect unification of these three in every moment of life.

The truth of non-substantiality is that, because phenomena appear and disappear solely as a result of their interrelationship with other phenomena, they themselves have no fixed or independent existence: their true nature is *ku*, the potential state that can be described neither as existence nor as nonexistence. The factor of nature – indicating life's invisible, spiritual aspect – corresponds to the truth of non-substantiality.

Nevertheless, while all things are non-substantial in nature, they have a provisional or temporary existence, which is in a state of constant flux. This is the truth of temporary existence. The factor of appearance – representing life's outward, visible aspect, including its form and behaviour – therefore corresponds to the truth of temporary existence.

The truth of the Middle Way is that, although all phenomena are characterized both by non-substantiality and by temporary existence, ultimately they can be defined as neither: the true nature of all phenomena cannot be grasped by conceptions and certainly not by mere words. Thus the factor of entity, meaning the essential aspect of life, correlates with the truth of the Middle Way.

When they are interpreted in terms of the life of a Buddha, the three truths can be correlated with the Buddha's three enlightened properties. First, the property of action, or the Buddha's physical property, denotes not only the Buddha's physical body but also the Buddha's compassionate actions directed towards saving other people. Since this is the Buddha's physical property it corresponds both to the factor of appearance and to the truth of temporary existence. Second, the property of wisdom enables the Buddha to perceive the truth: since this is the Buddha's spiritual property it corresponds both to the factor of nature and to the truth of non-substantiality. Third, the property of the Law is the truth to which the Buddha is enlightened: since it is the Buddha's essential property it can be correlated with both the factor of entity and the truth of the Middle Way.

So much for the three truths and the three properties. What do we mean when we talk about "the three virtues"?

The three virtues said to be possessed by a Buddha are emancipation, wisdom and the property of the Law. Emancipation – freedom from the sufferings of birth and death – clearly corresponds to the factor of appearance, the truth of temporary existence and the Buddha's physical property. The virtue of wisdom, whereby a Buddha realizes the truth, corresponds to the factor of nature, the truth of non-substantiality and the Buddha's spiritual property. The virtue that is the property of the Law is the truth which a Buddha has attained, or the true entity of life. This virtue can be correlated with the factor of entity, the truth of the Middle Way and the Buddha's essential property. According to Nichiren Daishonin, one immediately attains the reality of the three truths and manifests the three enlightened properties and three virtues of a Buddha within oneself when one embraces the Gohonzon, the embodiment of the Mystic Law.

The Ten Onenesses

There are other ways of looking at the ten factors. Taken all in all, they represent the oneness of the material and the spiritual, or oneness of body and mind. In his commentary on T'ien-t'ai's *Profound Meaning of the Lotus Sutra*, the Chinese Buddhist scholar Miao-lo (711-82) wrote:

> Appearance exists only in what is material; nature exists only in what is spiritual. Entity, power, influence and relation in principle combine both the material and the spiritual. Internal cause and latent effect are purely spiritual; manifest effect exists only in what is material.

Appearance is described as "material" in this passage because it represents the physical, outwardly manifest aspect of life. Nature is called "spiritual" because it is identified with the invisible inner aspect of life; internal cause and latent effect likewise denote something "spiritual" because they are dormant within life. Manifest effect has a perceivable form, and so it is defined as "material". Entity, power, influence and relation all entail both material and spiritual aspects of life. It goes almost without saying that all the other nine factors are integrated by the factor of consistency from beginning to end.

The term "oneness of body and mind" appears in Miao-lo's commentary. It is one of the ten onenesses, or "non-dualities", which are derived from T'ien-t'ai's systematization of the ten mystic principles of the Lotus Sutra. The ten onenesses are given as follows:

- The oneness of body and mind.
- The oneness of the internal and the external.
- The oneness of the inherent Buddha nature and the Buddhahood attained through practice.
- The oneness of cause and effect.

133

- The oneness of the pure and the impure – that is, of enlightenment and delusion.
- The oneness of life and its environment.
- The oneness of self and others – in other words, the oneness of the Buddha and common mortals.
- The oneness of thought, word and deed.
- The oneness of provisional and true teachings. A Buddha preaches both the provisional teachings and the true teaching – the one supreme vehicle – both of which spring from the Buddha's enlightened mind. To put it another way, all of a Buddha's teachings derive from the single Law of *Myoho-renge-kyo*.
- The oneness of benefit. This means that both the Buddha and the rest of the people ultimately enjoy the same benefit of Buddhahood: there is no fundamental distinction between the Buddha, who leads the people, and those who receive instruction from that Buddha, in that both are entities of *Myoho-renge-kyo*.

Thus the concept of oneness applies both to the relationship between body and mind and to those between humanity and nature, one person and another, mankind and society, and between all phenomena in the Universe.

Mind and Body
Since the early years of this century scientists and laypersons alike have become increasingly aware of the need to integrate the various fields of science in order to counter the growing emphasis on specialization. People who attempt this integration are sometimes called "systems scientists". The pioneers of systems science hoped to shed light on the complex interrelations of living organisms not just from an intuitive viewpoint but from a properly scientific one, and to this end they devised theories and specific methodologies; they were further able to demonstrate the applicability of their theories in a variety of areas of knowledge. This approach – emphasizing the reciprocal influences among phenomena – has been applied in many fields, including management, sociology, environmental engineering and even mechanical engineering.

The concept of the oneness of body and mind makes it clear that, even though the material and the spiritual are two separate classes of phenomena, they are nevertheless in essence indivisible, because they are both aspects of the same – ultimate – reality. When we talk about the "material" here we are referring to all physical, observable phenomena, including the human body; by the "spiritual" we mean all of the invisible, mental phenomena, such as the workings of reason, sense, emotion and volition. Modern researches in the fields of psychology and physiology have confirmed that there is an interaction between mind and body. Emotional stress gives rise to physical symptoms, such as ulcers or muscular tension, while physical factors such as vitamin deficiencies or changes in the level of the sugar in the blood can profoundly affect a person's emotional state. The Austrian pathologist Karl Rokitansky (1804-1878), for example, said that diseases of the stomach are a direct product of diseases of the brain, basing his statement on the fact that psychological stress affects the digestive process. Our rapidly increasing understanding of the subtlety of the reciprocal influence of mind and body has contributed to the development of a new science generally called "psychosomatic medicine".

The interrelationship between the material and the spiritual in terms of that between the human brain and the human mind is an important topic. The study of the brain and its functions is an important concern of modern medical science: it has been said that, while medicine's most important problem in the twentieth century is cancer, in the twenty-first its primary challenge will be the brain. Even today, there is considerable debate as to whether brain death or the cessation of heartbeat should be taken as the legal criterion for a human death.

The brain is often thought of as the site of the spirit and, as such, inseparably related to the mind. In his *Human Options* (1981) Norman Cousins, US peace activist and adjunct professor at the School of Medicine of the University of California, Los Angeles, has much to say on the topic of the amazing, unlimited powers of the human mind. Discussing the relationship between mind and brain, he claims that it is vital that we always choose to do what we believe is correct, because otherwise our choice adversely affects the physiological functioning of our brain. Cousins defines each individual's belief system as not just "a state of mind" but as "a prime physiological reality". He continues:

> Nothing is more wondrous about the fifteen billion neurons in the human brain than their ability to convert thoughts, hopes, ideas, and attitudes into chemical substances.[15]

Even a few neurons in the human brain can, in response to a subtle change in the mind, bring about a series of precise chemical reactions. The power contained within a single brain cell is indeed, to use Cousins' word, "wondrous".

The relationship between the mind and the brain is a principal subject of investigation in two different fields of science, psychopathology and neurophysiology. Researchers in the US, in particular, have studied the connection between changes in brain chemistry and emotional states such as joy, pleasure, misery and pain. For example, during the 1940s and early 1950s Harry Harlow, professor of psychology at Wisconsin University, explored the question of how the brain's secretions change in a person recently disappointed in love. Harlow's study was only one of many which documented the fact that brain secretions can be increased or diminished in response to such diverse factors as our thoughts, our behaviour and our environment.

However, even the closest scrutiny of our brain cells fails to reveal the nature of the spirit. Spiritual activity may be impossible without brain cells, but the brain is nevertheless only the *physical* seat of such activity. The Canadian neurosurgeon Wilder Penfield performed a long series of experiments during the 1930s and 1940s in an effort to determine whether or not the mind is located in the brain. He devised a surgical technique for the treatment of patients suffering from focal epilepsy and, while carrying out this technique, studied individuals' reactions to electrical stimulation of various parts of the brain. He discovered, for example, that when the visual or auditory areas of the brain were stimulated the patient would hallucinate; likewise, if one of the motor areas was stimulated, the person would find him- or herself involuntarily moving a limb. He showed that through electrical stimulation of the sensory areas in someone's brain one can cause that person to see, hear, smell, feel or taste, and in so doing he established an understanding of the way in which information received by the five sense organs is processed in the brain. But the most interesting thing of all about his experiments is that, when he asked the patients about their experience, they reported that they were surprised to find themselves responding con-sciously to the stimuli – they had not done so voluntarily, but rather had felt as if some outside force were compelling them, and they had followed its dictates. Penfield therefore came to the conclusion that the brain in and of itself is not responsible for all the workings of the human mind.

Further, he concluded that the highly evolved and sophisticated functions of the mind – functions such as belief, decision-making and value-judgement – can never be produced solely by the sort of electrical stimulation he used in his experiments. In his view, the brain is the physical vehicle of the psyche; or, more precisely, the physical locus of the manifestation of mental activity.

In addition, Penfield conducted research into the way that memories are stored in the brain, focusing his attention on the temporal lobe – an area of the brain a little smaller than a man's palm to be found just beneath the region of the temple and the ear. Penfield reported that, when this area of the brain was electrically stimulated, scenes from the patients' past reappeared in their mind's eye, and the thoughts and sensations that they had had originally likewise returned to them – much as if they were actually reliving the past experience. And people remembered things which had been long lost from their memories – for example, one man recollected his childhood acquaintances, other children with whom he had fought and a thief who had broken into his house. In light of Penfield's experiments it seems possible that the memories of *everything* we have experienced in the past are somehow stored in our brain.

137

Dr Yasunori Chiba, a Japanese neurophysiologist, has estimated that the number of data – in computer jargon, the number of bits – a single individual can commit to memory, both consciously and unconsciously, in the span of seventy years is approximately fifteen trillion. One Buddhist sutra states that, in the course of a single day, 800,004,000 thoughts cross an individual's mind; if we multiply this figure to get an estimate for a seventy-year period we end up with a figure of about twenty-one trillion. However, the sutra's precise figure of 800,004,000 should not be taken too literally; what is actually meant is simply "a large number". Nevertheless, in light of Chiba's figure it seems reasonable if one day, possibly, science will prove that each individual, at some level, has access to memories that extend right back to the origin of the human species – or even to the emergence of life itself, more than three billion years ago.

No one knows exactly where our memories are stored in the brain. Yet they emerge in response to stimuli from or in association with the external world. Neurophysiological studies have shown that the hypothalamus and the limbic system are associated with the primal responses, such as anger and fear, yet such emotions do not arise unless the relevant parts of the brain are stimulated: one could say that they lie dormant or latent within the human body.

Whatever the truth of these matters, the workings of the human brain are – again to use Cousins' term – "wondrous". We now know that the two cerebral hemispheres of the brain have different functions. The left hemisphere is associated with logic, calculation and language, while the right hemisphere is more concerned with sensitivity, intuition and imagination. The two hemispheres are joined by a "bridge" called the corpus callosum, which probably contains some two hundred million nerve fibres. Roger Sperry, a US professor of psychobiology and 1981 winner of the Nobel Prize for Physiology or Medicine, has developed experimental techniques whereby information can be fed into one or other of the cerebral hemispheres of so-called "split-brain" patients – people whose corpus callosum has for some reason been severed – so that the responses of the two hemispheres can be observed independently. The balanced development of the thought processes of both hemispheres is obviously essential if humanity is to progress harmoniously into the future. Some people say that the Japanese and other oriental cultures are right-brain, in that they are pictorial and imaginative, while Western culture, being directed towards logic and analysis, is left-brain. Clearly we need a sort of corpus callosum between the two different types of civilization!

In a sense, the modern computer can be considered as a by-product of neurophysiology: Norbert Wiener, the US mathematician regarded as the father of cybernetics, developed the science as a direct result of his researches into the functionings of memory in the human brain. The computer, just like the brain, can store, retrieve and process data. However, no one can yet create a computer able to take on all the functions of the human brain.

According to accepted theory in neuroscience, the amount of information contained in a single human brain approximates to that contained in the entire Universe. The Universe's information content at the moment of the Big Bang was sufficient to produce in due course all the stars and planets, including the Earth, as well as our own bodies and minds. It therefore seems reasonable to claim that the information contained within each of our brains is perfectly coextensive with that in the Universe as a whole.

In the *Record of the Orally Transmitted Teachings*, Nichiren Daishonin is quoted as stating that "Earth represents the physical, and space, the spiritual. These two categories of phenomena are inseparable."[16] Here, by "space" we mean the spiritual aspect of universal life, while the word "Earth" represents that part of the Universe visible to us – that is, the physical Universe. The Daishonin, therefore, taught that the Universe as a whole can be seen as an interplay between the material and the spiritual.

To sum up this section from a Buddhist viewpoint, we can say that all physical and mental phenomena are manifestations of the Mystic Law, which is the ultimate and unchanging reality of life and the Universe. The concept of the oneness of body and mind explains life in terms of the essential unity of these two aspects by clarifying the indivisibility of phenomena, on the one hand, and the ultimate reality, on the other. In Buddhism we describe this unity as "two but not two", meaning that there is a diversity of phenomena but only a single underlying reality. When we distinguish between the material and the spiritual we are operating on the level of phenomena; when we talk of their oneness we are talking in terms of the ultimate reality of life. In other words, to quote again from the *Record of the Orally Transmitted Teachings*, "that which embodies the oneness of body and mind is the single ultimate reality."[17]

"The oneness of body and mind" is therefore an expression which describes the ultimate reality of life.

The Three Realms of Existence

The one hundred worlds and the one thousand factors concern only the living, subjective individual: they cast no light upon his or her nonsentient environment. So, in themselves, they fall short of the full doctrine of *ichinen sanzen*, which applies not just to sentient beings but to nonsentient ones as well. However, with the revelation contained in the "Lifespan of the *Tathagata*" chapter of the Lotus Sutra, the doctrine of *ichinen sanzen* is rendered complete, the one hundred worlds and one thousand factors being multiplied by three, because of the three realms, to make a total of three thousand realms.

Of the three realms of existence only the realm of the environment is detailed in the "Lifespan of the *Tathagata*" (in its teaching about the True Land). However, the other realms are described in earlier sutras.

The "Lifespan of the *Tathagata*" expounds what T'ien-t'ai later formulated as the three mystic principles: True Cause, True Effect and True Land. By "True Effect" is meant Shakyamuni's original enlightenment; it is referred to by the sentence "Since I attained Buddhahood, an unimaginably long period has passed" – this reveals that Shakyamuni's world of Buddhahood is everlasting. The True Cause, or the practice whereby Shakyamuni gained his original enlightenment, is indicated by the statement that "once I also practised the bodhisattva austerities, and the life which I then acquired has yet to be exhausted"; this passage reveals the eternity of a Buddha's Nine Worlds, from Hell to Bodhisattva. The True Land, meaning the place where a Buddha preaches, is a concept derived from the passage: "Ever since then I have been constantly in this world, expounding the Law and instructing [the people]." This last passage reveals the eternal nature of the Buddha land, which is here identified with our ordinary, mundane world.

As noted, the mystic principle of the True Land leads us inevitably to the concept of the realm of the environment. The other two of the three realms are the realm of the five components and the realm of living beings: the five components are the constituents which, according to traditional Buddhist thought, unite temporarily to form a living being – that is, an individual who experiences one or other of the Ten Worlds. And it is in the environment that living beings carry out their various activities.

We can think of the three realms as the three different dimensions in which the Ten Worlds are manifest in the world of phenomena. Let us look at each of them individually.

The realm of the five components constitutes an analysis of life's physical and psychic functions. The five components, as we recall, are form, perception, conception, volition and consciousness. By "form" we mean the physical aspect of life – the body and the five sensory organs whereby we perceive the outside world. By "perception" we mean the function of reception of external information through the operation of the sense organs. "Conception" refers to the function whereby we form some idea or concept about what we have perceived. By "volition" we mean the will to initiate some action in response to what we have perceived and conceived. Finally, "consciousness" describes that discerning function of life which exercises value-judgements, distinguishes good from evil, and so on; it also supports and integrates the other four components. If we classify the five components in terms of life's material and spiritual aspects

141

we find that form alone corresponds to the physical aspect and the other four all correspond to the spiritual aspect. However, in line with the Buddhist belief that the spiritual and material aspects of life are essentially one, there can be no form without perception, conception, volition and consciousness, and equally there can be no consciousness without form, perception, conception and volition. The same goes for the other three components. In general, the five components should be understood not only individually but as a whole – that is, they should be understood in terms of their mutual interactions.

In contrast to the realm of the five components, which analyses living beings in terms of their physical and mental constituents, the realm of living beings sees them as integrated individuals who can experience the Ten Worlds and interact with other living beings. "No man is an island", as Donne pointed out: every one of us lives in a state of continual interrelationship and reciprocal influence. Looked at from this point of view, the realm of living beings can also be interpreted as the social environment, which includes all the other living beings with whom any given individual interacts.

The realm of the environment is easy to understand. All living beings dwell in some sort of an environment which supports their existence. The realm of the environment therefore includes all nonsentient life-forms, such as mountains, trees, grass and rivers.

Living beings in any of the Ten Worlds carry out their various activities as a result of the workings of the five components, but these will themselves be affected by whichever of the Ten Worlds the individual is currently experiencing. A person in the state of Hell, for example, will perceive, form a conception of and react to a particular event in a quite different way from someone who is in the state of Humanity. Moreover, differences in the states of living beings are reflected in the land they inhabit: the land may, depending upon its inhabitants, at different times manifest the states of Anger, Heaven and so on. All in all, the five components, living beings and their environments reflect the differences among each of the Ten Worlds.

While the Ten Worlds and the ten factors, taken together, describe aspects shared by all living beings, it is through the concept of the three realms that we can explain why no two beings are ever exactly alike. As we have just seen, the most basic differences expressed in the three realms are those of the Ten Worlds, but in addition to these we find also differences born from the life of each individual, for the workings of the five components differ from one person to the next. For example, even among people endowed with the same basic tendency towards Learning no two are endowed with exactly the same physical form, and no two will perceive, conceive or react to their environment in exactly the same way. Likewise no two people have exactly the same social or physical environment. The three realms, then, represent the actual world of the individual.

Life and Its Environment

We have already talked about the oneness of body and mind in terms of the ten factors. It is time to direct our attention to the oneness of life and its environment, a concept contained within that of the three realms.

As we have seen, a living being is formed from the temporary union of the five components. It constitutes a subjective self which experiences the karmic rewards for its past actions. However, there must also be an objective realm in which individuals' karmic rewards find expression. This objective world is the last of the three realms, the realm of the environment. In contrast, the five components and living beings – the first two of the three realms – correspond to "life".

Both life and its environment exhibit the manifest effect produced by the factors of internal cause, relation and latent effect. The effects of karma appear both in ourselves and in our objective environment, because self and environment are two integral aspects of any individual. When we use the word "environment" here we do not mean the overall context in which all beings live; rather, we are referring to the fact that each living being has its own unique environment in which the effects of its individual karma appear. In this sense, the formation of one's environment coincides with that person's birth into this world. Life and its environment – or, to put it another way, sentient beings and nonsentient beings – are often viewed as being totally distinct, but on the most fundamental level of life they are one and inseparable. It is to this principle that we are referring when we talk of the oneness of life and its environment.

So far, our Earth is the only home of life we know of in the entire Universe. It remains hospitable to life because of an extremely subtle environmental balance. Through the enormous power we have acquired as a result of technological advance, we have begun to have an influence on this delicate balance. As the science of ecology becomes more sophisticated, scientists' concern that people work more actively to preserve the biosphere grows stronger.

About ten thousand years ago what is now the Sahara Desert was blanketed in lush grass. It seems to have been a cultural centre, because a vast variety of ancient artefacts has been found scattered across it. Moreover, during the time of the Roman Empire part of the Sahara seems to have served as a granary. It is generally accepted that the Sahara region became a desert as a result of climatic changes and excessive grazing.

Today, such phenomena as droughts and floods seem to be occurring with even greater frequency than they did in the past, but added to these natural catastrophes there are man-made ones. These latter are the inevitable consequence of modern civilization's view that human beings and nature are two irreconcilably different entities.

Western societies have for centuries taken it as read that humanity's greatest challenge is the conquest and subjection of nature. The traditional oriental view could hardly be more different: it is that humanity is *a part* of nature, not a being in rivalry with it. It is possible that the difference between the two views is a result of the disparity between the oriental and occidental views of life itself.

Up until about the end of the nineteenth century Western

science was largely based on mechanistic ideas: the Universe was, in effect, a giant clock, and all phenomena could be explained in terms of "clockwork". Since the early decades of this century, however, attempts to integrate the findings of diverse specialized fields and to understand life in its totality have grown in both number and frequency. We can choose a couple of examples. The German zoologist Hans Driesch (1867-1941) concluded after years of research in the field of embryology that human behaviour cannot adequately be explained in purely mechanistic terms. He was a confirmed believer in the theory of vitalism, a theory which probably originated with Aristotle and which had it that there was a vital principle, or life force, present in living beings but absent from nonliving ones. Driesch borrowed Aristotle's term, *entelechy*, for this vital force, and suggested that it is at work in the regulation of cellular activity. Another of Driesch's hypotheses was that all living beings are interrelated to form a single living entity. Another scientist, the British physiologist and philosopher John Haldane (1860-1936), father of the great J.B.S. Haldane, specialized in the physiology of breathing and clarified much about the exchange of gases in the lungs during the process of respiration. Many of his studies were directed towards the cure or alleviation of lung diseases, especially those contracted by coal miners. Haldane demonstrated in these studies that life and its environment are inseparably related. A reading of his works confirms that his view of life was truly holistic.

Life can be understood only from a vantage point which integrates all of its activities as well as disciplines such as physics and chemistry. What we need most today is a philosophy and religion that can foster exactly this sort of holistic view – a view that encompasses not just the individual but the Cosmos as a whole.

In "On Omens" Nichiren Daishonin writes:

The ten directions are environment, and sentient beings are life. Environment is like the shadow, and life, the body. Without the body there can be no shadow. Similarly, without life, environment cannot exist, even though life is supported by its environment.[18]

When the Daishonin refers to the "ten directions" he is indicating the entire dimension of space, represented by the eight major points of the compass plus the zenith and the nadir. The subjective self, or "life", and the objective world, or "environment", share a symbiotic relationship.

The principle of the oneness of life and its environment further suggests that individuals can influence and reform their environments through inner change or through the elevation of their basic tendencies. Just as any living being contains the innate potential to dwell in any of the Ten Worlds, so does its environment: whatever the state we manifest in ourselves, that state will be simultaneously manifested in our surroundings. If our basic tendency is towards Hell we will evince anguish and misery from our surroundings, but if our basic state is Bodhisattva or Buddhahood we will enjoy the protection and support of the world around us. In other words, if we can elevate our basic state we can transform our external reality.

It is a common human failing always to blame our sufferings on things outside ourselves – other people, or circumstances beyond our control – rather than to make the effort to look for the causes within ourselves. However, if we take the oneness of life and its environment as a principle, and base our lives on this perception, we see that the fundamental cause of all our trials and tribulations lies not in the environment but in ourselves. In "On Attaining Buddhahood" Nichiren Daishonin writes:

If the minds of the people are impure, their land is also impure, but if their minds are pure, so is their land. There are not two lands, pure and impure in themselves. The difference lies solely in the good or evil of our minds.[19]

This passage tells us that there is a practical principle for the reformation of our world: a reformation of ourselves.

The previously quoted passage of the Daishonin includes the statement that "life is supported by its environment".

Aspects of the influence of the broader environment on human beings are studied in such sciences as bioclimatology, biometeorology and meteorological medicine. You can find frequent "alarmist" reports in the tabloid newspapers that, for example, a long period of cloudy weather may cause people to feel gloomy as a result of the fact that they are understimulated by ultraviolet rays, which have difficulty penetrating the clouds, or that the imminence of low atmospheric pressure will cause old wounds to ache. In fact, such claims seem to have a genuine physiological basis. Some West German radio stations feature daily broadcasts detailing the weather and its likely relationship to the listeners' health: they might warn, for example, that there is an unstable variation in low atmospheric pressure which could aggravate coronary and circulatory problems, or that northeasterly winds are making the air unusually dry and cool so that sufferers from asthma or migraines should take especial care.

Broadcasts like these could be termed a sort of meteorological medical report. Most of us recognize the subtle physiological changes brought about by differing atmospheric conditions. It is possibly for this reason that doctors prescribe a change of air. Recently, "woods bathing", or immersing oneself in nature, has become very popular in Japan: not only is it spiritually refreshing, it also clears one's head, because trees emit minute traces of substances called phytoncides, the inhalation of which enhances the capabilities of our nervous system and sharpens our thought processes.

The US neurosurgeon Harvey Cushing (1869-1939) once said: "A physician is obligated to consider more than a diseased organ, more even than the whole man – he must view the man in his world."[20] What he was suggesting – and what Buddhism suggests – is that in a sense our health depends on how we adapt ourselves to the challenges presented to us by our surroundings.

Even within the microcosm of our own body, the principle of the oneness of life and its environment is at work. If we look at ourselves as a single entity our *ichinen* – our life at

147

each moment – corresponds to life and the workings of our bodies' cells and molecules to our environment. In our every activity the two are inseparable. The cells and molecules – the environment that supports us – go on about their vital business as expressions of the three thousand realms at work in our lives at each moment. I think the very state of aliveness may be understood as a continuing relationship between life's generating power and the various components of the body. Nearly sixty trillion cells work independently – yet together! – to function as a single human being. But the human body is far more than just a collection of cells and organs. The various types of cells, organs and bodily systems maintain a creative balance between specialization and synthesis: they each display their individual character at the same time as they coordinate their activities into a harmonious unity.

The US social psychologist Kurt Lewin (1890-1947) coined the term "life space", by which he meant the individual's psychological environment as he or she perceives it. Lewin's approach bears many similarities to the concept of the oneness of life and its environment. His emphasis was on the internal, as opposed to the external, environment of living beings, and accordingly he saw the environment not just as the objective world but as an important component of the living beings that dwell in that world. He claimed that all life-forms on this planet have their own environment, meaning that there are as many environments as there are living beings. Even the cat or the dog that we keep as a pet has its own environment, in Lewin's view. In the course of creating their unique environment, each living being participates in a play of mutual influence with other living beings and with phenomena external to it.

Recent advances in medical technology have given us devices capable of exploring almost every aspect of a person's anatomy: the twin pinnacles of this achievement are perhaps the techniques known as X-ray computed tomography (CT) and nuclear magnetic resonance (NMR). Before the techniques of CT and NMR were developed bones often obscured X-ray scannings of the body, but today

148

every part of the body can be examined in remarkable detail. NMR gives what might be considered an example at the atomic level of the oneness of life and its environment. The technique works because, of the various atoms that constitute the human body, some nuclei – such as that of the hydrogen atom – resonate in a strong magnetic field, giving rise to a characteristic energy profile. The resulting signals are processed through a computer to produce a picture of the interior of the body. Although, at the naked-eye level, there is an obvious distinction between the human body and the external world, in the submicroscopic world of the atom there is no such obvious demarcation; both are composed of the same elements and atoms.

To give another example of the way the principle of the oneness of life and its environment works, we can look at the levels of salt in our own bodily fluids. This salt level is, apparently, close to that in seawater – something which evolutionary scientists say is a reflection of the fact that the life-forms from which we are descended evolved in the ocean. Towards the end of the nineteenth century the British physiologist Sydney Ringer (1835-1910) was working to create a laboratory solution of salts that would prolong the life of excised animal tissues immersed in it. He produced various combinations of organic salts, but still he was unsuccessful. Then, after much work, he discovered that – at last! – a frog's heart had kept on beating in one of his solutions. What had happened, as he discovered, was that one of his assistants had accidentally used tap water in the preparation of the solution, thereby introducing calcium and other inorganic substances. Thanks to this error, Ringer was able to establish the correct composition of a solution that would prolong the life of excised tissues: appropriately called Ringer's Solution, it is still in use today.

Our bodies are composed of various elements common throughout the Universe, such as hydrogen, oxygen and carbon. If you weigh 70kg, you are made up of roughly 44.1kg of oxygen, 13.3kg of carbon, 6.3kg of hydrogen, and 3.5kg of nitrogen; the other 2.8kg consists of potassium, calcium, phosphorus, sulphur and other trace elements

149

(including gold, which accounts for about 0.007g in the 70kg body). In this context a passage from one of Nichiren Daishonin's writings seems relevant:

> All phenomena are contained within one's life, down to the last particle of dust. The nine mountains and the eight seas are encompassed by one's body ...[21]

The "nine mountains and the eight seas" is a reference to the mountains and the seas which, according to ancient Indian cosmology, constitute the world. Another of the Daishonin's writings notes that "one's body imitates in detail the heaven and the Earth."[22]

The principle of the oneness of life and its environment applies not just to the microcosm of the human body but also to the macrocosm. Professor Tadanobu Tsunoda of Tokyo Medical and Dental University has produced evidence in favour of the idea that the motions of heavenly bodies – such as the Earth's revolution about the Sun and the Moon's revolution about the Earth – influence the functioning of the human brain. In his description of the relationship he uses the expression "changes in the microscopic brain which are synchronous with the cosmic environment".

The Daishonin teaches that the entire Universe is a single living entity, and that the cosmic life – the Law of *Myoho-renge-kyo* – manifests itself simultaneously both as living beings and as the environments in which they live. The two are one, united in the fact that they are both expressions of the fundamental Law of life.

The principle described simplistically as "the survival of the fittest" is generally regarded as the dominant factor in the evolution of life: according to this idea, certain living organisms, as a result of random mutations, become better adapted to their environment than others and so are more likely to survive and reproduce, passing on their improved characteristics to their offspring. However, in recent years scientists working in fields ranging from ecology to molecular biology have cast doubt on this scenario. One of the pioneers of this "new evolution" is the Japanese scientist Kinji Imanishi. He says that living beings play a dominant role in their own evolution, and suggests that all living beings not only select the location of their habitat but actually transform themselves in response to any changes of circumstance in that particular locale. His theory, therefore, proposes that the driving force of evolution consists not of random physical mutations but of the ability of living beings to make choices, and it emphasizes the inseparable relationship between evolution and the environment. In this respect, certainly, his theory comes close to the Buddhist view of life.

About 4.6 billion years ago the Earth was formed. During the following billion or two years the planet's ability to support life increased slowly until the most primitive life-forms developed. Exactly how they did so is still something of a mystery, but it is likely that volcanism on an unimaginable scale, the "organic soup" of the oceans and myriad chemical reactions in the atmosphere all played their part. If we view life as an essential force immanent in the Universe, we can put forward the idea that our planet had from the outset a tendency towards the emergence of life – a tendency that made primitive life possible while simultaneously bringing about the preconditions for its appearance. According to this view, all life-forms – including ourselves – were born from a nonsentient realm, the environment of the Universe; in his *Words and Phrases of the Lotus Sutra* T'ien-t'ai calls the place from which life emerges "the ultimate depth of life, that being the absolute reality". It is in these ideas that we find the great significance of the principle of the oneness of life and its environment. The Daishonin defines "the ultimate depth of life" as the most fundamental Law of life and the Universe – *Nam-myoho-renge-kyo* – which is itself the cosmic life force. It is, to put it another way, the Buddha nature inherent in all things, whether sentient or nonsentient, throughout the entire Universe.

Some Conclusions
How, in light of all of the above, does *ichinen sanzen* apply to our own societies?

151

Each individual life contains within itself all the various laws of the Universe, as well as the fundamental power that underlies all of the phenomena of the Universe and reveals itself through their workings. Each moment of our own individual life is exactly equivalent to the cosmic life. Far too often, though, we become fixated on the idea that we are separate entities, failing to realize that all life constitutes a single entity. We require a motivating force – the condition of Buddhahood – to direct our actions towards our neighbours, our country and indeed the entire world. Manifesting the state of Buddhahood implies the establishment of independence – that is, the ability to use our individual given circumstances as a means to growth, rather than being restricted or controlled by illusions and by the sufferings of life and death. In the light of the concept of the mutual possession of the Ten Worlds, we should try to establish the state of Buddhahood as the basis of everything we do.

Nichiren Daishonin's Buddhism defines true independence as our awakening to and fusion with the ultimate Law of life: the establishment of this independence is synonymous with the manifestation of Buddhahood from within our own life. When our inherent Buddhahood comes to the fore our innate power (one of the ten factors) of universal compassion and wisdom comes into action. Through the law of cause and effect (also included among the ten factors) the manifestation of Buddhahood will then be further strengthened so that it becomes integral to all our experience.

With the emergence of the Buddha nature, the individual's life manifests the four qualities of Buddhahood described in the Buddhist teachings – the four virtues of eternity, true self, happiness and purity. The virtue of eternity can be thought of as the state of boundless freedom attained when a person awakens to the eternity of life. By "true self" we mean the establishment of a genuine independence, one that is absolute and indestructible. The virtue of happiness implies a state of joy and fulfilment, educed from within, that cannot be destroyed by any outside influence. Finally, the virtue of purity is an essential purity of life, free from illusions and sufferings, which a person can maintain even while living and working in an impure society.

If we possess these qualities our existence will be joyful, happy, pure and secure despite any difficulties that may face us. Thus enriched, our voyage through the stormy seas of life and death will be free from illusions and directed towards the highest of objectives: the enlightenment of all.

If we establish Buddhahood as our basic state we are then able properly to harmonize the other Nine Worlds, and thereby to put them to positive use; moreover, we are able to give full play to the five components so that we can fully develop our individual qualities. We can build lasting happiness, invulnerable to any changes that might take place in our surroundings, and, with universal compassion, have a good influence on everyone whom we encounter, thereby transforming our environment for the better.

Nichiren Daishonin teaches that embracing the Gohonzon of *Nam-myoho-renge-kyo* makes possible the manifestation of the inherent Buddha nature. This fundamental truth of life – the Buddha nature – is further clarified by the concept of the nine consciousnesses, which will form the subject of the next chapter.

References

[1] *The Major Writings of Nichiren Daishonin*, vol. 3, page 199.
[2] *Nichiren Daishonin Gosho Zenshu*, pages 1239-40.
[3] *The Major Writings of Nichiren Daishonin*, vol. 1, page 3.
[4] *Nichiren Daishonin Gosho Zenshu*, page 724.
[5] *The Major Writings of Nichiren Daishonin*, vol. 1, page 45.
[6] Ibid., vol. 3, page 35.
[7] Ibid., vol. 1, page 52.
[8] Ibid., vol. 1, page 271.
[9] *Nichiren Daishonin Gosho Zenshu*, page 761.
[10] *Choose Life – A Dialogue*, Arnold Toynbee and Daisaku Ikeda, Oxford University Press, 1976, page 342.
[11] *The Major Writings of Nichiren Daishonin*, vol. 2, page 80.
[12] Ibid., vol. 1, page 53.
[13] *Nichiren Daishonin Gosho Zenshu*, page 1050.

[14] Ibid., page 410.
[15] *Human Options*, Norman Cousins, Berkley Books, 1981, page 205.
[16] *Nichiren Daishonin Gosho Zenshu*, page 742.
[17] Ibid., page 708.
[18] *The Major Writings of Nichiren Daishonin*, vol. 4, page 146.
[19] Ibid., vol. 1, page 4.
[20] Cited in *Man Adapting*, René Dubos, Yale University Press, New Haven, 1969, page 342.
[21] *Nichiren Daishonin Gosho Zenshu*, page 1473.
[22] Ibid., page 567.

6

Nine Consciousnesses –
Probing the Depths of Life

Every living being depends for its survival on its ability to perceive the nature of its surroundings and to respond accordingly. For instance, many plants survive the rigours of winter largely because they have the ability to adjust themselves to the difference between winter and summer weather; deciduous trees, to take a single example, would lose moisture through their large leaves in winter, and so they shed them. Trees, of course, have no thermometers to consult, but nevertheless they can detect temperature changes and take appropriate action.

In similar fashion, human beings have the ability to detect what is and what is not edible. For example, you might see a bowl of wax fruit. However tempting the false fruit might look, you can usually tell that it is wax just by looking at it; failing that, your sense of smell will almost inevitably give the game away. Finally, if your sense of smell and your tactile senses are deceived, you can taste a piece of the imitation fruit – and, of course, on finding that it is wax, spit it out. This is only one trivial example of the way in which the action of distinguishing or perception is the fundamental means whereby living beings can keep themselves alive.

In Sanskrit this ability of discernment, comprehension or perception is called *vijnana*. Usually the word is translated as "consciousness"; although this is a reasonable translation, we have to realize that, in using the term "consciousness" in this sense, we are referring to something rather different from what the word usually means.

The function of *vijnana* was included by Shakyamuni Buddha among the five components – form, perception, conception, volition and consciousness – which, all together, make up a living being. He developed the concept of the five

155

components as a means of analysing the lives of sentient beings in relation to their world. Each individual acts in tandem with its environment: it assimilates the information that it requires from its surroundings and then adjusts itself in accordance. This is among the vital functions of "consciousness" that we shall discuss in this chapter.

The Workings of Consciousness

Consciousness operates on several levels. The Buddhist doctrine of the nine consciousnesses, developed in the T'ien-t'ai and Hua-yen schools of sixth-century China, and given new significance in the Buddhism of Nichiren Daishonin, analyses the various strata of consciousness and thereby clarifies the entire spectrum of the operations of life itself.

Since the late years of the last century attempts have been made in the West to explore the different levels of human consciousness; these attempts have manifested themselves as the development of the sciences of psychoanalysis and depth psychology. The sciences of neurology and neurophysiology, too, in their analyses of the structure of the cerebral cortex, the site of our higher mental activities, have sought to examine objectively or inductively such functions as sensation, emotion, understanding and memory in connection with the workings of the brain.

Buddhism, by contrast, seeks to examine the depths of our lives in a more intuitive, deductive way. Although Western science and Buddhism may differ somewhat in their aims and basic conceptions, their different methods – objective analysis on the one hand and subjective inquiry on the other – are related, in that both attempt to tackle the problem of the differing strata of life, or consciousness. In this sense, the Buddhist theory of the nine consciousnesses has an importance comparable with, and analogous to, some of the hypotheses of modern scientific research.

The first five of the nine consciousnesses correspond to the conventional notion of the five senses – sight, hearing, smell, taste and touch. They arise as a result of the contact of the five sensory organs – eyes, ears, nose, tongue and skin – with

156

their respective objects. The five sense organs are pathways by which the external world is connected to the internal one, and are categorized as elements of the first of the five components, form, the physical aspect of life.

To understand how form relates to the other four components, let us use metaphor. Imagine you are strolling down a narrow back street, and that you hear the sound of a diesel engine. You look around and you see a truck approaching. The act of seeing, hearing or perceiving anything through one or more of the five senses corresponds to the second of the five components, perception. To judge whether or not it is safe to let a big lorry pass you on such a narrow street is the function of the third component, conception. The decision to step aside or to keep on walking involves a will to act based on the judgement you make: this will to act is the fourth component, volition. Consciousness, the fifth of the components, may be thought of as the component integrating perception, conception and volition in relation to form – that is, to the five sense organs and their respective objects.

In addition, each of the sense organs possesses – according to Buddhism – a consciousness of its own. What exactly do we mean when we say that a sense organ has a "consciousness"? Well, in physiological terms the sense organs do not pass on to the brain everything that they perceive; rather, they select the important things and transmit only these to the brain. So when we talk about the eyes' consciousness, for example, we are referring to their own power to discern – i.e., to select. Say we have lost our keys and are desperately searching for them. As usual in such situations, they are right in the centre of the living-room table, but still we do not see them. However frantically we hunt around, the keys remain lost because our eyes "select" the information that will be sent to our brain. Because we have a fixed belief that the keys could not possibly be in the middle of the living-room table – because we "would have seen them if they were" – the information picked up by our eyes, that that is indeed where the keys are, is not relayed on to our brain.

The eyes perceive images, the ears sounds, the nose odours, and so on. The function of consciousness that integrates this sensory input to form coherent images and distinguish among objects is the sixth consciousness.

Or, to take another approach, we can view the first six consciousnesses as functions emerging in response to the everyday external world of phenomena. We can easily recognize the workings of the six consciousnesses because they operate on the "outer surface" of our mind – that is, in our conscious realm. All six are undergoing perpetual change in response to their constant interaction with our surroundings, and yet there is no discontinuity in their functioning from one moment to the next, and so it is easy for us to fall into the trap of believing that we possess an unchanging self – perhaps even that this self oversees and controls the six consciousnesses. This function that produces a sense of a permanent self is called the seventh consciousness, or *mano*-consciousness. The word *mano* derives from the Sanskrit word *manas*, meaning mind, intellect or thought, and this consciousness owes its name to the fact that it performs the act of thinking. Unlike the sixth consciousness, which takes as its object the various circumstances of daily life and operates in response to them, the *mano*-consciousness operates from within, of its own accord and quite independently of any external circumstances. It represents the realm of abstract thought and examines the inner world, for example, distinguishing falsehood from truth. It is thanks to the power of the *mano*-consciousness to distinguish between good and evil that we are able to reflect upon our behaviour, decide whether or not it is worthy, and determine to improve our standards of conduct. Socrates' instruction, "Know thyself", may have been an attempt to awaken this consciousness in his contemporaries. The *mano*-consciousness, then, may be seen as indicating the functioning of thought in people who are no longer in the thrall of immediate matters but can view the everyday workings of the world with cool detachment, seeking to grasp the underlying truth of things.

Another characteristic of the *mano*-consciousness is a

strong attachment to the self; indeed, in addition to abstract thought and reflection, the basic function of this consciousness is that of attachment to one's own ego. Therefore the *mano*-consciousness is said to be always accompanied by four types of illusion: illusion that the self is absolute and unchanging, illusion leading to theories that the self is absolute and unchanging, illusion that leads to conceit, and illusion that leads to self-attachment. This consciousness, therefore, has a tendency to confine us within the framework of our own egos and thereby tempt us into arrogance and egoism. In sum, while the *mano*-consciousness is regarded as the locus of reason, it is simultaneously regarded as being invariably defiled by delusions concerning the self.

The attachment to self originating in the seventh consciousness is quite different from the awareness of self we form as a result of the workings of the first six consciousnesses. At some time between the third and the first centuries BC the *Abhidharma* schools of Hinayana Buddhism put forward the idea that the sixth consciousness was the ultimate basis of life and that the first five were its specific functions. However, this theory suffered from a number of significant flaws. For example, because the workings of the six consciousnesses all arise in response to external circumstances, we are faced with the problem of wherein lies the continuing subject that undergoes the cycle of birth and death. However, in the fourth or fifth century AD the Consciousness Only school of Mahayana Buddhism resolved this difficulty by postulating the existence of the *mano*-consciousness, saying that it operated below the level of the sixth consciousness. Unlike those of the first six consciousnesses, the functions of the *mano*-consciousness are considered by Buddhists to proceed unaffected by external events. We can see this sort of thing in operation when a person, perhaps through a car crash, ends up in a coma: despite the fact that the person is totally unconscious of what is going on, he or she nevertheless breathes and makes efforts to stay alive. The *mano*-consciousness, then, represents a very deep, unconscious awareness of self.

With the *mano*-consciousness we begin to move into the

realm beyond conscious awareness. However, it would be wrong to think that the operations of the *mano*-consciousness are entirely within the unconscious. Its powers of reasoning, like those of the sixth consciousness, are a phenomenon of the "outer surface" of the mind – i.e., the conscious. Nevertheless, we can view the *mano*-consciousness as a sort of transitional phase, spanning the border between the conscious and the unconscious.

In the West, understanding of the unconscious has advanced to a certain extent through the science of depth psychology. Sigmund Freud, the father of psychoanalysis, put forward the concept of the individual unconscious, and unearthed good evidence in favour of his theory that repressed sexual and aggressive drives give rise to hysteria and other neuroses. In terms of Buddhism, however, the sexual, aggressive and other instinctual drives at work via the *mano*-consciousness are defined as "earthly desires", such as greed, anger and stupidity. These three – the "three poisons" – are considered to be fundamental delusive passions, and to give rise to derivative ones, as we have seen (see pages 75-78). Anger, for example, gives rise to indignation, hatred, affliction, jealousy and irritability; greed brings on miserliness, arrogance and the desire to conceal one's personal defects; and stupidity, by which we mean ignorance of the true nature of life, leads to such derivative poisons as deception and flattery.

The *mano*-consciousness may give rise to delusions, but nevertheless it has positive qualities: for example, good faith, which forms the basis of mutual trust in relations between human beings; the capacity for repentance, or self-reflection, which spurs our conduct to a higher morality; and such intellectual faculties as concentration, wisdom, devotion and perseverance.

The Unconscious

All told, the *mano*-consciousness combines the functions of thought that have broken the confines of mere reactions to immediate matters with a strong unconscious awareness of self. The definition of the *mano*-consciousness gives us a clue as to where we should look for the continuing subject that perceives, thinks and so on, but it fails to provide us with a solution to the problem of how karma, which binds us to certain patterns of thought and behaviour, is transmitted and operates from the past through the present into the future. Because the notion of *mano*-consciousness could not solve these problems the "Consciousness Only" school proposed that there was an eighth layer of consciousness, the *alaya*-consciousness, which they said was to be found still deeper than the *mano*-consciousness. It is the *alaya*-consciousness that is believed to undergo the cycle of birth and death. The Sanskrit word *alaya* means a dwelling or a receptacle, and the *alaya*-consciousness gets its name because all of our actions – including thoughts, words and deeds, all of which come about through the workings of the first seven consciousnesses – are imprinted moment by moment into the unconscious realm of the *alaya*-consciousness as energies which have the potential to influence the future; these impressions are called "seeds", so the realm of the *alaya*-consciousness is sometimes described as the "storehouse consciousness" or the "repository of seeds". When we talk of "seeds" here we are thinking of them as analogous with the seeds of a plant, which sprout to produce branches and leaves: the seeds in the *alaya*-consciousness represent karma, or the latent power of our actions to produce future effects.

Karma stored in the *alaya*-consciousness has an effect on the workings of the first seven consciousnesses – we can see this, for instance, in the way that such factors as our country of birth, our native language, our social customs and our acquired knowledge and experience shape our personality. Different people recognize and respond to the same thing in different ways, depending upon the various elements that have gone into making up their personalities. A person who has lived in repressive circumstances, for example, may rebel in the face of even the most trivial of constraints, and therefore be unable to view life with objectivity.

Our perception of reality is – obviously – affected by our

161

past experiences. Suppose, for example, that you were bitten by a dog when you were a child. The event could well have been so traumatic that, even today, you are still haunted by it – to the extent that you feel genuine terror when confronted by even a small, friendly dog. Your reason tells you that your fear is without rational foundation, but nevertheless the impulse to avoid all dogs emerges from the depths of your unconscious every time you see one. This kind of reaction can be traced back to the original event you experienced and which has been stored in your *alaya*-consciousness. To go into this further, we find that in the depths of our *alaya*-consciousness there is an accumulation of the experience we have stored during our previous lifetimes, and that this accumulation limits our present existence. For example, inherent differences in personality among individuals can be ascribed to karmic causes which have their origins in previous lifetimes. Likewise, past karmic causes determine the condition in which each of us is born. In the Flower Garland Sutra we find the following passage:

> Regarding the ten evil acts, those who commit them most severely create the cause for falling into Hell, those who commit them less severely create the cause for falling into Hunger, and those who commit them least severely create the cause for falling into Animality. Among the ten, the sin of killing leads one to Hell, Hunger or Animality. Should he be reborn in Humanity, he would suffer from two kinds of retribution. First, he would be short-lived, and second, he would be sickly.

The sutra goes on to describe all of the various sufferings people will endure should they have committed one or all of the ten evil acts – the degree of suffering being determined by the act which they have chosen to commit and the way in which they have done so.

All our experiences and actions in both this lifetime and previous ones, whether they are good or evil or somewhere in between, are accumulated as seeds in the *alaya*-consciousness, and these seeds in turn direct our future actions. Since karmic seeds are to be found only at a very deep level of life, they are unaffected by the external world. Nevertheless, there is a reciprocal influence between the seeds lying deep in the *alaya*-consciousness and the surface levels of consciousness, where the three kinds of action – thinking, speaking and doing – manifest themselves.

Unlike the *mano*-consciousness, which is the realm of the individual ego, the *alaya*-consciousness has an aspect that links it up with the lives of other people. Karma is formed not only by the individual's actions but also by the actions he or she performs in conjunction with others. Karma created and experienced by a number of people, rather than just by one, is identified in Buddhism as "shared" or "general" karma. The Indian Mahayana scholar Nagarjuna, in his *Commentary on the Ten Stages*, interpreted this idea in relation to sentient and nonsentient existence: "Sentient beings are born by virtue of individual karma, and nonsentient beings, by virtue of shared karma." In other words, individual lives come into existence by way of their individual actions whereas nonsentient life-forms – such as mountains, rivers and the Earth itself – derive their existence from shared karma.

When we talk of "nonsentient life-forms" we are, in broad terms, referring to the nonsentient environment, which includes not just the natural world but also human social culture. We can say, in this context, that the sort of culture or country a people has is derived directly from their shared karma.

So the *alaya*-consciousness contains not only the individual's karma but also the karma common to his or her family and race, and even to humanity as a whole. The realm of *alaya*-consciousness therefore broadly links all living beings, and in this sense it can be said to embrace the notion of the "collective unconscious" proposed by C.G. Jung and elaborated upon in the science of depth psychology. Jung's theory was that every human being possesses the entirety of the human heritage within the recesses of his or her own psyche – that is, that each one of us shares with all our fellow humans a common psychic base, the collective unconscious.

C.S. Hall, one of Jung's disciples, examined the common

human fears of snakes and darkness and came to the conclusion that such fears could not be explained fully in terms of present-lifetime experiences alone; rather, he said, personal experiences seem merely to strengthen and reaffirm fears that are already within us. He suggested that the fears of snakes and of darkness are hereditary – that they are a legacy from our remote ancestors – and that this demonstrates that ancestral memories are in some way preserved in the deepest stratum of the individual human psyche. Taking this a step further, it may be that our unconscious contains not only the memories of our human ancestors but also those of our prehuman ancestors, too. Indeed, it might be that the footprint of each and every step in our past evolution is recorded in the deepest level of our individual minds.

However, Buddhism forays yet further into the depths of human existence, teaching that the human mind shares common ground with *all* phenomena – in that all phenomena are manifestations of the overall cosmic life force, which embodies itself in both sentient and nonsentient existences. The wisdom of Buddhism, therefore, illuminates not only the unconscious and the common foundation shared by humans and all other living beings but also the reality expressed through the totality of the Universe's phenomena.

In that the *alaya*-consciousness holds the potential effects of all of our actions, both good and evil, it in itself cannot be described as either intrinsically good or intrinsically evil. Encompassing as it does both purity and impurity, the *alaya*-consciousness is a realm in which the powers of good and evil do vigorous battle. It follows that, unless both good and evil in the realm of the *alaya*-consciousness are subsumed into some more profound dimension, they will be locked in eternal combat. This stand-off seems philosophically unacceptable, and so Buddhists of the T'ien-t'ai and Hua-yen schools were led to posit the existence of a ninth consciousness, the *amala*-consciousness, a level of the psyche even deeper than the *alaya*-consciousness. The Sanskrit word *amala* means pure, stainless or spotless, and so the *amala*-consciousness gets its name because it remains eternally untainted by karmic accretions. The *amala*-consciousness is itself the ultimate and unconditioned reality of all things, and thereby is equivalent to the universal Buddha nature. At this most profound level of the mind, our individual existences expand without limit to become one with the life of the Cosmos. In the light of Buddhist thought, we may regard the *amala*-consciousness as the "greater self", which is eternal and immutable: by awakening to and developing this fundamental pure consciousness we can resolve the ceaseless strife between good and evil represented by the *alaya*-consciousness and at the same time enable our other consciousnesses to function in an enlightened way.

Nichiren Daishonin gave concrete expression to the *amala*-consciousness – the fundamental reality of life – in the phrase *Nam-myoho-renge-kyo*, and he gave physical form to his enlightenment to the original cosmic life in the Gohonzon, the object of worship, thus opening a path whereby all people can achieve Buddhahood, manifesting the greater self that is latent within them. When we worship the Gohonzon we find joy and determination welling forth as we are brought face to face with the reality that our own existences are coextensive with the eternal life of the Universe. When we devote ourselves to and base our lives on this reality – the *amala*-consciousness – all the other eight consciousnesses work to express the immense power and the infinite wisdom of the Buddha nature.

This can be explained in terms of what Buddhism describes as the "five kinds of wisdom". When we tap the *amala*-consciousness, which corresponds to the "wisdom of the Dharma nature", the eighth (or *alaya*) consciousness manifests itself as the "great round mirror wisdom", which perceives the world without any distortions, in exactly the same way that a perfect mirror reflects all images with total accuracy. The *mano*-consciousness – the seventh consciousness – manifests itself as the "nondiscriminating wisdom" which perceives the essential nature common to all things without discriminating among them. The acquisition of this wisdom enables us to overcome our fervent attachment to the ego. The sixth consciousness manifests itself as the "wisdom of insight into the particular"; through it we are able to distinguish the individual aspects of all phenomena, so that we can take the appropriate actions in each and every situation. Finally, the five consciousnesses express themselves as the "wisdom of perfect practice": together they enable us to develop the power to benefit others as well as ourselves.

The Nine Consciousnesses and Death

The concept of the nine consciousnesses, analysing as it does the various layers of an individual's life and simultaneously throwing light on its totality, can surely contribute in some way to the solution of the problems that are facing us today, especially in the fields of medicine and psychiatry. In recent years many of the people involved in psychosomatic medicine have incorporated Buddhist or closely related ideas into their therapies. For example, Dr O. Carl Simonton, a radiation oncologist, uses a therapy that draws upon something close to the Buddhist concept of compassion in helping his patients to overcome feelings of resentment and ill will. First, Simonton has the patient form a clear mental image of the person towards whom he or she feels such deep resentment, and then he has the patient picture good things happening to that person – for example, imagining the person receiving love or attention or money, or whatever the patient feels the hate-object would most like. Often, as a result of this visualization technique, patients are able to overcome their own ill feelings. Shakyamuni, in his early years of preaching, taught a form of meditation in which a person first generates thoughts of compassion towards his or her loved ones and then extends these to the people whom he or she actively dislikes. In this way, the person can learn to master anger, a major source of delusion and of earthly desires.

It is my belief that, by presenting an integrated view of life and death spanning past, present and future, Buddhism has much to offer to the field of medical ethics in respect of such problems as the matter of informing people that their illness is terminal, voluntary euthanasia, organ transplants, *in vitro* fertilization and genetic engineering.

It is in this connection that we should discuss the workings of the nine consciousnesses in terms of the cycle of birth and death.

The *alaya*-consciousness is sometimes called "non-vanishing" because the karmic seeds stored within it do not disappear at death. Our individual lives, in the form of this eighth consciousness, continue even after death, in the state of *ku*, or latency, carrying with them the whole of our karma. However, the first seven consciousnesses, all of which function actively while we are alive, recede at the moment of death into a latent state within the *alaya*-consciousness. We can say that all of the memories, habits and karma stored in this consciousness as the moments tick by during our lives form the individual self, or the framework of individual existence that undergoes the cycle of death and rebirth. This consciousness may be thought of as the realm that interweaves all of the causes and effects that comprise each person's individual destiny.

While we are alive here on Earth all of the first seven consciousnesses function supported by the brain stem, limbic system and higher brain structures. In terms of neurophysiology we could perhaps associate the conscious activity of the *mano*-consciousness with the operations of the frontal lobe of the neocortex. Should the cerebral cortex for any reason be destroyed, we lose the means to manifest conscious mental activity although the brain stem is capable of maintaining life at its lowest level. A person who has lost the cerebral functions has no way to express emotions through either body or mind. All of the emotions – joy, sorrow, anger and so on – become submerged, receding from the domain of the conscious to find refuge in the unconscious. But they do not cease to operate. Although desire, impulse, sentiment, intelligence and the others are no longer active in the conscious realm, they remain very much alive – in the form of mental energy – in the unconscious. A person in a coma may not experience desires or emotions, but the depths of his or her psyche nevertheless

167

harbour a vast diversity of mental currents. Even when all conscious functions have been interrupted, there still exists in the depths of life the impulse to go on living.

Buddhism tells us that, at the time of death, life undergoes a change from the manifest to the latent state, or from sentience to nonsentience. There are three stages involved in this change. First, the operations of the five consciousnesses become latent, but the sixth consciousness continues to function. In the second stage, the sixth consciousness recedes into dormancy, but the *mano*-consciousness remains active, in the form of a passionate attachment to temporary existence. In the third stage the *mano*-consciousness lapses into latency within the *alaya*-consciousness.

In the previous chapter, when discussing the mutual possession of the Ten Worlds (see page 125), we saw the concept of a being's basic tendency, and this concept is crucial if we are to understand the experience of life after death. During the transition at death from sentience to nonsentience our capacity to respond to external stimuli becomes latent and our lives become fixed in whichever states we have established as our basic tendencies. So, as death approaches, we become less and less able to use worldly means to alter our conditions: at this time neither wealth, power, social standing nor the love of others can help us, and even great thoughts and philosophies, if we have understood them only superficially and failed to make them a part of our lives, will prove utterly useless to us in the face of imminent death. As life shifts from its manifest into its latent state, our power to influence the environment or to be influenced by it is lost and – just as fluid water becomes rigid ice – our basic tendencies become "frozen".

For example, the *alaya*-consciousness of someone who has established the tendency of Hell will, in death, merge into the realm of Hell inherent in the cosmic life and there undergo further agonies. A person continually governed by desire in this life will merge into the cosmic life's realm of Hunger, there to be tormented by frustration all the more, and a person inclined towards a state of Animality will, when his or her *alaya*-consciousness has merged into the

168

cosmic life, experience a state of uninterrupted animal fear.

On the other hand, a person who has created in his or her life on Earth the basic tendency of either Humanity or Heaven will be able to surmount the physical pain of death and experience a sense of elation. People with a basic tendency towards Learning or Realization will enjoy profound spiritual satisfaction, and persons in the state of Bodhisattva will retain their feelings of compassion and altruism in death as they did when they were alive, and may even see their own death as an opportunity to inspire or benefit others. Buddhahood, finally, is the wellspring of wisdom, courage and compassion, and a person who has firmly established this state, being fully awakened to the eternal nature of life, can subdue the fear of death to the point of being able to use his or her own as a way of leading other people to salvation.

However, the courage and compassion of Bodhisattva and Buddhahood cannot be faked. Death ruthlessly exposes cowardice, even if we have managed totally to conceal it throughout our life. It is too late, when we are looking death straight in the eyes, to regret the things we may have done or left undone. It is essential, then, that we strive to live each moment in the best possible way.

Buddhism notes three types of suffering: physical suffering, the product of physical pain; mental suffering, born from the destruction or thwarting of happiness; and fundamental (or existential) suffering, which arises from the impermanence of all phenomena. The fear of death, a problem which religion must inevitably tackle, is a prime representative of this third type of suffering. Buddhism aims to free people from the fear of death by leading them to realize the eternity of life. Those who have attained the realm of the ninth consciousness can face death with a deep sense of joy and satisfaction, having grasped the true implications of birth and death in terms of the scope of eternity and thus in full confidence of their eventual rebirth. Through Buddhist practice such an attitude is made possible.

The Nine Consciousnesses and the Human Self

The word "self" is often used in a negative sense, implying selfish or self-seeking behaviour, but this usage refers only to what Buddhism regards as the lesser, or smaller, self. There is in addition a greater self – the true self. This transcends the smaller self and expands to become one with the great sea of cosmic life. The whole of Buddhist philosophy centres on the idea of breaking out of the prison of the smaller self to attain the infinitely expanded true self. The theory of the nine consciousnesses was developed as a means of helping us to achieve this goal.

If we delve progressively deeper into the mind, from its outer surface to the inner psyche, or from the conscious to the deeper levels of the unconscious, we find that the self occupies a progressively greater amount of life-space. The first six consciousnesses, the everyday workings of the conscious mind, are those of the self experiencing only the first six of the Ten Worlds – a self whose subjective space is both shallow and transient. In these states we are completely caught up in our reactions to everyday events; any enjoyment we might experience in them can be easily destroyed in a storm of instinctive impulses, desires, emotions and karmic forces.

Dr Paul D. Maclean, a US Government research scientist and authority in the field of brain evolution and behaviour, has traced instinctive impulses and emotions to the workings of the reptilian brain, or paleocortex, and the mammalian brain, or archicortex. The function of the neocortex, he explains, is to exercise control over the outpourings of these instinctive impulses. It is my belief that Buddhist practice can enable us to elevate these impulses and develop the power to attain the higher worlds: Learning, Realization, Bodhisattva and Buddhahood.

The workings of the first six consciousnesses are confined within the limits of the smaller self. By contrast, the workings of the seventh consciousness, the *mano*-consciousness, allow us to rise above our immediate reactions to changing conditions within the Six Paths and to see things objectively, discovering a new state of life in which our

170

subjective space is greatly expanded. The workings of this consciousness, then, can be said to correspond to the functions of thought in people who are in the states of Learning and Realization – including, for example, the kind of thinking involved in abstract study and artistic creation; and they enable us to transcend the realm of everyday thoughts and the relatively shallow discerning power of the sixth consciousness. All through history the foremost scholars and artists have been people who have experienced the awakening of the *mano*-consciousness: the intelligence it generates has been a drive forcing them to seek out the laws governing society, history, the natural Universe and the modes of artistic expression. Yet the self that emerges from the seventh consciousness and the states of Learning and Realization is still not free from the impulses that govern and the catastrophes that beset a person dominated by the ego – quite the contrary: people in these states run the risk of becoming arrogant about their achievements, and easily become prisoners of the powerful tendency towards self-attachment developed by this consciousness.

The eighth consciousness, the *alaya*-consciousness, is a veritable whirlpool of karma, both good and bad. According to one Buddhist sutra, "We common mortals form karmic impediments each day and night amounting to 800,004,000 thoughts": as not only our thoughts but also our words and deeds are registered in this realm, we can see that it combines both good and evil, or enlightenment and delusion – opposing forces locked in never-ending combat. This perpetual contest cannot be resolved through the powers of thought available to people living in the worlds of Learning and Realization. In this sense, the realm of the Ten Worlds corresponding to the eighth consciousness is that of Bodhisattva, who battles the evil within through his or her efforts to lead others to Buddhahood. In other words, Bodhisattva is the state in which we arouse the power of compassion and, by forming the good karma of altruism, work to subdue the evil karma that has been imprinted on the inner layer of life – that is, we work towards self-reformation. Only in the Bodhisattva state, in which we

171

burst through the walls of egoism and dedicate our lives to the benefit of others, can we have any significant effect upon the *alaya*-consciousness. Even so, the *alaya*-consciousness can never be entirely free from delusion: complete purity is to be found only in the ninth consciousness, the *amala*-consciousness.

Nichiren Daishonin inscribed the Gohonzon as the embodiment of the *amala*-consciousness, or the ultimate reality. In his writing "The Real Aspect of the Gohonzon" he states:

> Never seek this Gohonzon outside yourself. The Gohonzon exists only within the mortal flesh of us ordinary people who embrace the Lotus Sutra and chant *Nam-myoho-renge-kyo*. The body is the palace of the ninth consciousness, the unchanging reality which reigns over all life's functions.[1]

The *amala*-consciousness, the ultimate reality, whose existence is potential within all life-forms, manifests itself when we believe in the Gohonzon and devote ourselves to the chanting of *Nam-myoho-renge-kyo*. The Gohonzon is the object of worship that embodies the *amala*-consciousness, and by embracing the Gohonzon, we tap this reality within ourselves. By tapping the life force of the *amala*-consciousness we are free to use the workings of the other eight consciousnesses in order to improve the lives of ourselves and of other people.

When our lives are rooted in the *amala*-consciousness they can draw on the power to transform totally the entire interlocking web of latent causes and effects that forms the *alaya*-consciousness, so that it is based on enlightenment, rather than delusion. Also, we cannot be carried away by the workings of the first eight consciousnesses. By way of analogy, a piece of wood floating in a stream is at the mercy of the current and will soon be swept away, but even the most powerful of currents cannot shift an island of rock.

The Daishonin writes: "Base your heart on the ninth consciousness and your practice on the six consciousnesses."[2] When we anchor our existences to our faith in the Gohonzon and devote ourselves to Buddhist practice in our

172

daily lives, we can manifest infinite wisdom, power and compassion and achieve a fundamental inner reformation. In this way, we can establish an unshakable foundation for true happiness.

References

[1] *The Major Writings of Nichiren Daishonin*, vol. 1, page 213.
[2] Ibid., vol. 2, page 244.

7

Nam-myoho-renge-kyo: *The Mystic Law and the Path of Attaining Buddhahood*

In the Buddhism of Nichiren Daishonin, if we are to attain enlightenment our primary practice must be the chanting of the phrase *Nam-myoho-renge-kyo*. The Daishonin writes about this phrase:

> To practise only the seven characters of *Nam-myoho-renge-kyo* may appear limited, yet since this Law is the master of all Buddhas of the past, present and future, the teacher of all Bodhisattvas in the Universe, and the guide that enables all human beings to attain Buddhahood, its practice is incomparably profound.[1]

Convinced that supreme enlightenment should be available to everyone, the Daishonin established this simple mode of Buddhist practice, whereby all human beings can make the ultimate truth their own.

Nam-myoho-renge-kyo is sometimes referred to as the *daimoku* (title) of the Lotus Sutra. In Sanskrit the sutra's title is *Saddharma-pundarika-sutra*, meaning literally "The Sutra of the Lotus Blossom of the Wonderful Law". In the year AD 406 the great scholar Kumarajiva (344-413), of Kucha in Central Asia, translated the sutra into Chinese with the title *Miao-fa-lien-hua-ching*, which in Japanese is rendered as *Myoho-renge-kyo*. Of all the six Chinese translations of the Lotus Sutra, Kumarajiva's superb version was the best known and by far the most popular: it came to be regarded as the definitive one, and helped win the sutra wide respect. He had exhaustively studied the doctrines and philosophy of Mahayana Buddhism as systematized by Nagarjuna and other great Indian scholars and, on the basis

174

of these doctrines, had contemplated and realized the meaning of "the lotus blossom of the wonderful Law". Kumarajiva's long spiritual odyssey finally gave him the power to grasp the ultimate reality implicit in the Lotus Sutra, and to express this realization through his brilliant translation, which formed the basis of many subsequent studies of the Lotus Sutra.

One of Kumarajiva's own disciples, Chu Tao-sheng, wrote the first extant Chinese commentary on the sutra: Chu devoted an entire section merely to an explanation of the title. More than a century later the great master T'ien-t'ai organized all the extant body of Chinese Buddhist scriptures and developed a complete codification, based on the Lotus Sutra, of Buddhist doctrine: he regarded the Lotus Sutra as the sutra that integrated all other Buddhist teachings. His ten-volume *Profound Meaning of the Lotus Sutra* is devoted largely to an explanation of the sutra's title, *Myoho-renge-kyo*, and is based on the premise that the essence of the entire sutra is to be found in its title.

So Nichiren Daishonin's assertion that the core of the Lotus Sutra is inherent in its title has a long and respectable history. In his writing "The One Essential Phrase" the Daishonin underscores the all-embracing nature of the sutra's title:

> Included within the title, *Nam-myoho-renge-kyo*, is the entire sutra consisting of all eight volumes, twenty-eight chapters and 69,384 characters ... Chanting *daimoku* twice is the same as reading the entire sutra twice, one hundred *daimoku* equal one hundred readings of the sutra, and one thousand *daimoku*, one thousand readings of the sutra.[2]

In another work he expands:

> Those who chant *Myoho-renge-kyo*, the title of the Lotus Sutra, even without understanding its meaning, realize not only the heart of the Lotus Sutra but also the essence of all the Buddha's teachings.[3]

In this connection it is vital to note, though, that for the

Daishonin the "five characters of *Myoho-renge-kyo*" were far more than just the title of a text: rather, they were the expression of the ultimate truth to which he was enlightened. As he writes:

> Our contemporaries think of the five characters of *Myoho-renge-kyo* only as a name, but this is not correct. It is the entity, that is, the heart, of the Lotus Sutra.[4]

In various of his writings the Daishonin identifies *Myoho-renge-kyo* equally with the true entity or aspect of all phenomena, the ultimate reality or absolute truth, and the Buddha nature that is inherent in all beings, whether sentient or nonsentient.

How, then, can we realize the truth of *Myoho-renge-kyo* for ourselves? The answer to this question leads us to the unique practice established by the Daishonin. An extract from a letter of his, "On Attaining Buddhahood", tells a follower that

> If you wish to free yourself from the sufferings of birth and death you have endured throughout eternity and attain supreme enlightenment in this lifetime, you must awaken to the mystic truth that has always been within your life. This truth is *Myoho-renge-kyo*. Chanting *Myoho-renge-kyo* will therefore enable you to grasp the mystic truth within you.[5]

For chanting, the Daishonin prefaces the five characters of *Myoho-renge-kyo* with *namu* or *nam* (between two "m"s the "*u*" is generally silent), a word which derives from the Sanskrit word *namas*, meaning "devotion". So, in the act of chanting *Nam-myoho-renge-kyo*, we devote ourselves to, or fuse our lives with, the fundamental Law of *Myoho-renge-kyo*, and in so doing immediately manifest our inherent Buddha nature.

Nam

In this chapter we shall discuss the meanings of the individual characters of the phrase *Nam-myoho-renge-kyo*.

First, as we have noted, *nam* is the Japanese transliteration of the Sanskrit word *namas*. In "The Gift of Rice" Nichiren Daishonin elaborates on the meaning of *nam*: "This word ... means to devote one's life. Ultimately it means to offer our lives to the Buddha."[6] And in the *Record of the Orally Transmitted Teachings* he explains that *nam* means devotion in both body and mind – that is, the physical and spiritual aspects of life. An immediate question arises: to what should we devote ourselves? In Nichiren Daishonin's Buddhism there are two ways of describing the object of devotion: the Law, or the ultimate truth, which is *Myoho-renge-kyo*, and the Person, or the Buddha who has manifested the Law in his life. In other words, the Person and the Law are fundamentally one: in Nichiren Daishonin's Buddhism the oneness of the Person – the Daishonin himself – and the Law – *Nam-myoho-renge-kyo* – is embodied in the mandala which he inscribed, the object of worship called the Gohonzon. (*Honzon*, in Japanese, means "object of worship", while *go* is an honorific prefix.)

In the Daishonin's Buddhism the term *nam* indicates our devotion to the Gohonzon. However, *nam* is two-directional: that is, one aspect of *nam* is that we devote our lives to or fuse our lives with the ultimate, unchanging reality, while the other is that, through this fusion, we are simultaneously capable of drawing forth an infinite wisdom that functions in accordance with our changing circumstances. This latter is the wisdom through which we human beings can experience boundless joy and freedom despite all the uncertainties of our daily lives.

As an aside, we can note that, while the word *nam* derives from the Sanskrit, *Myoho-renge-kyo* comes from Chinese. The amalgamation of both an Indo-European and an Eastern language in the phrase *Nam-myoho-renge-kyo* gives us an idea of the universality of Nichiren Daishonin's teaching.

Myoho

The word *myoho* means, literally, "the Mystic Law". The Law, or ultimate reality, is described as *myo* (mystic) because it is infinitely profound and beyond all the possible conceptions or formulations of the human mind. In "On Attaining Buddhahood" Nichiren Daishonin clarifies this point:

> What then does *myo* signify? It is simply the mysterious nature of our lives from moment to moment, which the mind cannot comprehend nor words express. When you look into your own mind at any moment, you perceive neither colour nor form to verify that it exists. Yet you still cannot say it does not exist, for many differing thoughts continually occur to you. Life is indeed an elusive reality that transcends both the words and concepts of existence and nonexistence. It is neither existence nor nonexistence, yet exhibits the qualities of both. It is the mystic entity of the Middle Way that is the reality of all things. *Myo* is the name given to the mystic nature of life, and *ho* to its manifestations.[7]

Here, then, the Daishonin is interpreting *myo* as the ultimate reality which is beyond our ability to perceive and *ho* as the world of phenomena in all its ever-changing forms. The union of these two concepts, as represented by the single word *myoho*, reflects the essential oneness of the ultimate reality and the manifest world. In other words, according to Buddhism there is no fundamental distinction between the ultimate reality and the everyday one. If we realize this we are enlightened; if we do not we are suffering from delusion. According to the Daishonin: "While deluded, one is called a common mortal, but once enlightened, he is called a Buddha."[8] In this context, "delusion" signifies all of the first nine of the Ten Worlds, from Hell to Bodhisattva, while "enlightenment" describes the world of Buddhahood. However, the Nine Worlds and Buddhahood, together, are inherent in every single moment. In the *Record of the Orally Transmitted Teachings* we find Nichiren Daishonin pointing out further that

> *Myo* indicates the nature of enlightenment [Buddhahood], while *ho* indicates darkness or delusion [the first nine of the Ten Worlds]. The oneness of delusion and enlightenment is called *myoho* or the Mystic Law.[9]

178

The meaning of the term "the oneness of delusion and enlightenment" can perhaps be illustrated by analogy to various phenomena of the physical world. For example, normal white blood corpuscles destroy germs and play a crucial role in the healing of wounds, and so are vital to our individual continued survival; however, should the growth of these corpuscles become perverted they can cause probably fatal diseases such as leukemia. We could perhaps express this dichotomy in the essential nature of white blood corpuscles as the oneness of the "enlightened aspect" and the "deluded aspect" of the corpuscles. This is a single example of the way that *all* phenomena have both positive and negative aspects.

"The oneness of delusion and enlightenment" means that, as potentials, delusion – the first nine of the Ten Worlds – and enlightenment – Buddhahood – coexist not just in individual lives but also in the Universe. However, as manifest realities, one rather than the other will be expressed, depending on whether or not we are awakened to the ultimate reality.

In "The Daimoku of the Lotus Sutra" Nichiren Daishonin further explains that the character *myo* of *Nam-myoho-renge-kyo* has in fact three distinct meanings: to open, to be endowed and perfect, and to revive. (We have touched on these on page 81.) When he wrote "to open" he meant opening out of or dispelling the darkness of delusion to reveal the Buddha nature: the life of a person who awakens to his or her own Buddha nature "opens" to become coextensive with the Universe. The phrase "to be endowed and perfect" implies that the Mystic Law encompasses all phenomena and is inherent in all things. The Mystic Law embraces all of the Ten Worlds and all of the three thousand realms, permeating and integrating the whole of phenomenal reality. So the expression "to be endowed and perfect" can be interpreted also to mean that the Mystic Law contains within itself all truths and blessings. The third of the definitions, "to revive", essentially means to enable the individual to attain Buddhahood. For example, everyone – even the worst of evildoers and all the other people whose

179

potential for Buddhahood was denied in the teachings prior to the Lotus Sutra – can attain the supreme enlightenment through the Mystic Law of *Myoho-renge-kyo*. If we look at the term "to revive" in a broader sense we can say that it means to create value. One sort of revival comes about when nonsentient materials such as wood and stone are transformed so that they create a building. Another form of revival comes about in the act of reforming our lives so that we can achieve enlightenment and contribute to the happiness of other people. Also, "to revive" signifies that all laws and teachings based upon the Mystic Law assume their correct perspective and reveal important aspects of the ultimate truth. Similarly, when we base our faith on the Mystic Law, all of our abilities, character traits and other personal qualities come to life, expressing themselves in a manner that not only contributes to our own growth but also benefits other people.

A final interpretation of *myoho* by Nichiren Daishonin occurs in his *Heritage of the Ultimate Law of Life*: "*Myo* represents death, and *ho* represents life." We cannot intellectually conceive of our lives in the state of death, and even less can we produce answers to the question of where life exists after death – and how. Even if we believe that our life merges back into the cosmic life, this is something that is difficult to understand. So death corresponds to *myo*, meaning "mystic" or "inconceivable". Life, by contrast, expresses itself in various visible forms, according to definite patterns, manifesting one or another of the Ten Worlds through the workings of the ten factors. For example, if we have nothing to eat for a long time we become ravenous and fall into the world of Hunger; likewise, if someone makes fun of us we are likely to lose our temper, displaying the world of Anger. This is the way that human life works.

Life, then, corresponds to *ho*, or law. Life and death are the two contrasting manifestations of the ultimate reality, or Mystic Law. Turning this around, we can say that the ultimate reality is manifested purely in the everyday realities of life and death.

Renge

The word *renge* literally means "lotus blossom". The lotus is a plant of remarkable antiquity, and has been admired as such in many cultures and traditions. The oldest lotus fossils date back as far as the Cretaceous, a period of geological time that lasted from about 135 million years ago to about 65 million years ago. A fossil lotus unearthed in the Kyoto area of Japan in 1933 is estimated to be ten thousand to twenty thousand years old: it seems to be identical with the lotus plant that we know today.

At Mohenjo Daro in the Indus Valley in Pakistan there are the ancient ruins of what was once a major city. Among these archaeologists have found an artefact known as the Great Bath which, it is assumed, was used for ritual ablution. An icon excavated there – and now on display at the Museum of Fine Arts in Boston – shows a woman wearing a headdress decorated with lotus flowers, a clear sign that the Indus Valley civilization strongly respected the lotus.

When I met in 1985 with Dr Karan Singh, a well known Indian scholar, our discussion touched on the lotus flower. I had assumed that it was found throughout India. Like many people, I had thought that, because Buddhism spread throughout ancient India, the lotus flower must be equally ubiquitous. I was astonished when Dr Singh told me that the lotus grows in India only in the region of the Himalayas, an area well travelled by Shakyamuni as he propounded his teaching.

Dr Singh went on to comment on the various implications of the symbol of the lotus throughout India's long history. First of all, he said, the flower signifies fertility, prosperity and longevity. Second, the creator of the Universe, Brahma, is said to have issued forth from a lotus. Third, the lotus flower grows in mud, which shows that beauty can emerge even from things which are not beautiful. Fourth, the lotus flower remains dry as it floats on the surface of the water, which symbolizes the virtue of remaining imperturbable amid the tribulations of life. Fifth, it was the practice in Sanskrit writings, if one wished to praise the beauties of a woman's eyes, to compare them to lotus flowers. Sixth, and last, the lotus flower closes at night and opens at dawn, a living metaphor of the way in which our minds can open to a divine and sublime philosophy.

The lotus flower is mentioned in the Rig Veda, the most ancient Indian scripture, and I believe that Dr Singh's various interpretations have their origins in the ancient Indian attitude towards the plant. In ancient India the lotus was appreciated in two primary ways: it was considered to be a flower that represented an ideal of beauty, and at the same time it was valued as a medicinal herb. In the latter context, we can note that its rhizomes were regarded as a source of nutrition and strength and were used in various medicines – it is said that Shariputra, one of Shakyamuni Buddha's disciples, was cured of a chronic illness through the use of the lotus's rhizomes. The flower itself was used as an herbal medicine for kidney and stomach troubles, while its leaves were used to staunch bleeding.

In China, too, the lotus is known to have flourished since antiquity, along the Yellow River and in other areas. Poems in praise of the lotus appear in *Shih ching* (the "Book of Poetry"), an anthology of some three hundred poems dating mostly from the early Chou dynasty, about three thousand years ago. The lotus flower, because of its appearance of nobility, has long been regarded by the Chinese as a symbol of a person's virtue – for example, in the essay "On the Love of the Lotus", by Chou Tun-i (1017-1073), who lived in the Sung dynasty. To present someone with a lotus seed was, therefore, to convey the message that you recognized that person's goodness and wished to keep company with him or her. The lotus flower has long been used in China on auspicious occasions to symbolize happiness – for example, its image was often emblazoned on the implements used in wedding ceremonies. The metaphor of the flower was also used to signify beautiful women.

In Egypt, hieroglyphs representing the lotus appear in murals and papyri discovered in the Pyramids. Parts of the hieroglyphic texts employ the lotus as a symbol for the deity who confers the blessing of immortality. From among the remains of ancient Egyptian temples have been excavated stone columns with capitals decorated with lotus flowers, and the lotus embellished many other ancient Egyptian works of art and architecture. It is likely that the lotus, which bloomed in profusion along the Nile, suggested itself to the ancient Egyptians, as it opened its flowers in the dawn, as a symbol for the renewal of life.

In ancient Greece the symbol of the lotus was used to adorn temple sanctuaries. Excavations of ancient temple sites in the Olympus massif in northeastern Greece have brought to light architectural decorations which include arabesque patterns interwoven with images of lotus flowers.

The expedition of Alexander the Great to India around 326 BC initiated the synthesis of Buddhist culture and Hellenic civilization which eventually produced the artistic riches of the Gandhara region in what is now northern Pakistan and eastern Afghanistan. The Gandharan artistic influence travelled eastwards along the Silk Road, and eventually, *via* China and the Korean Peninsula, reached Japan, where, during the sixth to eighth centuries (the Asuka, Hakuho and Tempyo periods), it made great contributions to the development of Japanese art. In the diverse works of art from ancient Gandhara, China and Japan the image of patterns of lotus petals appears again and again. A few years ago I was given by the Dunhuang Institute of China a reproduction of a painting from the ceiling of one of the famous Mogao Caves of Dunhuang, in western Gansu Province, north of Tibet: I was delighted to note that this painting, too, featured a beautiful lotus-flower pattern.

The lotus flower is mentioned in the famous Buddhist text *Questions of King Milinda*, which takes the form of a dialogue between the Indo-Greek king Menander and the Buddhist monk Nagasena – a conversation said to have taken place some time after Alexander's expedition to India. In this dialogue the lotus flower appears as a metaphor for the greatness of the Law, or of the Buddhist teachings. The *Treatise on the Sutra of the Perfection of Wisdom*, an exhaustive Mahayana work attributed to Nagarjuna, says that the reason images of the Buddha are adorned by lotus pedestals is that the lotus plant dignifies the seat of the Mystic Law.

The lotus flower was also extolled in Japanese literature, in works such as the eighth-century *Record of Ancient Matters* and the poetry anthology known as the *Collection of Ten Thousand Leaves*. Sei Shonagon refers to the lotus blossom in her eleventh-century *Pillow Book* as being superior to all other flowers. Later, in the Edo period (1600-1867), the poetic form known as *haiku* became popular, and these poems contain frequent favourable references to the beautiful flowers and large round leaves of the lotus. Indeed, to the Japanese, the lotus flower has an image somewhat different from that of the more earthly cherry or plum blossoms: it represents a purity and a universal principle that underlies the entirety of existence. As an aside, Mount Fuji is often likened to the eight-petalled lotus, since this is exactly what its caldera looks like when viewed from the air.

The seeds of the lotus are known to be very long-lived. Seeds discovered in a peat deposit in Chiba Prefecture, Japan, by the late Dr Ichiro Oga of the University of Tokyo have been assessed as being about two thousand years old, and yet some of them were successfully germinated and their descendants are now under cultivation in many parts of the country. It is as though lotus seeds provide a sort of testament to the eternity of life.

We can say, then, that it seems as if the qualities of purity and eternity implicit in the image of the lotus blossom have appealed to human beings all over the Earth since ancient times. Perhaps it was this connotation of purity and eternity that led to the use of the lotus blossom as a symbol for the Law or for the teachings of Shakyamuni Buddha. In his *Profound Meaning of the Lotus Sutra* T'ien-t'ai explains that the word "lotus" in the sutra's title should be understood not only as a metaphor for the Mystic Law but also as the Law itself:

Now the name lotus is not intended as a symbol of anything. It is the teaching expounded in the Lotus Sutra. The teaching expounded in the Lotus Sutra is pure and undefiled and explains

184

the subtleties of cause and effect. Therefore, it is called lotus. The name designates the essence of the meditation on the Law of the Lotus Sutra, and is not a metaphor or figurative term ... But because the lotus of the Law is difficult to understand, the metaphor of the lotus plant is introduced ... Thus the easily understood metaphor of an actual lotus plant is used to make clear the difficult-to-understand lotus that is the essence of the Lotus Sutra.[10]

Nichiren Daishonin elaborates on the profound principle indicated by the lotus:

Myoho-renge-kyo is likened to the lotus ... Of all the flowers, he [the Buddha] selected the lotus blossom to symbolize the Lotus Sutra. There is a reason for this. Some plants first flower and then produce fruit, while in others fruit comes forth before flowers. Some bear only one flower but many fruit, others send forth many flowers but only one fruit, and still others produce fruit without flowering. Thus there are all manner of plants, but the lotus is the only one which bears flowers and fruit simultaneously. The benefit of all the other sutras is uncertain, because they teach that one must first make good causes and then only at some later time can one become a Buddha. The Lotus Sutra is completely different. A hand which takes it up immediately attains enlightenment, and a mouth which chants it instantly enters Buddhahood, just as the Moon is reflected in the water the moment it appears from behind the eastern mountains, or as a sound and its echo arise simultaneously.[11]

Elsewhere, the Daishonin further states:

The supreme principle was originally without a name. When the sage was observing principles and assigning names to all things, he perceived that there is this wonderful single Law that simultaneously possesses both cause and effect, and he named it *Myoho-renge*, the lotus of the Mystic Law. This single Law of *Myoho-renge* encompasses within itself all the laws or phenomena comprising the Ten Worlds and the three thousand realms, and is lacking in none of them. Anyone who practises this Law will simultaneously obtain both the cause and the effect of Buddhahood.[12]

The lotus plant produces its blossoms and its seedpods at the same time, thereby representing "the wonderful single Law that simultaneously possesses both cause and effect". This principle, the simultaneity of cause and effect, means that both the Nine Worlds (cause) and the world of Buddhahood (effect) exist simultaneously in every moment of life, and so there is no essential, fundamental difference between a Buddha and an ordinary person. In terms of practice, the Daishonin taught that when a person chants *Nam-myoho-renge-kyo* with faith (cause) in the Gohonzon, the state of Buddhahood (effect) instantaneously emerges from within that person's life. Hence his statement that "Anyone who practises this Law will simultaneously obtain both the cause and the effect of Buddhahood".

Underlying all existences, whether sentient or nonsentient, is the Law embodying the simultaneity of cause and effect: it is the central theme of Buddhism, and parallels to it are to be found in modern scientific theories, too. As an illustration, we can use a puzzle from the world of physics. What is it that gave rise to the Universe of hundreds of billions of galaxies each containing tens or hundreds of billions of stars and planets? It is generally accepted that the physical Universe had its origins in the Big Bang, an unimaginable explosion believed to have taken place as much as twenty billion years ago, and as a result of which the Universe is still expanding. Because the Universe began to expand at the very moment it came into existence, we can say that this is an instance in the physical realm that serves to illustrate cause and effect occurring simultaneously.

Turning to another marvel, we can look at the fertilized human egg, the product of the male and female gametes. This is no more than a tenth of a millimetre around, and yet it nevertheless contains all of the genetic information required for it to develop into a full-sized adult human being. At the moment of conception, the egg can be seen as simultaneously embodying both the "effect" and the "cause" of a new human existence. The seed of a plant likewise exemplifies the oneness of cause and effect. Seeds are usually sown in Spring and bear fruit in Autumn but,

186

from a perspective rather different from the purely temporal one, we can say that inherent within the seed already are both cause (sowing) and effect (harvest). A profound contemplation of the causal law at work in life inevitably leads us to acceptance of the oneness of cause and effect.

At the same time, though, we must bear in mind that the examples cited above deal with the question of causality in the world of phenomena, the realm accessible to scientific investigation and confirmation. The Buddhist principle of causality, however, probes much deeper, penetrating the innermost nooks and crannies of life. It deals with a realm that transcends both space and time in which, for that very reason, it is meaningless to talk of cause preceding effect: both exist simultaneously.

People sometimes tend to equate causality – either the scientific or the karmic concept – with determinism, because of the idea that a given cause must inevitably produce a given effect, and that one cannot do much about this. However, this criticism fails to take into account our potential to alter the effects of our past deeds through the causes or actions we initiate from now on. Buddhism tells us that there is an indispensable element necessary if we are to bring to the surface the causality that lies dormant in the depths of our being. This element is an external cause which, when it unites with the latent cause, produces a manifest effect. Without the appropriate external cause the latent cause and the latent effect coexisting with it will remain forever dormant. Moreover, depending upon the nature of the external cause – i.e., our interaction with the environment – the form in which latent effects become manifest may vary greatly. As we bring forth the supreme condition of Buddhahood from within ourselves, the entire network of causes and effects which constitutes our own personal karma is dramatically transformed, becoming based on enlightenment rather than delusion and working to advance our development as a human being.

Another attribute of the lotus that lends itself to Buddhist symbolism is the fact that, as we saw, the plant grows and blooms in muddy water, yet its blossoms are pure and beautiful. This leads one to think of the emergence of the pure Buddha nature from within the life of the ordinary person, despite its defilement by delusions and earthly desires. "Emergence from the Earth", the fifteenth chapter of the Lotus Sutra, describes people who embrace the Mystic Law as "untainted by the affairs of the world, like a lotus blossom in the water".

It is worth looking further at this concept, since it involves one of the cardinal concerns of Buddhism.

Human existence is often seen as a seething whirlpool of desires, drives and impulses, which give rise to vices and suffering. It is true that a person dominated solely by his or her own desires and impulses can enjoy neither true self-identity nor freedom but will, instead, always be at the mercy of changing conditions in his or her life. For exactly this reason some religious teachings have claimed that the eradication of one's desires is the sole path to salvation. However, desire is an inherent function of life, and in the final analysis one cannot extinguish desire without extinguishing life itself. Desire, as an innate function of our individual lives, can be thought of not as necessarily damaging but as neutral, in that it has the potential either to harm or to benefit human existence. The real question is not the suppression of our desires but how to control and direct them so that they can work to enhance human virtues. This is where Buddhism comes in. According to Buddhist teachings, once we activate the supreme state of Buddhahood inherent in every one of us it elevates and redirects the workings of our desires so that they further our individual growth and enlightenment. If, by contrast, we give our desires free rein without first orienting them in a higher state of life, they will operate only in a destructive fashion, bringing us anguish and perhaps even threatening our continued existence.

The significance of Buddhism lies both in its discovery of the Buddha nature in all beings and in the establishment of a practical method whereby it can be brought out, so that human beings can derive the maximum possible meaning from their individual existences. Both of these features are of special relevance to modern civilization, which for some while now has been trapped in a sort of spiritual quicksand. The key to our escape from the quicksand is the calling forth of the supreme human potential that is available to each of us. Most of us have to struggle to attain a higher state of mind and to find a deeper meaning in our lives, at the same time having to cope with the various difficulties of everyday existence. However, once our lives are firmly rooted in the Buddha nature we can direct all our problems and sufferings in such a way that they actually contribute to our further spiritual development. Earthly desires, then, can if properly channelled help us as we develop spiritually: it is only if they are improperly channelled that they become such a liability.

Buddhist scriptures often talk of the "eight-petalled" lotus, whereas in reality lotuses have between twenty and twenty-five petals – often more, up to a hundred, if the lotus plant in question has double or manifold petals. When the number eight is used in this context in the Buddhist scriptures, what is meant is that the lotus blossom has *many* petals, rather than that it has a precise number. The number eight also has had a traditional meaning of "fullness" or "completeness", a significance which is recognized when the scriptures talk of the eight-petalled lotus.

So, what is the significance of the eight-petalled lotus? Nichikan Shonin, the twenty-sixth high priest of Nichiren Shoshu, argues in his commentary on the Daishonin's "The Entity of the Mystic Law" that the eight-petalled lotus exists within each of us. He points to the resemblance between the appearance of the human arrangement of the lungs, heart and other organs in the human breast and petals of the lotus, and describes the former as a physical expression within our bodies of the lotus of the Mystic Law inherent in our lives. These two concepts of the entity of the lotus – its physical expression in our own bodies and the lotus of the Mystic Law – were in fact first brought together by T'ien-t'ai – it was from a follower of his that the Japanese priest Dengyo learned the concepts and, in AD 805, brought them back to his country, Japan. Nichikan Shonin used these metaphors to help his contemporaries understand that their lives were one with the entity of the Mystic Law.

In one of his writings Nichiren Daishonin says: "As for the wonderful entity of *Myoho-renge-kyo*, when we inquire into what sort of entity it is, we find it is the eight-petalled white lotus inherent in our lives."[13] In other words, the eight-petalled white lotus represents the entity of *Myoho-renge-kyo*. Here the idea of the lotus blossom is used not as a metaphor but indicates the "wonderful single Law that simultaneously possesses both cause and effect" – or *Myoho-renge-kyo*. To this Nichikan Shonin adds:

> It follows therefore that life and its environment, as well as cause and effect, all constitute the eight-petalled white lotus inherent in our lives, that is, the object of worship hidden in the depths of the essential teaching of the Lotus Sutra.[14]

The Mystic Law, or the ultimate reality of all things, expressed in this extract as the "eight-petalled white lotus inherent in our lives", was embodied by Nichiren Daishonin in the form of a mandala, the Gohonzon – the object of worship in his teaching.

An explanation of the meaning of the words "the Lotus Blossom of the Wonderful Law", which comprise the original Sanskrit title of the Lotus Sutra, may to some extent be gleaned from a reading of the text itself, but nowhere in the sutra do we find a definitive statement of the Law referred to in the title. It is in this fact that the significance of Nichiren Daishonin's Buddhism lies: he gave the Law concrete expression as *Nam-myoho-renge-kyo*. Some of the Chinese priests who came to know the Lotus Sutra through Kumarajiva's translation recognized its spiritual profundity. For example, Kumarajiva's disciple Chu Tao-sheng wrote in his commentary on the sutra that it encompassed all principles and all good. Later, T'ien-t'ai delivered detailed and systematized teachings based on the sutra. Nevertheless, despite all the attention the Lotus Sutra has attracted, it is clear if you examine the text that some truth still remains hidden.

It was only after I had taken faith in and studied Nichiren Daishonin's Buddhism that I understood this. The

Daishonin interprets all of the twenty-eight chapters of the Lotus Sutra as an elucidation of the Mystic Law, expressed by him as *Nam-myoho-renge-kyo*, and of the enlightenment of Shakyamuni Buddha, who had himself awakened to this Law. However, because this Law is beyond ordinary comprehension the Daishonin embodied it in the form of a mandala; he taught that, by chanting *Nam-myoho-renge-kyo* while having faith in this mandala, each and every one of us can attain enlightenment.

To digress briefly, the relationship between the lotus and the ultimate reality reminds me of an anecdote concerning the French impressionist Claude Monet. It was told to me by René Huyghe, the French art critic and historian. In 1890 Monet purchased a strip of marshland across the road from his house and flower garden. Through this strip of land flowed the Epte, a tributary of the Seine. Monet diverted this stream and constructed a water-lily pond and a "Japanese" bridge spanning it. This was the exotic "lotus land" in which, during his later years, he meditated and painted. He used to sit by the pond, leaning over and gazing at the water's surface which, like a mirror, reflected the sky – but, in Monet's eyes, it had *become* the sky: he saw a union of clumps of clouds moving and water plants rippling. His eyes saw clusters of lily pads and blossoms dotting the water's surface – which by this time to him had merged with everything around it. According to his mind's eye, all of these things were a unified whole: there was no longer any clear distinction between the water and the land or between the water and the sky. We are lucky enough to see the fruits of his speculations in his water-lily paintings. Huyghe remarked that, if we compare these paintings of Monet with the drawings produced by Chinese artists in the eighth and ninth centuries, we can see that Monet, although he was obviously occidental in terms of both birth and tradition, nevertheless shared the unified worldview that characterizes Chinese art.

Kyo
The word *kyo* is the Japanese translation of the word "sutra". By "sutra" we mean a teaching of Shakyamuni

Buddha and, because the Buddha taught through the medium of preaching – that is, he used his own voice – the word *kyo* has sometimes been interpreted to mean "sound". For example, T'ien-t'ai writes in his *Profound Meaning of the Lotus Sutra* that "The voice does the Buddha's work and is therefore termed *kyo*". Nichiren Daishonin, in the *Record of the Orally Transmitted Teachings*, also states: "*Kyo* means the words and speech, sounds and voices of all living beings."[15] He thereby indicated that the ultimate Law to which a Buddha is enlightened is inherent in all living beings.

The Chinese character used for *kyo* originally meant the warp of a length of cloth; possibly because this creates the image of continuity, *kyo* came also to mean a teaching that should be preserved and handed down to posterity. The character was used in China to mean "books" or "classics", such as those of Confucianism or Taoism; when the Buddhist scriptures were introduced from India the character was used to mean "sutra". It is in this sense that the Daishonin interprets the word when he says, in the same work: "That which is eternal, spanning the three existences, is called *kyo*."[16]

A Buddha's enlightenment, expressed in the voice of his preaching, is *kyo*, and the truth to which he has been enlightened is eternal, spanning past, present and future. When we awaken to this truth we realize the eternal aspect of our own individual lives, an aspect that transcends the changes of the physical world and the cycle of birth and death.

The Mystic Law

As we have seen, Nichiren Daishonin embodied the Mystic Law as a mandala called the Gohonzon. His teaching was that through belief in the Gohonzon and the chanting of *Nam-myoho-renge-kyo* we can manifest the Mystic Law that is the ultimate reality of each of our lives; thus the Mystic Law is on the one hand the object of worship and, on the other and more generally, the truth that is inherent in ourselves. The Daishonin explains this in a letter to one of his followers, Abutsu-bo:

> Now the entire body of Abutsu Shonin is composed of the five universal elements of earth, water, fire, wind and space. These five elements are also the five characters of the *daimoku*. Therefore, Abutsu-bo is the Treasure Tower itself, and the Treasure Tower is Abutsu-bo himself. No other knowledge is purposeful. It is the Treasure Tower adorned with seven kinds of gems – listening to the true teaching, believing it, keeping the precept, attaining peace of mind, practising assiduously, unselfishly devoting oneself, and forever seeking self-improvement.[17]

In this passage the Daishonin relates "the entire body of Abutsu Shonin" to *Myoho-renge-kyo*, or the Mystic Law. As we saw in chapter five, the Mystic Law has no existence outside the world of phenomena – or, according to the Daishonin, the world of the five universal elements, in which case we cannot help but conclude that the Mystic Law is inseparable from our bodies. Indeed, our bodies – as the manifestations of our lives – are also the entities of the Mystic Law. In Buddhism the body and the mind are inseparable and essentially indistinguishable: they are a single psychosomatic entity. So, when we refer to "the human body", we mean not the physical body as distinct from the mind but the whole entity which incorporates both mind and body. However, it is difficult to believe that our body really is, itself, the Mystic Law, and so far too often we waste our efforts trying to find it elsewhere. The fact is that our own lives are each a Treasure Tower. We discussed the Treasure Tower mentioned in the Lotus Sutra earlier (see page 13). In the sutra, the tower is said to be adorned with seven different types of precious stones, as we saw, but the Daishonin reinterprets these as being the seven aspects of Buddhist practice required if we are to perceive that our own lives are indeed the entity of *Nam-myoho-renge-kyo*. He explains that the Treasure Tower represents both the Gohonzon and the lives of those who embrace it and thereby manifest their innate Buddha nature. Elsewhere he writes

193

that, because the Gohonzon embodies a truth that exists latent within us:

> Never seek this Gohonzon outside yourself. The Gohonzon exists only within the mortal flesh of us ordinary people who embrace the Lotus Sutra and chant *Nam-myoho-renge-kyo*.[18]

In conclusion, we can say that the general aim of Buddhism is the freeing of human beings from the sufferings of birth and death by enabling them to awaken to the unchanging truth, which is their own Buddha nature. An important difference between the Daishonin's Buddhism and earlier systems is that, while they showed how people could be brought to enlightenment through the exertion of tremendous effort in terms of doctrinal studies and meditative disciplines, thereby restricting enlightenment to a monastic elite, the teachings of Nichiren Daishonin provide a way which allows all of us, whatever our ability or circumstances, access to the ultimate truth.

References

[1] *The Major Writings of Nichiren Daishonin*, vol. 2, page 228.
[2] Ibid., vol. 1, page 222.
[3] Ibid., vol. 3, page 246.
[4] Ibid., vol. 3, page 248.
[5] Ibid., vol. 1, page 3.
[6] Ibid., vol. 1, page 267.
[7] Ibid., vol. 1, page 5.
[8] Ibid., vol. 1, pages 4-5.
[9] *Nichiren Daishonin Gosho Zenshu*, page 708.
[10] Ibid., pages 512-13.
[11] *The Major Writings of Nichiren Daishonin*, vol. 4, pages 305-6.
[12] *Nichiren Daishonin Gosho Zenshu*, page 513.
[13] Ibid., page 411.
[14] *Nichikan Shonin Mondanshu*, page 666.
[15] *Nichiren Daishonin Gosho Zenshu*, page 708.
[16] Ibid., page 708.
[17] *The Major Writings of Nichiren Daishonin*, vol. 1, page 30.
[18] Ibid., vol. 1, page 213.

Glossary

Abhidharma The *Abhidharma* is one of the three divisions of the Buddhist canon, comprising doctrinal commentary. The name comes from two Sanskrit words – *dharma* meaning "the Law" or "truth" and *abhi* meaning "towards" or "upon". *Abhidarma* therefore means study of the Law – in other words, doctrinal study of the sutras. From the fourth century BC there were repeated schisms in the Buddhist Order and eighteen or twenty *Abhidharma* schools were eventually formed, many of which made considerable efforts to systematically interpret the sutras. Especially prominent among them was the Sarvastivada ("All Exists") school. Among the many *abhidharma* texts the *Great Commentary on the Abhidharma* and *A Treasury of Analyses of the Law* are especially famous. *See also* **Great Commentary on the *Abhidharma*, Treasury of Analyses of the Law**.

Alaya-consciousness (Sanskrit *alaya-vijnana* The *alaya*-consciousness is known also as the "storehouse consciousness" or the "karmic repository". This is the eighth of the Nine Consciousnesses, and is located below the realm of conscious awareness. All karma created in the present and previous lifetimes is stored here. All the actions and experiences of life that take place through the operations of the first seven consciousnesses are accumulated as karmic seeds in the *alaya*-consciousness, which at the same time exerts an influence on the workings of the seven consciousnesses. *See also* **karma, nine consciousnesses**.

Amala-consciousness (Sanskrit *amala-vijnana* The *amala*-consciousness is the ninth of the nine consciousnesses. This is the "fundamental pure consciousness" and is identical to the universal Buddha nature. *See also* **nine consciousnesses**.

Anger (Sanskrit *asura*, Japanese *shura*) Anger is the fourth of the Ten Worlds and one of the four evil paths. It is a state dominated by a selfish ego that values oneself alone and holds others in contempt. A person in this state is attached to the idea of his or her own superiority and cannot bear to be inferior to others in anything. *Asuras*, contentious demons in Indian mythology, were regarded as typifying the condition of life in the world of Anger.

Animality (Sanskrit *tiryanch*, Japanese *chikusho*) Animality is the third of the Ten Worlds and one of the three evil paths. It is a state in which one is swayed by instinctive desires and has no sense of reason or morality. *See also* **Ten Worlds, three evil paths**.

Appearance (Japanese *nyozeso*) Appearance is one of the ten factors of life, and represents that aspect of things that can be discerned from the outside, pointing to the material and physical side of existence, and includes such attributes as colour, form, shape and behaviour. *See also* **ten factors of life**.

Bodhisattva (1) A Bodhisattva is a person who aspires to Buddhahood. In Hinayana Buddhism the term is used almost exclusively to mean Shakyamuni in his previous lifetimes, when he was striving for enlightenment. However, after the rise of Mahayana Buddhism, the term "Bodhisattva" came to mean anyone aspiring to enlightenment and performing altruistic deeds. (2) Bodhisattva is also the ninth of the Ten Worlds, a state characterized by compassion in which people seek enlightenment both for themselves and for others. *See also* **Ten Worlds**.

Buddha A Buddha is a person who perceives the ultimate reality, and who leads others to the attainment of the same enlightenment. The word *buddha* was in India originally a common noun meaning "enlightened one", but was later used also to indicate Shakyamuni, the historical founder of Buddhism.

Buddhahood Buddhahood is the highest of the Ten Worlds. It is characterized by infinite wisdom and infinite compassion, and is regarded as a state of perfect freedom in which one is awakened to the eternal and ultimate truth that is the reality of all things.

Buddhist gods Buddhist gods, also called "heavenly beings" or "benevolent deities", are the gods who assembled from all parts of the Universe in order to listen to Shakyamuni preach the Lotus Sutra, and who vowed to guard its proselytisers. However, the term "Buddhist gods" may also be understood to symbolize the powers of protection inherent in the natural phenomena of the Universe and in society, powers which are activated and strengthened by the individual's Buddhist practice.

Consciousness Only school (Sanskrit *Vijnanavada*) The Consciousness Only school is known also as the Yogachara school. It was one of the two major Mahayana schools in India, the other being the Madhyamika school. The founder of the Consciousness Only school is generally regarded as having been Maitreya (*c.*270-350). The school's doctrine was developed by Maitreya's disciple Asanga and by Vasubandhu in the first half of the fifth century. The Consciousness Only school upholds the idea that all phenomena arise from the *vijnana*, or consciousness, and that the basis of all functions of consciousness is the *alaya*-consciousness. The Consciousness Only doctrine probably constituted the mainstream of Buddhist study in the Nalanda Monastery, which was one of the foremost centres of Buddhist learning in ancient India. The Fa-hsiang (Japanese Hosso) school carried on the Consciousness Only school's philosophy in both China and Japan. *See also* **alaya-consciousness**.

Consistency from beginning to end (Japanese *nyoze hommatsu kukyoto*) Consistency from beginning to end is one of the ten factors of life. It is the integrating factor that unifies the other nine – from "appearance" to "manifest effect" – in every moment of life. This factor also explains that, when the first three factors are collectively defined as "entity" (beginning) and the following six factors as "function" (end), both beginning and end

– or the entity of all phenomena and the functions of that entity – are inseparable. *See also* **ten factors of life**.

Daimoku (1) *Daimoku* is the title of a sutra – specifically, the title of the Lotus Sutra, *Myoho-renge-kyo* (Chinese *Miao-fa-lien-hua-ching*). (2) *Daimoku* is also the invocation of *Nam-myoho-renge-kyo* in the Buddhism of Nichiren Daishonin.

Dharma nature Dharma nature is the eternal and unchanging truth inherent in all things, the enlightened nature which all life innately possesses. It is the opposite of darkness or illusion.

Eagle Peak (Sanskrit Gridhrakuta) Eagle Peak, sometimes called Vulture Peak, was a mountain located to the northeast of Rajagriha, the capital of Magadha in ancient India. Here Shakyamuni is said to have expounded the Lotus Sutra and other teachings. The expression "Eagle Peak" is also used figuratively to refer to the Buddha land or the state of Buddhahood.

Earthly desires Earthly desires (also called "defilements", "impurities" or simply "desires") is a generic term for all of those workings of life – including desires and illusions in a general sense – that cause us spiritual and physical suffering and impede our quest for enlightenment. There are various ways of classifying earthly desires. The *Treatise on the Sutra of the Perfection of Wisdom*, a Mahayana doctrinal commentary, says that the three poisons – greed, anger and stupidity – give rise to all of the other earthly desires; whereas another Mahayana commentary, the *Establishment of the Consciousness Only Doctrine* (Sanskrit *Vijnaptimatratasiddhi-shastra*, Chinese *Ch'eng-wei-shih-lun*, Japanese *Joyuishiki Ron*), divides earthly desires into two categories, fundamental and derivative. The ten fundamental desires consist of the five delusive passions (greed, anger, stupidity, arrogance and doubt) and the five false views (regarding the self as absolute, believing either that life ends at death or that it continues in some eternally unchanging form, failing to recognize the law of cause and effect, regarding inferior things as superior, and viewing erroneous practices as the true way to enlightenment). Moreover, twenty derivative desires arise from and accompany the fundamental ones: for example, irritability, the tendency to bear grudges and the desire to inflict harm all derive from the fundamental earthly desire of anger. T'ien-t'ai classified earthly desires into three categories of illusions: illusions of thought and desire; illusions innumerable as particles of dust and sand; and illusions about the true nature of existence.

Earthly desires are enlightenment "Earthly desires are enlightenment" is a principle which teaches that delusion and enlightenment are both innate in life, and that one attains Buddhahood not by extinguishing illusions and earthly desires but by awakening to one's inherent Buddha nature.

Eighth consciousness *See alaya*-consciousness, **nine consciousnesses**.

Eighty-four thousand teachings The eighty-four thousand teachings are known also as the "eighty thousand teachings". This expression refers to the totality of the teachings that Shakyamuni Buddha expounded during his lifetime. The figure is not to be taken literally: it means simply "a large number".

197

Entity (Japanese *nyozetai*) Entity is one of the ten factors of life. Entity is an aspect of things which permeates and integrates external appearance and internal nature. It is one of the first three factors of life, which explain the reality of life. *See also* **ten factors of life**.

External cause *See* **relation**.

Esho-funi See **oneness of life and its environment**.

Five components of life (Sanskrit *pancha skandha*) The five components of life are the physical and psychic factors into which living beings may be analysed. They are form, perception, conception (or conceptualization), volition and consciousness. This fifth component, consciousness, also integrates the other four. Form indicates the physical aspect of life, while the other four components refer to life's spiritual aspect.

Five elements The five elements are earth, water, fire, wind and space. *See also* **four elements**.

Flower Garland Sutra (Sanskrit *Buddhavatamsaka-nama-mahavaipulya-sutra*, Chinese *Hua-yen-ching*, Japanese *Kegon Kyo*) The Flower Garland Sutra, often called by its abbreviated Sanskrit name, the *Avatamsaka* Sutra, is the basic text of the Kegon (Chinese Hua-yen) sect and is traditionally thought to have been the teaching which Shakyamuni Buddha expounded immediately after his enlightenment. The sutra teaches that all phenomena constantly interrelate with and give rise to one another: one permeates all, all are contained in one, and so on. The sutra also delineates many stages of Bodhisattva practice. *See also* **Hua-yen school**.

Four bodily humours The four bodily humours are blood, phlegm, choler (yellow bile) and melancholy (black bile).

Four elements The four elements are earth, water, fire and wind. *See also* **five elements**.

Four Heavenly Kings The Four Heavenly Kings are Jikokuten (Sanskrit Dhritarashtra), Komokuten (Virupaksha), Bishamonten (Vaishravana) and Zojoten (Virudhaka). They are the lords of the four heavens who are believed to protect Buddhists and the land in which they practise.

Four meetings The four meetings are encounters that awoke Shakyamuni Buddha to the impermanence of all things and led him to renounce his secular life and start on his religious pursuit of the truth. The encounters were with an old man, a sick person, a corpse and a religious ascetic. *See also* **four sufferings**.

Four noble truths The four noble truths are found in a teaching of Shakyamuni Buddha expounded soon after his enlightenment. The four are: the truth of suffering, the truth of the origin of suffering, the truth of the cessation of suffering, and the truth of the path to the cessation of suffering.

Four Noble Worlds The Four Noble Worlds are the top four of the Ten Worlds – Learning, Realization, Bodhisattva and Buddhahood. The term is used to make a contrast with the Six Paths, or six lower worlds. The Four Noble Worlds are the states in which a person tries to transcend the uncertainties of the six lower worlds – which are controlled by earthly

198

desires and governed by an ever-changing environment – and to establish independence. *See also* **earthly desires, Six Paths** and **Ten Worlds**.

Four sufferings The four sufferings are the sufferings of birth, old age, sickness and death. They represent sufferings arising from the transience of all phenomena.

Four virtues The four virtues are the four noble qualities of a Buddha's life, as expounded in the Nirvana Sutra. They are eternity, happiness, true self and purity. Because every human being possesses the Buddha nature, all of us can develop the four virtues if, through fulfilling the Buddhist teaching, we attain Buddhahood.

Fundamental darkness Fundamental darkness is the most fundamental illusion. It is inherent in life, and gives rise to all the other illusions and desires. The term "fundamental darkness" is used to contrast with fundamental enlightenment, or the innate Buddha nature.

Gohonzon The Gohonzon is the object of worship in Nichiren Daishonin's Buddhism. The Japanese word for an object of worship is *honzon*, meaning an "object of fundamental respect"; *go* is an honorific prefix. Nichiren Daishonin defined the ultimate Law permeating life and the Universe as *Nam-myoho-renge-kyo*, and embodied his enlightenment to this Law in the form of a mandala that was perfectly endowed with all of the Ten Worlds. He taught that one should have faith in this mandala – the Gohonzon – as the object of worship whereby one could attain Buddhahood. *See also* **mandala, Ten Worlds**.

***Great Commentary on the* Abhidharma** (Sanskrit *Abhidharma-mahavibhasha-shastra*, Japanese *Abidatsuma Daibibasha Ron*) The *Great Commentary on the Abhidharma* is an exhaustive commentary on the Hinayana doctrines in two hundred fascicles compiled in Kashmir in the former half of the second century AD. The compilation is said to have been carried out by five hundred monks under the guidance of Parshva and Vasumitra at the time of the Fourth Buddhist Council. It was translated into Chinese by Hsüan-tsang and other priests and exerted a great influence on Mahayana Buddhism in later ages. *See also* **Abhidarma**.

Great Concentration and Insight (Chinese *Mo-ho-chih-kuan*, Japanese *Maka Shikan*) *Great Concentration and Insight* is one of T'ien-t'ai's three major works. *Great Concentration and Insight* is actually a compilation of lectures delivered by T'ien-t'ai at Yü-ch'üan-ssu temple in Ching-chou in AD 594, completed in ten volumes by his disciple Chang-an. It elucidates the principle of *ichinen sanzen* based on the Lotus Sutra, and teaches the method of practice for observing one's mind in order to realize this truth within oneself. *See also* **T'ien-t'ai**.

Heaven (Sanskrit *deva-loka*, Japanese *ten*) Heaven is also known as Rapture. It is the sixth of the Ten Worlds and one of the Six Paths. It is the condition of joy or rapture we experience when, for example, we achieve the satisfaction of our desires or are released from pain. According to the original concept, there were twenty-eight subdivisions in the realm of Heaven: six heavens in the world of desire, eighteen in the world of form, and four in the world of formlessness. If Heaven is viewed as a state of life, these divisions of the threefold world can be taken as representing various kinds of joy. *See also* **Six Paths, Ten Worlds**.

Hell (Sanskrit *naraka* or *niraya*, Japanese *jigoku*) Hell is the first and lowest of the three evil paths, the Six Paths and the Ten Worlds. It is the realm of utmost suffering. According to the sutras, there are various kinds of hells, of which the best known are probably the eight hot hells and the eight cold hells. As a state of life, Hell is a condition of extreme mental or physical suffering characterized by the furious impulse to destroy oneself and, in the process, everything else. *See also* **Six Paths, Ten Worlds**.

Hinayana Hinayana (literally, the "lesser vehicle") is one of the two major branches of Buddhism. Hinayana is a collective name applied disparagingly to the several *Abhidharma* schools that arose after the Buddha's death by proponents of the Mahayana ("great vehicle"), a new Buddhist movement thought to have begun around the beginning of the first century AD. Hinayana generally stressed attainment of personal liberation by eradicating desire and escaping the cycle of birth and death, and maintained a chiefly monastic orientation. The Mahayanists criticized the adherents of these schools for what they perceived as a tendency towards sterile academicism and monastic elitism, emphasizing instead the importance of practice among the laity and efforts for the salvation of all. Only one of the original schools, Theravada, still survives; it flourishes in Sri Lanka, Burma, Thailand, Cambodia and Laos. *See also Abhidharma*, **Mahayana, two vehicles**.

Hua-yen school The Hua-yen school is a school based on the Flower Garland Sutra. Its founder is thought to be Tu-shun (557-640), of the Chinese early T'ang dynasty. In 736 the T'ang priest Tao-hsüan brought the Hua-yen texts to Japan. In 740 a priest called Shinjo (Korean, Simsang) from Silla in what is now the Korean Peninsula gave lectures in Japan on the Flower Garland Sutra, and he is regarded as the founder of the Japanese branch of the school, known as the Kegon sect. The school teaches that, since the true nature of all things is non-substantiality, then, from the standpoint of a Buddha's enlightenment all phenomena are identified with one another and interpenetrate each other completely: one permeates all, and all are contained within one. *See also* **Flower Garland Sutra, T'ien-t'ai school**.

Humanity (Sanskrit *manusya*, Japanese *nin*) Humanity is known also as Tranquillity. This is the fifth of the Ten Worlds. The realm of human beings, it also represents a state in which one can control one's instinctive desires through the use of reason and can act humanely. *See also* **Ten Worlds**.

Hundred worlds *See ichinen sanzen*.

Hunger (Sanskrit *preta*, Japanese *gaki*) Hunger is the second of the Ten Worlds and one of the three evil paths. It represents a state in which one is governed by one's insatiable desire for food, wealth, fame, power or anything else. A person in this state is physically and spiritually tormented by constant craving. The causes of Hunger are such traits as greed, miserliness and jealousy.

Ichinen sanzen *Ichinen sanzen* is the principle, taught by T'ien-t'ai in his *Great Concentration and Insight*, that all phenomena are inherent at each moment in the life of each individual; his argument is based on the Lotus Sutra. *Ichinen sanzen* can be translated as "a single life, at each moment, possesses three thousand realms". T'ien-t'ai's analysis explains the mutually inclusive relationship between the ultimate truth and the phenomenal world. *Ichinen* ("one mind") is the ultimate reality, which is manifest in each instant of an individual's existence, while *sanzen* ("three thousand") represents the varying aspects and phases that it assumes. The figure of three thousand is reached by multiplying the Ten Worlds, their mutual inclusion, the ten factors and the three realms of existence.

Ichinen sanzen has two interpretations, actual *ichinen sanzen* and theoretical *ichinen sanzen*. Actual *ichinen sanzen* represents the life of a Buddha, in which the world of Buddhahood is fully active and manifest, while theoretical *ichinen sanzen* indicates the life of common mortals among the Nine Worlds, in which the world of Buddhahood remains dormant.

Influence (Japanese *nyozesa*) Influence is one of the ten factors of life. It is the movement or action produced when latent power is activated. *See also* **ten factors of life**.

Internal cause (Japanese *nyozein*) Internal cause is one of the ten factors of life. It is the cause latent within life that produces an effect of the same nature as itself, either good or evil. Internal cause is formed through influence or actions, and each internal cause simultaneously contains a latent effect. *See also* **latent effect, ten factors of life**.

Karma Karma is the collection of potential effects residing in the inner realm of life which manifest themselves in various ways at some point in the future. Buddhism teaches that every action imprints a latent influence on one's life with the power to bring about an effect at some later time. Accordingly, our actions in the past have shaped our present reality, and in turn our actions in the present shape our future. This law of karmic causality operates over past, present and future. Karma formed in past lifetimes is responsible for the differences already existing among us when we are born into this one.

Kegon sect *See* **Hua-yen school**.

Ku (Sanskrit *shunya* or *shunyata*) *Ku* is a fundamental Buddhist concept, variously rendered in English as "non-substantiality", "Emptiness", "Void", "latency", "relativity" and so on. It is the concept that no phenomena have a fixed or independent existence. The word *ku* also refers to a potential state that is considered as being neither existence nor nonexistence.

Latent effect (Japanese *nyozeka*) Latent effect is one of the ten factors of life. It is the effect produced in the depths of life when an internal cause is activated by the factor of relation (or external cause). Nichikan Shonin, the twenty-sixth high priest of Nichiren Shoshu, writes: "Whether the mind produces good or evil depends on whether it has produced good or evil before. In this sense, what the mind has produced is internal cause and what it will produce is latent effect." Since both internal cause and latent effect are inherent in life they exist simultaneously; that is, there is no time lapse between them, as often occurs between an action and its manifest effect. *See also* **internal cause, manifest effect, relation, ten factors of life.**

Learning (Sanskrit *shravaka*, Japanese *shomon*) Learning is the seventh of the Ten Worlds and one of the two vehicles (the other is Realization). "Men of Learning" originally meant those who had heard the Buddha preach the four noble truths and who strove to attain enlightenment through the eradication of earthly desires. Learning is now viewed also as a condition of life, the state in which one perceives the impermanence of all things and attempts to free oneself from the sufferings of the Six Paths through seeking some lasting truth in the teachings of people who have already attained enlightenment. *See also* **Realization, Ten Worlds, two vehicles.**

"Lifespan of the Tathagata" (Japanese *Juryo*) "Lifespan of the Tathagata" is the sixteenth – and key – chapter of the Lotus Sutra, which discusses Shakyamuni's Buddhahood in terms both of its cause and effect and of the land. Shakyamuni reveals that he first attained Buddhahood in the remote past and ever since has remained in the mundane world teaching the Law; thus a Buddha retains the Nine Worlds of a common mortal, and the Buddha land and the mundane world are essentially one. Shakyamuni demonstrated that no fundamental difference exists between the Buddha and the ordinary person. *See also* **Lotus Sutra.**

Lotus Sutra (Sanskrit *Saddharma-pundarika-sutra*, Japanese *Hokekyo*) The Lotus Sutra explains that the potential for Buddhahood exists within all living beings, and reveals that Shakyamuni originally attained his enlightenment in the inconceivably remote past. Among the three extant Chinese translations the *Myoho-renge-kyo* (Chinese *Miao-fa-lien-hua-ching*), translated in twenty-eight chapters by Kumarajiva in AD 406, was the most widely read and had the greatest influence; in China and Japan, therefore, when one talks of the Lotus Sutra one is usually referring to the *Myoho-renge-kyo*. *See also* ***Myoho-renge-kyo*, *Nam-myoho-renge-kyo*.**

Madhyamika school *See* **Consciousness Only school.**

Mahayana Mahayana (literally, the "great vehicle") is one of the two major streams of Buddhism. The word "vehicle" here indicates a teaching or a means to convey people to enlightenment. Mahayana teachings are concerned not only with individual salvation but with the importance of bringing *everyone* to enlightenment. The Mahayana movement is said to have begun in India about the beginning of the first century; subsequently it spread to Central Asia, China, Korea and Japan. *See also* **Hinayana.**

Mandala A mandala is an object of worship upon which Buddhas and bodhisattvas are depicted or on which the mystic doctrine is expressed. The Sanskrit word *mandala* originally meant a round or square altar on which depictions of the Buddha were placed; the word was translated from Sanskrit into Chinese with expressions meaning "perfectly endowed" or "cluster of blessings". *See also* **Gohonzon.**

202

Manifest effect (Japanese *nyozeho*) Manifest effect is one of the ten factors of life. It is the concrete, perceivable result that, as a consequence of internal cause and latent effect, emerges as time passes. *See also* **internal cause, latent effect, ten factors of life.**

Mano-**consciousness** (Sanskrit *mano-vijnana*) *Mano*-consciousness is the seventh of the nine consciousnesses. The Sanskrit word *manas*, from which *mano* derives, means mind or intellect. This consciousness performs the function of abstract thought and discerns the inner world. Awareness of self is said to originate at this level. The passionate attachment to the ego which functions to create evil karma is also regarded as the working of the *mano*-consciousness, influenced by the eighth or *alaya*-consciousness. *See also* **alaya-consciousness, nine consciousnesses.**

"Means" "Means" is the second chapter of the Lotus Sutra. In this chapter Shakyamuni says that the sole reason for every Buddha to appear in the world is to awaken in every human being the Buddha wisdom, help them realize it, and enable them to attain Buddhahood. He also explains that his earlier teachings, expounded before the Lotus Sutra, were all his "skilful means" to lead people towards the realization of their own Buddha nature. "Means", together with the sixteenth chapter, the "Lifespan of the Tathagata", is one of the two pivotal chapters of the sutra. *See also* **"Lifespan of the Tathagata", Lotus Sutra.**

Miao-lo (711-782) Miao-lo is the sixth patriarch in the lineage of the T'ien-t'ai school in China, counting from the Great Teacher T'ien-t'ai. At the age of twenty Miao-lo studied the doctrine of the T'ien-t'ai school under Hsüan-lang, the fifth patriarch, and at the age of thirty-eight he entered the priesthood. Miao-lo reasserted the supremacy of the Lotus Sutra and wrote commentaries on T'ien-t'ai's three major works, thus bringing about a revival of interest in T'ien-t'ai Buddhism. He is revered as the restorer of the school.

Mutual possession of the Ten Worlds Mutual possession of the Ten Worlds is a principle formulated by T'ien-t'ai on the basis of the Lotus Sutra; it states that each of the Ten Worlds contains within itself the potential for all ten; it is one of the component principles of *ichinen sanzen*. This mutual possession means that life is not fixed in any one of the Ten Worlds but, at any given moment, can manifest any of the ten, from Hell to Buddhahood. Its most important implication is that any ordinary human being of the Nine Worlds has the potential to attain Buddhahood, and that therefore a Buddha, who retains the nine lower worlds, is in no genuine way distinct from ordinary human beings. *See also* **ichinen sanzen, Ten Worlds.**

Myoho-renge-kyo (Sanskrit *Saddharma-pundarika-sutra*, Chinese *Miao-fa-lien-hua-ching*) (1) *Myoho-renge-kyo* is a Chinese translation of the Lotus Sutra (*see* **Lotus Sutra**). (2) *Myoho-renge-kyo* is also the entity of the Mystic Law itself, or *Nam-myoho-renge-kyo* (*see* **Nam-myoho-renge-kyo**).

Mystic Law The Mystic Law is the Law of *Nam-myoho-renge-kyo*, the *ultimate Law of life and the Universe. See* **Lotus Sutra**, *Nam-myoho-renge-kyo.*

Nagarjuna Nagarjuna is a Mahayana scholar in southern India thought to have lived between AD 150 and AD 250. He is counted as the fourteenth of Shakyamuni's twenty-four successors. Born to a Brahman family, he at first studied Hinayana Buddhism but later converted to Mahayana. Thereafter Nagarjuna travelled throughout India to master all Mahayana sutras. He wrote commentaries on a great number of Mahayana sutras and organized the theoretical foundation of Mahayana thought, thus making an inestimable contribution to its development. He is especially known for his systematization of the doctrine of Emptiness or non-substantiality (*ku*). Since his doctrine is integral to Mahayana Buddhism, Nagarjuna is revered as the founder of the eight sects (Kusha, Jojitsu, Ritsu, Hosso, Sanron, Kegon, Tendai and Shingon). *See also* **ku**.

Nam-myoho-renge-kyo *Nam-myoho-renge-kyo* is the ultimate Law or absolute reality that permeates every object or event in the Universe; also, the invocation or *daimoku* of Nichiren Daishonin's Buddhism. The prefix *nam* or *namu* derives from Sanskrit and means "to devote one's life" – i.e., to fuse one's life with the eternal truth of *Myoho-renge-kyo*, and also to draw forth, through this fusion, the Buddha wisdom. *See also* *daimoku*, **Lotus Sutra**, *Myoho-renge-kyo*.

Nature (Japanese *nyozesho*) Nature is one of the ten factors of life; it is that aspect of things which comprises an individual's inherent disposition or quality and which cannot be perceived directly from the outside. For example, in terms of human life nature corresponds to such spiritual aspects as mind and consciousness. *See also* **ten factors of life**.

Nichiren Daishonin (1222-1282) Nichiren Daishonin is the founder of the school of Buddhism now known as Nichiren Shoshu, whose doctrine regards him as the Buddha of the Latter Day of the Law. He stated that the ultimate Law permeating life and every event in the Universe is the essence of the Lotus Sutra, the Mystic Law, or *Nam-myoho-renge-kyo*. *See also* **Lotus Sutra**, *Nam-myoho-renge-kyo*, **Nichiren Shoshu**.

Nichiren Shoshu Nichiren Shoshu is a school of Buddhism – the "orthodox Nichiren sect" – which regards Nichiren Daishonin as its founder and Nikko Shonin as his immediate successor. Its head temple is Taiseki-ji, in Shizuoka Prefecture, Japan, and its largest lay organization is the Soka Gakkai. *See also* **Soka Gakkai**.

Nine consciousnesses The nine consciousnesses are the nine kinds of discernment: sight-consciousness, hearing-consciousness, smell-consciousness, taste-consciousness, touch-consciousness, mind-consciousness, *mano*-consciousness, *alaya*-consciousness and *amala*-consciousness.

Nine great ordeals The nine great ordeals are the nine attempts which people made to kill or discredit Shakyamuni. For example, Devadatta tried to drop a boulder on him from the top of a cliff, and King Ajatashatru attempted to kill him by releasing a drunken elephant near him.

Nine Worlds The Nine Worlds are often contrasted with the world of

Buddhahood. They are the nine conditions from Hell to Bodhisattva that indicate deluded states of life. *See also* **Ten Worlds**.

Ninth consciousness *See amala-*consciousness.

Nirvana Nirvana is, in the Hinayana sutras, the attainment of enlightenment through the extinction of earthly desires and escape from the cycle of birth and death. In Nichiren Shoshu the word "nirvana" means an enlightened condition, based on faith in the Mystic Law, experienced in the real world. *See also* **Hinayana, Mystic Law, Nichiren Shoshu**.

Non-substantiality *See ku*.

Oneness of body and mind The oneness of body and mind is a principle that the two apparently distinct entities of body (the physical aspect of life) and mind (life's spiritual aspect) are in fact two integral and integrated aspects of the same entity. This is one of the ten onenesses formulated by Miao-lo in his *Annotations on the Profound Meaning of the Lotus Sutra*, which is predicated on T'ien-t'ai's discussion of the ten mystic principles of the Lotus Sutra in the *Profound Meaning of the Lotus Sutra*.

Oneness of life and its environment The oneness of life and its environment is a principle which states that the self and its environment are two integral aspects of the same entity. This is one of the ten onenesses – each stemming from the unity of all phenomena – formulated by Miao-lo in his *Annotations on the Profound Meaning of the Lotus Sutra*. *See also* **ten onenesses**

Power (Japanese *nyozeriki*) Power is one of the ten factors of life. It is life's inherent strength or energy to achieve something. Nichikan Shonin, the twenty-sixth high priest of Nichiren Shoshu, defines it as the capacity which life possesses in each of the Ten Worlds, and explained, for example, that those in the state of Humanity have the power to carry out the five precepts – not to kill, not to steal, not to commit unlawful sexual intercourse, not to lie and not to drink intoxicants. *See also* **ten factors of life**.

Profound Meaning of the Lotus Sutra (Chinese *Fa-hua-hsüan-i*, Japanese *Myoho-renge-kyo Gengi*) The *Profound Meaning of the Lotus Sutra* is a lecture given by T'ien-t'ai at Yü-chüan-ssu temple in Ching-chou in AD 593, during the Sui dynasty, and compiled in ten fascicles by Chang-an, the second patriarch of the T'ien-t'ai school. On the premise that the essence of the entire sutra is expressed in the title, T'ien-t'ai discusses the title of the Lotus Sutra, *Myoho-renge-kyo*, in light of the five major principles of name, entity, quality, function and teaching. From the viewpoint of name, for example, he gives an exhaustive interpretation of each of the five characters *myo, ho, ren, ge* and *kyo*.

Pure Land The Pure Land is a land of bliss in which a Buddha is thought to dwell. Provisional teachings such as those of the Jodo (Pure Land) sect hold that the Pure Land is far from the mundane world, but the Buddhism of Nichiren Daishonin teaches that it is wherever a person devotes him- or herself to the practice and propagation of the Mystic Law.

Realization (Sanskrit *pratyekabuddha*, Japanese *engaku*) Realization is the eighth of the Ten Worlds and one of the two vehicles (the other being Learning). The expression "men of Realization" originally meant those who had awakened to the impermanence of all phenomena through perceiving the twelve-linked chain of causation or through observing the phenomena of the physical world. As a condition of life, Realization is a state in which one perceives the transience of life and tries to free oneself from the sufferings of the Six Paths by seeking some eternal truth through one's own observations and efforts. *See also* **Learning, Six Paths, Ten Worlds, two vehicles.**

Realm of living beings The realm of living beings is one of the three realms of existence. The realm of living beings is that of the individual, formed by a temporary union of the five components. Since a living being is simply the temporary union of the five components, the realm of living beings is sometimes called the "realm in name only"; however, this realm is considered to be the integrated individual, capable of interacting with other individuals and with its surroundings, and is contrasted with the realm of the five components, which analyses the living being from the viewpoint of its component physical and spiritual functions. The realm of living beings can also be interpreted in the plural, to mean a group of living beings. *See also* **three realms of existence.**

Realm of the environment The realm of the environment is one of the three realms of existence; it is the place where living beings dwell and act. The differences among the Ten Worlds manifest themselves in the realm of the environment according to the people who inhabit it. *See also* **three realms of existence.**

Realm of the five components The realm of the five components is one of the three realms of existence. *See* **five components, realm of living beings, three realms of existence.**

Record of the Orally Transmitted Teachings (Japanese *Ongi Kuden*) The *Record of the Orally Transmitted Teachings* is a compilation of Nichiren Daishonin's lectures on the Lotus Sutra.

Relation (Japanese *nyozeen*) Relation is sometimes referred to as "external cause"; it is one of the ten factors of life. Relation is the auxiliary cause or external stimulus that helps an internal cause produce its effect. Relation should not be thought of as the environment itself; rather, it is the function which relates life to its environment. *See also* **internal cause, ten factors of life.**

Shakyamuni Shakyamuni ("Sage of the Shakyas") is the founder of Buddhism. East Asian Buddhist tradition says that Shakyamuni was born in 1029 BC and died in 949 BC, but Western historians set his birthdate some 500 years later: no definite conclusion has been reached, but two Western schools of thought say, respectively, that he lived 560-480 BC or 460-380 BC. His family name was Gautama, meaning "best cow", and his given name was Siddhartha, "goal achieved", though some think this may have been an epithet given him by later Buddhists. He was born in the Lumbini Gardens, in what is now Nepal, as the son of the king of the Shakyas, a minor tribe of ancient India. In youth he renounced his princely status and set off in search of a resolution to the four inescapable sufferings of birth, old age, sickness and death. He studied the influential philosophies of his day and practised various austerities but, finding it impossible to reach enlightenment through self-mortification, he eventually rejected these practices. Near the town of Gaya he sat under the Bodhi (Bo) tree, entered meditation, and attained enlightenment. During the succeeding fifty years he expounded numerous teachings to many different people, seeking to lead them from their various sufferings to freedom. His teachings were later compiled in the form of the Buddhist sutras; among them, the Lotus Sutra was traditionally revered by East Asian Buddhists as the highest. He died at the age of eighty.

Shikishin funi See **oneness of body and mind**.

Siddhartha *See* **Shakyamuni**.

Six Paths The Six Paths are the first six of the Ten Worlds: Hell, Hunger, Animality, Anger, Humanity (Tranquillity) and Heaven (Rapture). Taken together, the Six Paths indicate the state of delusion or suffering. *See also* **Ten Worlds**.

Soka Gakkai The Soka Gakkai is a religious society – the name translates as "value-creation society" – founded in 1930 as an organization of lay believers in Nichiren Shoshu. Its purpose is to propagate the teachings of Nichiren Daishonin and promote international cultural and educational exchanges in order to secure the happiness of every individual human being and to establish world peace. *See also* **Nichiren Shoshu**.

Sutra of Infinite Meaning (Chinese *Wu-liang-i-ching*, Japanase *Muryogi Kyo*) The Sutra of Infinite Meaning is a sutra regarded as a teaching introductory to the Lotus Sutra. The sutra unfolds on Eagle Peak and consists of three chapters. In the first chapter, "Virtuous Practice", Bodhisattva Great Splendour, on behalf of the assembly, praises Shakyamuni Buddha in verse. This verse section contains the passage of the thirty-four negations referring to the entity of the Buddha. In the second chapter, "Preaching", the Buddha states that all principles and meanings derive from one Law, although he does not clarify what this Law is. He then declares, "For the past more than forty years, I have not yet revealed the truth", indicating that his prior teachings were all provisional and expedient. The final chapter, "Ten Blessings", explains that by practising this sutra one can obtain ten kinds of blessings. *See also* **Lotus Sutra**.

Sutra of Meditation on the True Law (Sanskrit *Saddharma-smrity-upasthana*, Chinese *Cheng-fa-nien-ch'u-ching*, Japanese *Shobonenjo kyo*) The Sutra of Meditation on the True Law is often called the Shobonen Sutra; it is one of the *Agama* (Hinayana) sutras and elucidates the cause and effect of birth and death in the Six Paths.

Taho (Sanskrit Prabhutaratna) "Taho" means "Many Treasures", and describes a Buddha referred to in the Lotus Sutra: he appears seated in the Treasure Tower at the Ceremony in the Air to bear witness to the truth of Shakyamuni's teachings. *See also* **Treasure Tower**.

Tathagata See **"Thus Come One"**.

Ten factors of life The ten factors of life together comprise an analysis of the unchanging aspects of life common to all mutable phenomena. The ten factors are mentioned in "Means", the second chapter of the Lotus Sutra, which states:

> The true entity of all phenomena can only be understood and shared between Buddhas. This reality consists of the appearance, nature, entity, power, influence, internal cause, relation, latent effect, manifest effect, and their consistency from beginning to end.

This passage provides a theoretical basis whereby any individual may attain Buddhahood: since the ten factors are common to all existence, there can be no fundamental distinction between a Buddha and any other human being.

Ten Goddesses The Ten Goddesses are the ten daughters of a female demon called Kishimojin (Sanskrit Hariti). Kishimojin and her daughters are mentioned in the twenty-sixth chapter of the Lotus Sutra, where they pledge to protect the sutra's votaries.

Ten onenesses The ten onenesses are also called the ten non-dualities, and are principles set forth by Miao-lo in his commentary on T'ien-t'ai's *Profound Meaning of the Lotus Sutra*. They are: (1) the oneness of body and mind; (2) the oneness of the internal and the external; (3) the oneness of the inherent Buddha nature and the Buddhahood attained through practice; (4) the oneness of cause and effect; (5) the oneness of the pure and the impure (i.e., of enlightenment and delusion); (6) the oneness of life and its environment; (7) the oneness of self and others (i.e., of the Buddha and common mortals); (8) the oneness of thought, word and deed; (9) the oneness of the provisional and the true teachings; and (10) the oneness of benefit (i.e., both the Buddha and common mortals ultimately enjoy the same blessing of Buddhahood). *See also* **oneness of body and mind, oneness of life and its environment**.

Ten Worlds The Ten Worlds are the ten conditions manifested by a single living entity. They are Hell, Hunger, Animality, Anger, Humanity (or Tranquillity), Heaven (or Rapture), Learning, Realization, Bodhisattva and Buddhahood. The first three are the three evil paths; the first four are the four evil paths; the first six are the Six Paths; the first nine are the Nine Worlds; and the final four are the Four Noble Worlds. *See also* **Four Noble Worlds, Nine Worlds, Six Paths**.

Threefold world The threefold world is the world of unenlightened beings who dwell among the Six Paths. According to Vasubandhu's *A Treasury of Analyses of the Law* this world consists of three parts: the world of desires; the world of form, whose inhabitants, while free from desires, are still bound by material restrictions; and the world of spirit or formlessness, whose inhabitants have escaped from desires and material restrictions. *See also* **Six Paths**.

Three mystic principles The three mystic principles are the True Cause, the True Effect and the True Land, formulated by T'ien-t'ai on the basis of the sixteenth chapter of the Lotus Sutra. The True Cause is the practice Shakyamuni undertook in order to reach his original enlightenment; the True Effect is the original enlightenment he attained; and the True Land is the place where the Buddha has been expounding his teachings since he attained his original enlightenment. In Nichiren Shoshu the three mystic principles are interpreted as the Three Great Secret Laws: the True Cause for attaining Buddhahood is the *daimoku*; the True Effect is the enlightenment of the original Buddha Nichiren Daishonin, as embodied in the Gohonzon; and the True Land is the high sanctuary where the Gohonzon, the object of worship, is enshrined. *See also* **Gohonzon, True Cause, True Effect, True Land.**

Three poisons The three poisons are greed, anger and stupidity, the fundamental evils inherent in life which give rise to human suffering; they are described as "poisons" because they pollute people's lives. They are said also to be the underlying causes of the three calamities: greed brings about famine, anger brings about war, and stupidity leads to pestilence.

Three properties (Sanskrit *trikaya*, Japanese *sanjin*) The three properties are known also as the "three bodies" or the "three enlightened properties". They are the three kinds of body a Buddha may possess; the concept was adopted in Mahayana Buddhism as a way of organizing the different views of the Buddha that appear in the sutras. The three bodies are:

- The Dharma body, or body of the Law (Sanskrit *dharma-kaya*, Japanese *hosshin*): the fundamental truth or Law to which the Buddha is enlightened.
- The bliss body (Sanskrit *sambhoga-kaya*, Japanese *hoshin*), sometimes called the reward body, which is received as the reward for having completed Bodhisattva practice and obtained the Buddha wisdom.
- The manifested body (Sanskrit *nirmana-kaya*, Japanese *ojin*), or the physical form in which a Buddha appears in this world in order to save the people.

It was generally held that these represented three different kinds of Buddhas. However, on the basis of the Lotus Sutra and *ichinen sanzen*, the principle he derived from it, T'ien-t'ai says that the three bodies – or properties – are not separate entities: they are three integral aspects or properties of a single Buddha. In this light, they may be understood as follows:

- The property of the Law, or the essential property of the Buddha's life, which is the truth to which the Buddha has become enlightened.
- The property of wisdom, or the spiritual property of a Buddha's life, which enables him or her to perceive the truth.
- The property of action, or the physical property of a Buddha's life. The property of action is the Buddha's body, with which he acts compassionately in order to save other people, or it can be seen as the actions themselves.

Three realms of existence The three realms of existence are the realm of the five components, the realm of living beings and the realm of the

209

environment. The concept originally appeared in the *Treatise on the Sutra of the Perfection of Wisdom*, written by Nagarjuna (*c*.150-250), and was adopted and developed by T'ien-t'ai during the sixth century in China as a component principle of *ichinen sanzen*. In his interpretation, the three realms are the three dimensions of the phenomenal world in which the Ten Worlds manifest themselves. Thus the five components are the physical and psychic elements which constitute a living being; a living being is an individual existence which in each moment experiences one or other of the Ten Worlds; and the environment is the place in which living beings dwell. *See also* **five components**, *ichinen sanzen*, **realm of living beings**, **realm of the environment**, **realm of the five components**, **Ten Worlds**.

Three truths (Japanese *santai*) The three truths are the three integral aspects of the truth formulated by T'ien-t'ai in his *Profound Meaning of the Lotus Sutra* and *Great Concentration and Insight*. They are the truth of non-substantiality (Japanese *kutai*), the truth of temporary existence (Japanese *ketai*) and the truth of the Middle Way (Japanese *chutai*). Because they are not really separate, but instead indicate three facets of a single truth, they are sometimes together described as the "threefold truth", the "triple truth" or the "three perceptions of the truth". *See also* **ku**.

Three virtues (Japanese *santoku*) (1) The three virtues are the property of the Law (Sanskrit *dharma-kaya*, Japanese *hosshin*), wisdom (Sanskrit *prajna*, Japanese *hannya*) and emancipation or freedom (Sanskrit *vimukti* or *vimoksha*, Japanese *gedatsu*) – possessed by a Buddha. The property of the Law is the truth which the Buddha has realized, or the true aspect of all phenomena; wisdom is the ability to realize this truth; and emancipation is the state in which one is free from the sufferings of birth and death. The three virtues thus correspond with the three properties. *See also* **three properties**.

(2) The expression "the three virtues" can also refer to the attributes of sovereign, teacher and parent – i.e., the qualifications of a Buddha. The virtue of the sovereign is the power to protect all living beings; that of the teacher is the wisdom to instruct them and lead them to enlightenment; and that of the parent is the compassion to nurture and support them.

"Thus Come One" (Sanskrit *tathagata*) "Thus Come One" is one of the ten honorific titles of a Buddha, meaning a person who has arrived from the world of truth. A Buddha embodies the fundamental truth of all phenomena and has grasped the law of causality that spans past, present and future.

T'ien-t'ai (538-597) T'ien-t'ai is the founder of the Chinese T'ien-t'ai school, and is commonly referred to as the Great Teacher T'ien-t'ai. His name and title were taken from Mount T'ien-t'ai, where he lived. He lived during the Northern and Southern Dynasties period and the Sui dynasty. He refuted the spiritual classifications formulated by the ten major Buddhist schools of his day, which based themselves either on the Flower Garland Sutra or on the Nirvana Sutra, and devised the classification of the five periods and eight teachings, thereby establishing the supremacy of the Lotus Sutra. He also expounded the theory of *ichinen sanzen*. Because he systematized both its doctrine and its method of practice, he is revered as the founder of the school, although the lineage of the teaching itself is considered to have begun with Nagarjuna. T'ien-t'ai's lectures were recorded by his disciple and successor Chang-an. *See also ichinen sanzen*, Lotus Sutra, *Profound Meaning of the Lotus Sutra*, **T'ien-t'ai school**.

T'ien-t'ai school The T'ien-t'ai school is a school of Buddhism founded by T'ien-t'ai. The school maintains that enlightenment is achieved by meditation to "observe one's mind" and perceive the truth *(ichinen sanzen)* therein. T'ien-t'ai refuted the views of the schools which believed in the supremacy of either the Flower Garland Sutra or the Nirvana Sutra, and asserted that Shakyamuni's ultimate teaching is to be found in the Lotus Sutra. His lectures on the Lotus Sutra were written down and collected by his successor, Chang-an: they are the *Profound Meaning of the Lotus Sutra*, the *Words and Phrases of the Lotus Sutra* and the *Great Concentration and Insight*. Miao-lo, the sixth leader of the school, wrote commentaries on the three major writings and was responsible for the school being restored after a period of decline. His disciples Tao-sui and Hsing-man transmitted T'ien-t'ai's teachings to Dengyo. who later founded the Tendai sect, the Japanese version of the T'ien-t'ai school. *See also ichinen sanzen*, **Miao-lo, T'ien-t'ai**.

Treasure Tower (Japanese *hoto*) The Treasure Tower is the tower of Taho Buddha which, according to the eleventh chapter of the Lotus Sutra, "Treasure Tower", appeared from beneath the surface of the Earth. It was adorned by seven kinds of gems. In Nichiren Shoshu it is taken to mean the Gohonzon itself and also the lives of those who believe in the Gohonzon. *See also* **Gohonzon, Taho Buddha**.

Treasury of Analyses of the Law (Sanskrit *Abidharma-kosha-shastra*, Japanese *Abidatsuma Kusha Ron*) A *Treasury of Analyses of the Law* is an exhaustive study written by Vasubandhu and translated into Chinese during the period between 563 and 567, and again from 651 to 654. This work includes a comprehensive discussion of Buddhist themes in nine chapters: (1) "On the Elements [dharmas]", (2) "On the Sense Organs", (3) "On Realms", (4) "On Actions", (5) "On Earthly Desires", (6) "On the Noble Stages", (7) "On Wisdom", (8) "On Meditation", and (9) "On Refutation of the Idea of the Self".

True Cause The True Cause is one of the three mystic principles: in terms of Shakyamuni's Buddhism, it is the practice carried out by Shakyamuni in order to attain his original enlightenment. However, in the text of the Lotus Sutra, the actual Law which Shakyamuni practised remains unclear. Nichiren Daishonin identified the True Cause or fundamental Law which enables all Buddhas to attain their enlightenment as the Law of *Nam-myoho-renge-kyo*. *See also* **three mystic principles**.

True Effect The True Effect is one of the three mystic principles: in terms of Shakyamuni's Buddhism, it is the original enlightenment which he attained at a time in the inconceivably remote past. In Nichiren

Daishonin's Buddhism the term "True Effect" means the enlightenment – which is without beginning or end – of the original Buddha. *See also* **three mystic principles.**

True Land The True Land is one of the three mystic principles: it is where Shakyamuni has always been, teaching the Law, since the time of his original enlightenment. In many of the teachings predating the Lotus Sutra the Buddha's land is described as being in a realm apart from this world, but in the sixteenth chapter of the Lotus Sutra it is made explicit that the True Land is in fact this world itself, and it is here that the Buddha has dwelt since his original enlightenment. In Nichiren Shoshu the True Land is interpreted also as the place where the Gohonzon is enshrined. *See also* **Gohonzon, three mystic principles.**

True Law *See* **Mystic Law.**

Truths, three *See* **three truths.**

Two Heavenly Gods The Two Heavenly Gods are Bishamonten and Jikokuten, two of the Four Heavenly Kings. *See also* **Four Heavenly Kings.**

Two saints The two saints are the two bodhisattvas referred to in the writings of Nichiren Daishonin. They are Yakuo (Sanskrit Bhaishajyaraja, meaning "medicine king") and Yuze (Sanskrit Pradanashura, meaning "brave donor").

Two vehicles (Japanese *nijo*) The two vehicles are the two kinds of teaching, together corresponding to Hinayana Buddhism, expounded for, respectively, people of Learning and Realization; the two vehicles can also be thought of as those two groups of people themselves. *See also* **Hinayana, Learning, Realization.**

Vasubandhu Vasubandhu is a Buddhist scholar in India thought to have lived around the fourth or fifth century AD. He is counted as the twenty-first of Shakyamuni's twenty-four successors. He became the undisputed master of Hinayana philosophy in the India of his day. Vasubandhu first criticized Mahayana but later converted to it under the influence of his elder brother Asanga, whom he assisted thereafter in promoting the Yogachara or Consciousness Only school of Mahayana. Vasubandhu is said to have written a thousand works, five hundred related to Hinayana and five hundred to Mahayana.

Words and Phrases of the Lotus Sutra (Chinese *Fa-hua-wen-chü*, Japanese *Myoho-renge-kyo Mongu*) *Words and Phrases of the Lotus Sutra* is a ten-fascicle commentary on the Lotus Sutra expounded by T'ien-t'ai and recorded by Chang-an during the Sui dynasty.

Index

Kumarajiva, 174-5, 190
kyo, 191-2
Kyoshin, Soya, 127

Land of Tranquil Light, 95, 98
latent cause, 187
latent effect (factor), 96-7, 114, 128, 129-30, 133, 143, 187
Law *see* Mystic Law
"Leader of People", 123
Learning, 10, 114, 117, 121-2, 124
"Letter from Sado", 32, 99-100
"Letter to the Brothers", 100
Lewin, Kurt, 148
life force, 1
"Lifespan of the Tathagata", 103, 112, 116, 140
longevity *see* age
Lorenz, Konrad, 126
lotus, 181-6, 187-8
  eight-petalled, 189-90
Lotus Sutra (*Myoho-renge-kyo*), 6, 7, 13-14, 28, 82, 84, 92, 99, 111, 115, 172, 174-94 *passim*
  Nichiren Daishonin and, 15, 38, 47, 50
  on ageing, 50
  on childlessness, 47
  on illness, 81
  on plants, 106-107
  supremacy of, 65
  T'ien-t'ai on, 109, 131
  Treasure Tower reference in, 13
  see also "Lifespan of the Tathagata", "Means"
Lovelock, Jim E., 20-21

Maclean, Paul D., 170
Mahayana, 6, 8, 63
manifest effect (factor), 96, 97, 114, 128, 129-30, 133, 143, 187
mano-consciousness, 90, 158-61, 163, 165, 167, 168, 170-71
Margulis, Lynn, 20-21
Maudgalyayana, 101
"Means", 116, 128
medicine
  ancient, 54-7
  Buddhist, 52-3, 57-66
  occidental, 23, 27, 31, 52-83 *passim*, 97, 166
Menaker, W. and A., 19
Menander, 183
Mendel, Gregor, 36
metampsychosis *see* transmigration
Miao-lo, 31, 68, 82, 133
Middle Way, 131, 132, 178
mind, 134-40

mind-consciousness, 90
Mohenjo Daro, 181
Monet, Claude, 191
monosomy, 22
Moon, phases of, 19
moxa cautery, 62
myo, 81-2, 88, 177-8, 179, 180
myoho, 81, 88, 177-80
Myoho-renge-kyo 13, 134, 150, 174-94 *passim*
  see also Lotus Sutra, Mystic Law, Nam-myoho-renge-kyo
Mystic Law (Law, True Law), 37, 65, 81-3, 88-9, 90, 91-2, 99, 100, 107, 113, 116, 117, 131, 133, 134, 139, 150, 152, 174-94 *passim*
  see also Myoho-renge-kyo, Nam-myoho-renge-kyo

Nagarjuna, 52-3, 61, 69, 88, 122-3, 163, 174, 183-4
Nagasaki, 23
Nagasena, 183
nam, 176-7
Nam-myoho-renge-kyo, 12-15, 81, 116, 117, 153, 165, 174-94
  chanting, 13, 15, 84, 90, 91-2, 93, 94, 95, 117, 172, 174-94 *passim*
  see also Mystic Law
nature (factor), 128-9, 130, 131, 133
near-death experience, 85-6
"New Age" science, 28
Nichimyo, Lady, 107
Nichiren Shoshu, 15
nine consciousnesses, 8, 68, 155-73
Nine Worlds, 11, 15, 98, 116, 122, 125, 127, 178, 186
nirvana, 6, 7, 95, 112-13
Nirvana Sutra, 29, 100, 101-102
NMR, 148-9
non-substantiality *see ku*
Nung, Shen, 75
Nyudo, Ko, 46-7

Oga, Ichiro, 184
"On Attaining Buddhahood", 109-10, 146, 176, 178
"One Essential Phrase, The", 175
oneness of body and mind (*shikishin funi*), 108, 133, 135, 140, 143
oneness of life and its environment (*esho funi*), 19-21, 108, 134, 143-51
"On Omens", 145-6
"On Practising the Buddha's Teachings", 94-5
"On the Love of the Lotus", 182
"On the Ten Factors of Life", 131

216

218